T0413414

CALVINISM, REFORM AND THE ABSOLUTIST STATE IN ELIZABETHAN IRELAND

Religious Cultures in the Early Modern World

Series Editors: *Fernando Cervantes*
Peter Marshall
Philip Soergel

Titles in this Series

1 Possession, Puritanism and Print: Darrell, Harsnett, Shakespeare and the Elizabethan Exorcism Controversy
Marion Gibson

2 Visions of an Unseen World: Ghost Beliefs and Ghost Stories in Eighteenth-Century England
Sasha Handley

3 Diabolism in Colonial Peru, 1560–1750
Andrew Redden

4 Sacred History and National Identity: Comparisons between Early Modern Wales and Brittany
Jason Nice

5 Monstrous Births and Visual Culture in Sixteenth-Century Germany
Jennifer Spinks

6 The Religious Culture of Marian England
David Loades

7 Angels and Belief in England, 1480–1700
Laura Sangha

8 The Laudians and the Elizabethan Church: History, Conformity and Religious Identity in Post-Reformation England
Calvin Lane

9 Religious Space in Reformation England: Contesting the Past
Susan Guinn-Chipman

10 Anglo-German Relations and the Protestant Cause: Elizabethan Foreign Policy and Pan-Protestantism
David Scott Gehring

11 John Bale and Religious Conversion in Reformation England
Oliver Wort

12 Religious Diaspora in Early Modern Europe: Strategies of Exile
Timothy G. Fehler, Greta Grace Kroeker, Charles H. Parker and Jonathan Ray (eds)

13 Celestial Wonders in Reformation Germany
Ken Kurihara

14 Jews and the Renaissance of Synagogue Architecture, 1450–1750
Barry L. Stiefel

15 Priestly Resistance to the Early Reformation in Germany
Jourden Travis Moger

16 Images of Islam, 1453–1600: Turks in Germany and Central Europe
Charlotte Colding Smith

17 Female Piety and the Catholic Reformation in France
Jennifer Hillman

18 Exile and Religious Identity, 1500–1800
Jesse Spohnholz and Gary Waite (eds)

19 The Renaissance Ethics of Music: Singing, Contemplation and *Musica Humana*
Hyun-Ah Kim

Forthcoming Titles

Indulgences after Luther: Pardons in Counter-Reformation France, 1520–1720
Elizabeth C. Tingle

Ceremony, Ritual and Kingcraft at the Court of Charles I
Nile K. Blunt

Missionary Strategies in the New World, 1610–1690: An Intellectual History
Catherine Ballériaux

www.pickeringchatto.com/religious

CALVINISM, REFORM AND THE ABSOLUTIST STATE IN ELIZABETHAN IRELAND

BY

Mark A. Hutchinson

PICKERING & CHATTO
2015

Published by Pickering & Chatto (Publishers) Limited
21 Bloomsbury Way, London WC1A 2TH

2252 Ridge Road, Brookfield, Vermont 05036–9704, USA

www.pickeringchatto.com

All rights reserved.
No part of this publication may be reproduced,
stored in a retrieval system, or transmitted in any form or by any means,
electronic, mechanical, photocopying, recording, or otherwise
without prior permission of the publisher.

© Pickering & Chatto (Publishers) Ltd 2015
© Mark A. Hutchinson 2015

To the best of the Publisher's knowledge every effort has been made to contact relevant copyright holders and to clear any relevant copyright issues. Any omissions that come to their attention will be remedied in future editions.

BRITISH LIBRARY CATALOGUING IN PUBLICATION DATA

Hutchinson, Mark A., author.
Calvinism, reform and the absolutist state in Elizabethan Ireland. – (Religious cultures in the early modern world)
1. Reformation – Ireland. 2. Calvinism – Ireland – History – 16th century. 3. Ireland – Religion – 16th century. 4. Ireland – History – 1558–1603. 5. Great Britain – Religion – 16th century. 6. Great Britain – Politics and government – 1558–1603.
I. Title II. Series
274.1'506-dc23

ISBN-13: 9781848935488
Web-PDF ISBN: 9781781447406
ePUB ISBN: 9781781447413

∞

This publication is printed on acid-free paper that conforms to the American National Standard for the Permanence of Paper for Printed Library Materials.

Content Management Platform by Librios™
Typeset by Pickering & Chatto (Publishers) Limited
Printed and bound in the United Kingdom by CPI Books

CONTENTS

In memory of my mother Linda

ACKNOWLEDGEMENTS

At some level this book has been a long time in the making. I began thinking about reformation views of man and about Ireland's place in a wider British and European world when I was an undergraduate in Dublin. This was in no small part due to my teachers there, Ciaran Brady and Helga Robinson-Hammerstein. Their scholarship, as well as their friendship, since my undergraduate days, has remained a guide. After Dublin I spent a year in St Andrews and after that I began my doctoral work in Canterbury where the supervision of Jackie Eales, along with a three-year research studentship, allowed me to lay the basis for much of the thinking which underpins this study. I cannot thank Jackie enough for her support, friendship and rigorous reading of my thesis. A lot of what was good in the initial work came from her nudges in various directions.

In England I also benefited from small grants from the Royal Historical Society, which allowed me to complete some of my archival research and to attend various conferences. In particular, at the annual Early Modern Studies conference in Reading I have had the pleasure to become acquainted with my counterparts in Tudor and Stuart Britain. I have always tried to talk directly to them about Ireland and such motivation informs part of this book.

Another key moment in my research came with my attendance at the Elizabeth I and Ireland conference in Connecticut, Storrs, which was organized by Valerie McGowan-Doyle and Brendan Kane. I appreciate the support and encouragement both have continued to provide, especially the opportunity to develop an aspect of my thinking in a collection of essays they edited on *Elizabeth I and Ireland*. Similarly, comments made by Thomas Herron and Willy Maley on an earlier piece I contributed to a special edition of the *Sidney Journal*, as well as useful criticism along the way from David Edwards and Andrew Hadfield, have been very helpful. Jane Dawson provided me with her transcriptions of various letters from a previously unknown letter book kept by the radical cleric Christopher Goodman, which has strengthened the case I have tried to make concerning the more radical Protestantism in Ireland, whilst Alan Ford has been generous in his support and advice.

Furthermore, in finishing the research for this book I have had the privilege to hold an Irish Research Council Postdoctoral Fellowship in the Humanities and Social Sciences at University College Cork. Cork is an inspiring place, as all natives of Cork city know, and I cannot disagree. My colleagues Jason Harris, Emma Nic Cárthaigh, Clare O'Halloran, Jennifer Browne, Nóirín Ní Bheaglaoi, Áine Sheehan, Simon Egan, and in particular Emer Purcell and Diarmuid Scully, have provided a wonderful intellectual environment, which is underpinned by friendship and much drinking.

But it was at the Lichtenberg-Kolleg, the University of Göttingen Institute of Advanced Study, that this book was finished. It was out in Wolfenbüttel that I met Philip Soergel who expressed an interest in the book, and I am very glad he did. It has also been a pleasure to work with the wider team at Pickering and Chatto. Moreover, at the Kolleg, the team of Dominik Hünniger, Kora Baumbach and Turan Lackschewitz have been very supportive; whilst working alongside my colleagues as part of the 'Religious Toleration and Modernity Group' I have benefited greatly from conversations with Haim Mahlev and in particular Tim Stanton and the Director here, Martin van Gelderen, whose own work on early modern republicanism underpins various aspects of this book. My many conversations with Catherine Ballériaux on the topic of grace and covenant theology have also benefited me more than she knows.

I would also like to mention my other friends who over the years have housed me in London, Dublin and other places as I visited archives (and more) and then bored them at least a little with my topic of research: Matthew Neuberger, Aisling Fitzpatrick, Celia Cranfield, Irene O'Daly, Kevin Byrne, Walter Jayawardene, Nora Mahony, Eavan Crehan, Neil Craig and Sally Manikian. Jonathan Jones has also been helpful in explaining some aspects of English common law.

But, then, the last shall be first. The individual to whom I owe the biggest intellectual debt is my IRC mentor at Cork, Hiram Morgan. Hiram is the best of critics, always understanding where the work means to go and identifying the various points that link it together more clearly than the author himself; and then there is the wonderful Dorothy Convery who, along with Hiram, read and commented on an earlier draft of this book. It is much the better for their comments. I am very happy I ended up in Cork for two years.

Finally, David Calvert now knows more about Elizabethan Ireland (and early modern Europe) than anyone can without wanting such knowledge, whilst preventing the author from absorbing too much of the vocabulary of a deranged early modern protestant. My two sisters Claire and Rebecca have always been supportive in their own sisterly ways and I am genuinely glad I have them.

The last two individuals I should mention, however, are the most at fault. My father Robert has been and remains my best teacher. The lady to whom this book is dedicated was always dogmatic in her support.

M. A. H.
Lichtenberg-Kolleg, Göttingen
Herzog August Bibliothek, Wolfenbüttel
October 2014

LIST OF FIGURES

NOTE ON THE TEXT

Spelling has been standardized in quotations from manuscript and other primary source material. Original spelling has been maintained in quotations taken from contemporaneous printed treatises and Spenser's *View*. In terms of references to 'the state', by the accession of James I & VI the term does start to be capitalized as 'the State', indicating that term had established itself firmly within English and Irish parlance. This shift started to take place in Irish government correspondence near the end of the 1580s and because spelling has been standardized this change in statist vocabulary is not recorded here.

INTRODUCTION

In a *Discourse of Civill Life* (1606), Lodowick Bryskett, the former clerk to the council in Ireland, had retired to a cottage on the outskirts of Dublin, where a group of colleagues or friends arrived in order to discuss the active life and the broader question of civility or civil education. Bryskett's visitors included, amongst others, the archbishop of Armagh, Dr John Long, the poet Edmund Spenser, the army captains Warham St Leger and Christopher Carleil, and the Irish councillor Sir Robert Dillon. Bryskett's account of this meeting served as a literary device in order to set the scene for his dialogue, though it reflects something of the reality of his Irish life.[1] It also parallels a similar event in England where Humphrey Gilbert, an English explorer, who had seen military service in Ireland, met to discuss the work of the Roman historian Livy with Sir Thomas Smith, a leading legal scholar and diplomat, and also Gabriel Harvey, Spenser's mentor.[2]

In both accounts an idea of Ireland is instrumental. The discussion Gilbert and Smith had over civil society was largely theoretical, but it was Gilbert's Irish experience and Smith's plan to colonize part of Ulster that led them to critique Livy. In the more settled environment of Elizabethan England the potential scope for remaking civil society was limited. Similarly, for Bryskett and his colleagues or friends, their engagement with ideas about civility and man's reform had immediate practical implications. Elizabeth's Irish kingdom was in a condition of perceived widespread civil disorder and the question of the island's longer-term reform dominated discussion for most of Elizabeth's reign.

Ireland's great Old English lords headed large clientage networks. These networks formed the basis of semi-independent military forces, which allowed these lords to govern their lordships according to their own will. In Ireland's Gaelic lordships, English law and landholding practice were ignored and instead these lords governed their followers according to Gaelic customary norms, thus claiming an independent sovereign jurisdiction. Alongside this, within Ireland's Old English gentry community, government's attempts to raise some form of tax met with increasingly vocal protests; whilst Irish medieval Catholicism, in its different forms, was thought deviant, with such criticism only intensifying with the perceived need for protestant reform. Ireland, then, was an arena where English political thought, where English ideas over the nature of civil society, came to be practically applied in a heated and unstable environment. Ireland, more so than England, would shape the intellectual trajectory of Elizabethan political thought, where political violence and rebellion were commonplace.

Within Irish government correspondence quite a precocious shift in ideas and vocabulary can be identified. Bryskett, Spenser, Long and St Leger were part of a wider Calvinist or reformed protestant grouping that staffed Irish government. Such a grouping also included Lord Deputy Henry Sidney and his chancellor Robert Weston, Lord Deputies Arthur Grey and John Perrot, and provincial administrators such as Edward Fitton, Richard Bingham and William Herbert. Their counterparts in England included William Cecil (Lord Burghley), Sir Francis Walsingham and the earl of Leicester.[3] Leicester supported the appointment of various lord deputies including his brother-in-law Henry Sidney.[4] Here the idea of civility or reform that was outlined did not simply involve civil education, but an idea of godly reform.

The network of reformed protestants in England sought a more fully reformed church, where medieval liturgy would be dispensed with and more importantly God's word fully preached. This encompassed a notion of renewal, whereby society would come to be in communion with God once it had fully shaken off the spiritual darkness of the medieval church.[5] In many ways, the question of Irish civil disobedience drew out the full detail of an English godly vision for society, which remained more contained within the more settled environment of Elizabethan England; whilst Ireland provided an arena further away from conservative intervention by Elizabeth giving godly protestants something of a free hand. A connection was drawn between the dissemination of God's word, the operation of grace and the reform of individual consciences, which, it was argued, would establish 'true obedience' and godly political relationships. As a result the preaching of God's word was thought of as a principal component in Irish political reform.

Beside this, however, by 1578 quite a startling shift in vocabulary began to take place. Within Irish government correspondence an early and marked use of the term 'the state' can be identified. The term had been used to refer to the state or condition of the island; but policy discussion came to be framed in terms of the need to maintain the sovereign authority and institutions of the state. Here Irish government drew on language and ideas we would associate with the Italian republican thought of Machiavelli and Guicciardini, or the absolutism of Bodin. The use of term 'state', moreover, predated developments in England by around a decade or so and was conceptually advanced. Its deployment gave tentative shape to the two principal assumptions associated with a modern abstract notion of the state, expressing both the idea that the authority of government was absolute and so distinct from the wider polity, and the idea that such authority was distinct from the person of the prince and so inherent in the institutions or offices of government.[6]

This raises an important set of questions which form the backbone of this study. Why had this set of Irish reformers suddenly turned to discuss the maintenance of secular state institutions, as opposed to furthering godly reform? Why had Irish government decided to deploy a new non-godly vocabulary? It is in attempting to answer these questions that the study seeks to re-evaluate the connection between protestant thought and the emergence of statist ideas, as well as re-examining English protestant involvement in Irish government.

The study starts from the position that there is a need to re-consider reformation thought, its political implications and a subsequent need to conceptualize the state. It also sees Ireland as an important case study in such an investigation, where various English and European ideas about good government and civil life were exposed to open discussion because these models broke down in Ireland due to stress and strain. Such a shift in ideas compels us to reassess the impact of protestant thought on Irish government, where within Irish historical scholarship a link has been drawn between the idea of original sin and a more coercive position, which ignores in its entirety the protestant evangelical motive.[7] More importantly, it raises questions about a tendency within modern scholarship to treat the emergence of an idea of the state within a strictly political sphere, where an emerging statist position simply involved constitutional rights and the position of sovereignty within the community. Do we not need to address a preceding notion of Christian friendship- and grace-based political relationships which had begun to break down?

God's Grace and Civil Life

To begin with, there is a tendency within modern scholarship to downplay or sidestep the implications reformation thought had for established views of normative political relationships, where an emphasis within reformed theology on sin, grace and individual conscience challenged a whole set of notions about the perfectibility of man. Quite a modern notion of civic or political life pervades English and European historiography where the political space is viewed as an area in which man could seek his betterment (whatever that might entail). Here writing on protestant political thought in England, Margo Todd argues that Christian humanism remained to the fore – that 'protestants of all sorts adopted the hope of catholic humanists like Erasmus for a godly social order established through education and discipline'.[8] Similarly, Markku Peltonen, in discussing the broader basis for English political thinking, argues that civic humanism and an active republicanism informed how the Elizabethans thought about the political community.[9]

However, if a protestant conception of God's word and grace is re-examined, the emphasis on the continuity between a humanist and a protestant position does begin to break down. In the first place, there is a sharp divide between an Erasmian view of man's reform and that held by Luther or Calvin. For Erasmus

God's word is educative, whereby man's intellect responds to the good news of the Gospel, grace then meeting the intellect halfway and helping to perfect man. In contrast, for protestants the intellect has very little to contribute. Instead, God's word acts through grace (as an aspect of God's will) reforming man's conscience, thus bringing man to know God and what is good.[10] Such a position rests upon a completely different conception of man, where through the Fall man's will is fully corrupt, where man cannot contribute anything towards his own redemption – thus it is by the action of grace alone (regardless of intellect) that man is reformed.[11] In these terms grace should be seen as the redemptive power of God's love, expressing each individual's direct relationship with God unmediated through church or priest.

This begins to suggest that ideas around civic life and active virtue could become highly contested; and part of the misinterpretation of protestant thought stems from a misreading of what an emphasis on God's word implies. It is too readily assumed that God's word, and the establishment of a preaching ministry, expresses a straightforward educative enterprise, when in fact it invokes a completely different grace-based category or idea of reform and wider relationships. Beside this the establishment of a preaching ministry is usually treated as an entirely religious concern, when in fact the dissemination of God's word was viewed as a critical factor in the reform of man and the construction of a godly political order, where, once redeemed, subjects and citizens would naturally act for the wider good.[12] This in turn points to a series of potential problems because of the various difficulties encountered in England and more so in Ireland when it came to the construction of a functional church. This raised questions about whether a man who lacked grace might in fact be capable of acting well (especially if God's word had not been widely preached). How did such a position affect notions about the unity of a Christian polity? How did reformed protestants respond if they thought God's grace was absent from political life, and how could protestants judge the internal disposition of individual citizens or subjects? Moreover, to what extent was a modern notion of 'the state' conditioned by such problems?

European State Theory

When we consider the broader pattern of developments set out in Quentin Skinner's *Foundations of Modern Political Thought*, where a statist discussion is seen as emerging, in part, out of a discussion begun by protestant resistance theorists over their right to act against the ruler, a godly dimension does seem to be at play. This raises the question as to what exactly a notion of 'the state' is meant to do. For Skinner, as for Todd and Peltonen, there is nothing distinctly Calvinist about the political thinking of reformed protestants. For Skinner the reformation provided a context that required protestants to reconsider, reformulate and redeploy an earlier medieval vocabulary; it did not add any new ideas or new justifications for political action.[13] Resistance theorists simply pillaged a medieval heritage, which dealt with notions of popular sovereignty and the rights of inferior magistrates, in order to justify arming themselves against an ungodly ruler.

But what should we make of the fact that protestants tended to adhere to the idea of the mixed polity, whereby sovereign authority was seen as being shared throughout the political community, thus providing inferior magistrates with the right to act against the ruler? A mixed polity was thought to consist of aspects of three forms of government, democracy, aristocracy and monarchy, with sovereign authority being shared between each estate. After all, for Calvin a mixed polity was the best form of government in a godly society, where magistrate and preacher should work together in order to preserve and strengthen a godly order. In effect, the best form of church government was the best form of civil government. Calvin even referred to such a conjunction of ideas as a 'Christian polity'.[14]

This suggests that a notion of grace and godly friendship may have been more instrumental in such thinking, where the community was brought into direct communion with God and as a consequence all were mandated to work together in the 'building up' of God's kingdom. That in contrast with a more hierarchical model, where the prince simply upholds a Christian order, a godly community required a political structure that allowed all to participate in political life because grace brought all to act well and mandated that all serve God.

However, this is by no means simple, because in a broader European debate, a more directly political or practical outlook can be argued to have been in play. In France, Huguenots adopted such a view in order to argue for freedom of worship within a kingdom that was predominantly catholic.[15] In England, such a view underlay what Patrick Collinson terms 'the monarchical republic', where Elizabeth's more convinced protestant councillors argued for a right to a voice in government in order to insist that more church reform was necessary, this being conditioned by local self-governing gentry republics as found in England's villages and towns.[16] In contrast, it was the French catholic writer Jean Bodin in his *Six Books of the Commonwealth* who adopted an absolutist position, arguing that sovereignty as an indivisible power had to be located within a particular estate in society, and preferably with the prince, thus undermining the mixed polity which saw sovereignty as being shared throughout the community. Bodin adopted his view in order to unpick Huguenot arguments, which he saw destabilizing civil society.[17]

In relation to a specifically Irish context, this raises an awkward question, because those protestants involved in Irish government came to adopt an absolutist definition of sovereign authority (as delegated to them), thus denying the validity of the various customary rights of Elizabeth's Irish subjects. In doing so, not only did Irish government adhere to a position it knew to be antithetical in wider European protestant thought; in England these individuals held the opposite view, supporting adamantly a mixed polity position. Part of the answer to such a question lies in properly reconsidering the theological context surrounding the development of statist thought. In fact, the inversion of the usual pattern found in European political debate helps us examine such a link, because it demands that we reconsider the relationship between a protestant view of civil society and an emerging state theory. It demands that we consider how notions of grace-based friendship, which linked the polity together, relate to a set of institutional structures.

Interestingly, in this regard, J. G. A. Pocock argues in *The Machiavellian Moment* that Italian republican writing, in a pre-reformation context, was responding to the failure of a radical vision of redemption and reform to materialize in Florence as offered by Savonarola. Here the state and its institutions emerge as an alternative basis for a political community in a context where it was no longer possible to think of citizens being guided by knowledge of the *summum bonum*, namely God, and therefore naturally acting for the good of the community.[18] In particular, a notion of *fortuna* was deployed in order to describe the disorderly nature of the temporal political sphere when a clear providential vision for society was lacking. A focus on external state institutions, then, allowed those involved in government to talk about a more contingent set of political relationships in the absence of the more eternal bonds of grace-based friendship. In other words, a focus on institutional structures (either in a mixed or absolutist state) provided a way of talking about political relationships when the internal bonds of unity had gone, whereby individuals could act for 'the state' as opposed to a common or greater good which was now contested.

Very much akin to this, within the Irish kingdom a general need to speak about a set of external political relationships took place in a context where a similar set of ideas concerning man's internal condition and his capacity to act well had begun to fall apart. Leaving aside the question of an Irish proto-absolutism at this point, by generally recasting political relationships as involving the offices and apparatus of the state, government, it would appear, sought to regulate those relationships through institutional controls instead of relying on loyalty or fidelity to the prince, which became problematic if consciences were deemed suspect. More specifically, by placing limits on office holding and by constructing regional institutions of government (i.e., provincial presidencies in Ireland) sovereignty would be positioned within state institutions and not necessarily with the gentry community or within lordships when the wider community was thought unreformed.

Normative Political and Religious Vocabulary

Once, then, 'the state' is seen as responding to a vision of man suspect in conscience, if not fallen, the political space that the state opens up becomes very different. In other words, what propels a broadly statist model is not a Christian humanist vision of man, who naturally seeks out avenues available for his own betterment, but a more difficult vision of man born in sin but redeemed by grace. Here the study of Elizabethan Ireland presents itself as an important corrective, because of the particular conditions of the island. First, Irish policy debate exposes the detail of a discussion concerning the nature of man and his reform, because the primary task of government was to construct a civil society from the ground up. Secondly, Ireland helps demonstrate how difficult it was for a sense of modernity and political freedom to emerge from a combination of protestant thought and early modern state theory.

Quentin Skinner argues that in understanding the ideas of major political thinkers and philosophers, these thinkers need to be understood as responding to a particular set of historical problems. Political thinkers were not voicing some universal, timeless, principle, but were responding to contemporaneous circumstances. Secondly, how individuals spoke about and justified political action depended upon, or was conditioned by, available normative vocabulary and ideas, since we can only speak and express ourselves using the vocabulary we have near at hand. Thus the emergence and development of political thought is indicative of attempts to push the boundaries of pre-existing vocabulary in order to articulate a new set of ideas; and by implication these ideas are limited by normative terminology and by the context in which they emerge.[19]

In relation to Irish historiography, an awareness of normative political and religious vocabulary demands a significant level of reinterpretation. Irish historians stress the growing violence and arbitrariness of government, but within a limited interpretative framework. There is a sense of Irish peculiarity and 'the colonial', where the formation of various Irish identities, Old English, Gaelic Irish and New English, has been understood in terms of 'the outsider' (the colonial newcomer) who dispossessed the native.[20] Alongside this, Rory Rapple and David Edwards now point to the startling use of martial law and other extra legal measures.[21] Here, however, government's disregard for the due process of law demands an explanation beyond simply arguing that violence became normalized, that the New English saw the Irish as different and less deserving of rights, or that panic set in.

It is also not sufficient to simply dismiss references to religious reformation as empty rhetoric, when church reform usually headed government reform programmes, or to dismiss reformation 'ontology' as irrelevant when the idea of God and Christ were most certainly fundamental to the outlook of all.[22] Nor is it good enough to argue that protestants, on the basis of their theology, simply condemned the Irish as beyond help. Brendan Bradshaw in 'Sword, Word and Strategy' suggested that Christian humanists in Ireland saw preaching as effective because they thought man's intellect sufficiently intact; whilst reformed protestants, seeing a corrupt will overpowering the intellect, discounted preaching and embraced the sword.[23] For Bradshaw this meant that those more radical protestants involved in Irish government simply condemned the Irish and quickly embraced a more coercive policy. A similar view was adopted by

Nicholas Canny in both *The Elizabethan Conquest* (1976) and *Making Ireland British* (2003).[24] Such a position, however, ignores the fact that an emphasis on the Fall was universally applicable and that the more important corollary of reformation thought was an emphasis on redemption offered to all. Here Ciaran Brady and James Murray have also pointed to a disjuncture within Irish history writing between the recognition that efforts had actually been made to evangelize and the darker political narrative outlined. Although in their attempt at a corrective they define reformation as simply part and parcel of an attempt to extend English law throughout the Irish kingdom as mandated by reformation statute. As a result they too end up ignoring the evangelical motive by treating religious reformation as a predominately institutional process.[25]

Instead, we should work from the position that Irish government had to justify and understand its actions within the confines of English political and religious ideas. If it stepped beyond what was permitted it had to find a way to justify and think about such behaviour within that framework (and this was far from straightforward). As Hiram Morgan, and more recently Nicholas Canny, observed, Ireland may be better understood within a far broader European pattern, where a similar problem of inter-community violence had to be rationalized, explained and justified, as opposed to being contextualized as colonial and so different.[26]

But at a more important level, Ireland, in far broader terms, allows us to move beyond a focus on political tracts by allowing us to examine shifts in everyday policy discussion. Not only do we need to understand major political thinkers as being in dialogue with a set of lesser figures and writers, as Skinner argues, we need to contextualize shifts in thinking as being part of a far wider exchange of information and ideas which took place on the ground. For instance, a lot of policy discussion within the English privy council occurred *sole voce*, because those involved in government met in person; whilst in contrast in Ireland the same type of everyday discussion had to take place in the regular exchange of letters between those in Ireland and the privy council in England. Irish government correspondence generally consists of various lord deputies, lord presidents and other minor office holders reporting on the condition of Irish society, sometimes on a weekly or more regular basis, where the various problems described were conditioned by the immediate circumstances faced and the breakdown in models for religious and political reform.

Such correspondence allows us, then, to trace incremental shifts in everyday terminology and to see how practical reality drove the articulation of new ideas. Actually, if it is considered that there are over 200 volumes of official state papers dealing with the specific question of Irish government under Elizabeth, which have been artificially separated from the main body of English state papers, the presence of quite a significant Irish accent in English thought becomes all too apparent – though English historians tend to see Ireland as somewhat irrelevant.

Furthermore, because of the widespread dysfunction of Irish civil life, in Ireland a whole set of assumptions about man, sin, grace and 'the good life', which usually went unspoken, can be seen interacting and informing an attempt to speak about 'the state'. This suggests that what we see taking place in Ireland has a far wider European significance. After all, various operative assumptions are sometimes hard to grasp. When someone writes about the establishment of a preaching ministry, or the need for reform, they invoke a whole body of unspoken assumptions which lie below those terms. In particular, many protestants involved in early modern government saw no reason to spell out a set of relationships they assumed to be highly normative, when they wrote or spoke about a godly vision for society. The same can be said about other aspects of European government, such as the imposition of English or even civil law.

But then the operative assumptions which lie underneath various concepts of law tend to be closer to modern thinking. Thus there is not the same disjuncture between past and present operative assumptions. It is also the case that many political thinkers focused on institutional structures in order to avoid discussing the very problematic relationships that such a focus on institutions was meant to solve. They discussed customary rights or the limits on office holding, instead of a contested view of the nature of man, and an unsettling breakdown in trust, in order to make sense of fractured relationships. Thus the wider theological context, in many instances, is purposefully obfuscated. In Ireland, however, the near total dysfunction of the Elizabethan church, where God's word had not been widely preached, as well as the continued failure to resolve this problem, meant that the position of God's word in the reform of society became contested to such a degree that exactly how God's word was thought to operate had to be discussed. Alongside this, the continued breakdown in political conditions, the crisis that resulted from perceived widespread civil disobedience, also meant that the nature of those relationships had to be directly critiqued. In effect Ireland draws out a whole set of ideas which remained unstated, and what we see in Ireland has implications for the way we view English and European Protestantism and the manner in which protestants came to conceive of the godly polity and subsequently 'the state'.

Re-interpreting State Theory

After all, within other European political communities there are indications that a particularly godly if not Calvinist dimension did form part of protestant resistance writing. Martin van Gelderen, in his account of the political thought of the Dutch revolt, points to a conscience-based argument for resistance, which sat below a broader constitutionalist position. Dutch writers drew a link between the health of an individual's conscience and the moral rectitude of acting to defend the traditional rights and privileges of the Netherlands.[27] Anne McLaren has also drawn attention to the way in which godly conscience or the disposition of Elizabeth's protestant councillors was equated with political virtue. This, it was argued, would compensate for the natural deficiencies of Elizabeth as a female prince. For McLaren this represented an attempt to repackage the resistance arguments used against the rule of Mary Tudor as an argument in favour of godly female rule.[28]

These positions would lead to a shift in focus onto state structures, and as before this is suggestive of a need to find a different model for the community. For example, van Gelderen notes that Dutch writers equated traditional or customary rights with calls for freedom of conscience in order to unite a religiously fragmented polity in opposition to tyrannical Spanish rule. The objective of political action was not the furthering of religious reformation but the need to maintain traditional state institutions in the Netherlands as a means of regulating and preserving customary rights.[29] There is a sense of negative freedom here, whereby those institutions act as an external check on an individual's behaviour, therefore protecting the rights and liberties of every citizen and allowing some level of freedom of worship. This contrasts with an idea of positive freedom associated with a unified Christian community, whereby the action of grace frees an individual internally from sin, and in being free every godly citizen will act in the same godly way.[30]

A similar pattern can also be identified with regard to French absolutist thinking, although the confessional context was very different. Mack P. Holt, writing of the French Wars of Religion, points to the unmaking of the French body politic as the Galician church, which was synonymous with the French political community, became fractured, and it was within this context that the catholic Bodin in his *Six Books* outlined an absolutist notion of state authority.[31] As mentioned, Bodin defined sovereign authority as an 'absolute and perpetual power' and argued that such authority was located with a particular estate in society.[32] This was meant to provide a point of political action and unity which sat above confessional division, as well as undermining the arguments of Huguenot resistance writers.[33]

But what remains in play in these various accounts is an emphasis on a more strictly secular political sphere, where confessional division and the problem of conscience drives or compels the emergence of a modern political space. There is a clear sense of early modernity where man can act as a political figure or a *politique* without the question of confession simply stymieing any possibility of his participation in political life – either in the freer context of the Netherlands, where a concept of individual liberty emerged, or in the narrower confines of 'absolutist' France. In contrast, what Ireland helps demonstrate is the extent to which such emerging institutions remained conditioned by notions of sin and a concern over the absence of grace. Thus whilst state institutions, in whatever form, may have been designed to open up and regulate a more secular political space, paradoxically their meaning and purpose remained defined by a preceding Christian model of the community, where state institutions sought to remake relationships that in the absence of Christian friendship were in many ways unwanted and conditioned by a sense of distrust.

This becomes more apparent if shifts in Irish thinking are read against a more tentative shift in thought and outlook identified in England by John Guy and latterly by Anne McLaren. Guy writes of Elizabeth's two reigns, where an early sense of protestant collegiately within the English privy council gave way to a more arbitrary style of government. By the late 1580s an ageing Elizabeth and an inner circle, which included Lord Burghley and a new archbishop of Canterbury, John Whitgift, sought to impose their will from above whilst denying the claims of various catholic and protestant parties that they had a constitutional or customary right to a voice in government.[34] Building on this, McLaren not only points to an initial grace-based model, she hints that the failure of this model, which arose out of the fracturing of that community (into episcopal, puritan and catholic outlooks) was instrumental in encouraging a less collegiate and more absolutist style of government.[35] It is here that we return to the question of Irish proto-absolutism and its more tentative English twin.

Again part of the difficulty in finding a satisfactory explanation as to why a set of English protestants could embrace such an absolutist position stems from the way in which such a shift in thought tends to be contextualized. Whilst Collinson saw 'the monarchical republic' as expressing a level of godly intent, for Collinson what drove a protestant English interest in mixed polity thinking was simply their need for a voice in government so they could argue for more religious reform. In many ways, the more radical English protestant grabbed a set of established political ideas in order to argue for the dissemination of God's word and the reform of the liturgy of the church, but an idea of a godly England (reformed in conscience) did not really change how the protestant Englishman thought of those political relationships. Building on this, for Stephen Alford, what motivated or informed protestant collegiality under William Cecil was the threat posed by Mary Queen of Scots, which bound protestant councillors together, as well as an earlier conciliarist tradition which had developed due to the minority rule of Edward VI. With the execution of Mary Queen of Scots, and the appointment of a second generation of privy councillors, such collegiality, it is suggested, waned. [36] Thus religious thinking may have informed 'the political' but it did not alter what it meant. What Ireland reveals, however, because of the nature of the policy debate, is the sheer extent to which something more fundamental was in play, where 'the political' actually did come to be redefined by religious thought and motivation.

The various underlying assumptions identified in Ireland can be found in parallel in England – though England's more settled condition meant they were not as pronounced. Here, I would argue, that the end of an emphasis on the mixed polity was not simply about a change in political circumstances, but was also informed by a notion of Christian unity based on word, grace and conscience. Here the end of the viability of the mixed polity arose (around the 1580s) because of the fact that word and grace were actually thought absent and so the godly relationships which informed a notion of active virtue and a level of political equality fell apart. What drove proto-absolutism, then, was the emerging invalidity of the preceding model, which suggested an alternative non-godly political order was required. Proto-absolutism allowed dysfunctional political relationships to be regulated by excluding (at least temporarily) those not thought to be godly or of right behaviour from political life.

In this way civic republicanism, when the godly community was absent, quickly became absolutism, and to understand this shift in thought in England these ideas need to be contextualized beside a more open and explicit discussion of underlying assumptions found in Ireland.[37] We might even suggest that in the various contexts where mixed monarchy remained valid, there is also a need to draw a distinction between a mixed polity, where custom and trust governed relationships, and a mixed state, where a more defined institutional conception of the distribution of authority took over, very much akin to an absolutist turn in thinking.

'Commonwealth', 'Grace' and 'the State'

The study, then, will trace the shifting use of terminology within Irish government correspondence. Chapter 1 examines initial moves away from an earlier 'commonwealth' model, which assumed man capable of furthering his own reform, in addition to the emergence of quite a blunt definition of basic civil obedience as being reliant on the threat of government violence. Alongside this the chapter examines the initial emergence of a protestant redefinition of political relationships which was denoted by the vocabulary of 'true obedience'. Here an inversion of protestant resistance theory took place. In the context of ungodly rule protestants equated 'true obedience' to God with acts of civil disobedience. In Ireland, however, 'true obedience' was equated with long-term civil obedience.

Chapters 1 and 2 also explore the political implications of this position, in light of a failure to establish a functional preaching ministry and the connection drawn between the dissemination of God's word, the action of grace on conscience and a long-term civil obedience. This sat beside an increasingly evident counter-reformation note in Irish rebellion (in particular in the second Desmond rebellion of 1579 and the Nugent and Baltinglass risings in the Pale of 1580). Here a series of strained references to a notion of 'true obedience' can be identified in the letters of Lord Deputy Henry Sidney, Lord Deputy Arthur Grey and Archbishop John Long, amongst others. Critically, a godly model had not been implemented, and thus it had not been tested, meaning that any new way of thinking about political relationships and political stability remained caught within a godly frame. Within both these chapters the various ideas identified in Ireland will be read against a parallel and more muted discussion in England.

Chapter 3 considers the initial deployment of a non-godly vocabulary of 'the state' which tended to be broadly absolutist in character. The chapter concentrates on Irish constitutional peculiarity, which primed Irish policy debate so an emerging notion of the state was near at hand. Here the study examines how geographical distance from the person of the prince, along with the perceived corruption of the wider community, encouraged government to think of sovereign authority as distinct from the person of the prince and a corrupt Irish polity thus encouraging a level of double abstraction. Beside this a diminished sense of *lèse majesté*, which arose because of Elizabeth's physical absence from the island, meant the various constitutional assumptions made tended to be openly examined, whilst constant references to the state or condition of the island meant the material for an easy linguistic shift could be grabbed. The confidence of the Old English community was also critical in the critique which emerged.

Chapters 4 and 5 explore how the notion of 'the state' was deployed in Ireland as a means of articulating an alternative non-godly model for political action and the wider political community. Here the study begins to address a particularly pertinent question. Why did a set of English reformed protestants in Ireland deploy the language of an abstract and absolutist 'state', when such a position in continental Europe was used to deny their protestant or Calvinist associates not only a right to a voice in government, but the possibility of freedom of worship? An important figure in this respect is Philip Sidney, the son of the Irish Lord Deputy Henry Sidney, who defended his father's absolutist interpretation of crown prerogative powers and deployed an emerging language of 'the state' in the Anjou marriage debate in England. Once again events in Ireland are paralleled in England, though it is in the Irish kingdom that these ideas are given early and advanced form and that the full context surrounding their development is laid bare.

Also important is Geoffrey Fenton who translated a large body of European religious and political thought and served as Irish secretary of state. Of particular interest in chapter 4 is the way in which the phrase 'broken state' was used by Fenton and others to refer to contingent, sinful and unstable political relationships, which then slide into references to 'the state' to denote the institutions of government and the exclusion of the wider community from participation in political life (especially the Old English of the Pale).

Chapter 5 gives an account of the manner in which the notion of 'the state' also framed the more general re-organization of political relationships in Ireland. At one level, an idea of political contingency or *fortuna* broadened out, and man's internal passions and appetites, his physical desires and reactions, became the subject of attention. Some individuals involved in government began to think of the way in which the natural body might react in a disordered world and in turn how man might be trained through custom and habit to act well in the absence of a grace based internal reform. Beside this, there was an attempt to deconstruct lordships and the position of the freeholder altered in the perceived absence of a viable gentry community. The freeholder was not necessarily to serve the commonwealth through active participation in political life, but he became more a structural component of the institutional state helping in the atomization of society and the positioning of political authority in state institutions (and its removal from great lordships). With the earl of Tyrone, Hugh O'Neill, the components of an alternative catholic body political and state can also be identified.

Finally, chapter 6 gives an account of the emergence of an Irish language of the state in John Hooker's contribution to the Irish section of the second edition of *Holinshed's Chronicles* (1587), as well as in Richard Beacon's *Solon his Follie* (1594) and Edmund Spenser's *A View of the Present State of Ireland* (1597). With Hooker a marked contrast between an earlier protestant mixed polity view and an absolutist position emerges. Hooker details in many respects a version of the narrative that this book traces, where a certain amount of emphasis is placed on the fact that consciences in Ireland are corrupt which conditions his assertion that the Irish community does not have the right to question the crown's prerogative powers.

With Beacon and Spenser, however, something more significant takes place. On the one hand a slightly more institutional sense of the state is set out. But alongside this, with the separation of the state from the polity a space opens up for the re-conception of the political community which exists below the state and its institutions. Here the polity starts to be thought of as a natural body with passions and appetites, formed by custom and habit, as opposed to the body of Christ bound by grace. Nevertheless, the critical point remains that the terminology associated with a natural body simply provided a different, slightly more productive, way of discussing sin and its political implications. The state in Ireland remained conditioned by a failure to construct a redeemed and reformed political community.

1 BUILDING A GODLY POLITY IN IRELAND

The tone of early policy discussion in Ireland tended to suggest that the norms of civil society were so evidently true, that in the face of such civility the shackles of Irish barbarism would simply fall away. Various political treatises written in the 1520s and '30s emphasized how the introduction of settled arable farming, primogeniture, English medieval religious practice, and the due process of law would naturally alter the behaviour of Ireland's disobedient lords and allow government to establish friendly and stable political relationships within the polity or kingdom.[1] Brendan Bradshaw, in the *Irish Constitutional Revolution*, saw this renewed vigour as coinciding with the introduction or use of the term 'commonwealth'. This invoked the category of the moral good, which in turn required government to look to the reform of the whole island, to analysis the 'inadequacies of the system of political organization' and to seek to alter such circumstances.[2] What happened, however, when these self-evident truths failed to materialize?

It is the failure to further societal reform in Ireland, whereby current political conditions remained unaltered, that the first two chapters of this book take as their point of departure. What these chapters ask is how a group of reformed protestants involved in Irish government, from the mid-1560s onwards, understood the widespread civil disorder they confronted and what this might tell us about a wider reformed protestant or Calvinist re-conception of notions of civil obedience, the common good and political relationships within a polity or kingdom. How did Calvinists respond when their theology suggested that man's ability to act well was dependent on grace, when grace was thought to act separately on each individual? Gone was the assumption that redemption depended on participation in the rituals of the medieval church, where the simple fact of the community's involvement in the life of the church meant no awkward questions needed to be asked concerning the presence of grace in political life.[3] How did Ireland's political condition, where the question of the island's reform to a long-term civil obedience dominated discussion, affect how reformed protestants read and applied their theology?

In exploring these questions, this chapter begins by assessing the optimism of commonwealth thought and the challenges posed by an Irish context. It examines how notions of civil obedience, as found in protestant resistance theory of the period, informed Irish policy. 'True obedience' was equated with good conscience, which in turn was argued to be dependent on the action of God's grace. Here Ireland inverts the paradigm for resistance, because those Calvinists involved in government did not ask when they might justifiably disobey an ungodly ruler, but how they might bring a kingdom to obey a godly prince. The rest of the chapter addresses initial attempts to implement such a model, where emphasis was placed on the need to disseminate God's word. It was as a consequence of a continued failure to make any marked progress that an underlying definition of godly civil obedience was outlined in open political debate.

Commonwealth Thought

If Ireland was to expose a godly view of political life to scrutiny, an earlier 'commonwealth' position had already been tested. In Bradshaw's *Constitutional Revolution*, it was the combination of English Christian humanism of the 1520s and '30s, with its Irish counterpart, that drove an attempt to restructure Henry VIII's lordship of Ireland. A central plank of this policy was the 1541 act of kingly title and the now ubiquitous policy of surrender and regrant, which had its basis in a renewed interest in statute law and government's ability to tackle social and political ills through prescribed solutions. Here Bradshaw moved beyond the commonplace observation that the act of kingly title simply tackled an awkward point arising from Henry's break with Rome.[4] Instead, it was argued that the act was meant to do far more, because it provided the constitutional mechanism by which Irish lords could become subjects of the crown in Ireland.[5]

The act of kingly title established the basis upon which those lords who held land with no legal right under English law could surrender their estates and retake them from the prince. This was meant to establish the basis upon which civil society, 'the good life', could be furthered in the Irish kingdom. The analysis as applied consisted of two components. The first part was structural, where Brehon law (that used amongst the Gaelic Irish) was seen as fostering retributive justice, where it was material loss as opposed to the morality of the act that underlay decisions, whilst customary Gaelic exactions encouraged the maintenance of private armies and exploitation. Secondly, such structural analysis lay on top of an optimistic assessment of the nature of man, who, made in the image of God, it was suggested, would naturally act for the common and greater good if given the opportunity.[6] Thus changing the structure of society would naturally draw out man's good character, where a more equitable justice would encourage honesty and reasoned discussion, *negotium*, which would become the basis for political relationships. This was very much in line with the optimism of the Northern European Renaissance, where man was assumed capable of self-fashioning.[7]

From this perspective, as with much Irish historical scholarship, events in Ireland remain conditioned by a larger English or European narrative. *The Irish Constitutional Revolution* drew directly upon Geoffrey Elton's *Reform and Renewal* which had identified a concurrent statute based movement for reform in England. For Elton 'Tudor writers were troubled by the state of the world, by its lack of honest spirituality and by social differences, and they brought [to bear] ... some ... basic ideas concerning the political perfectibility of man's condition and a naively sanguine trust in the power of edicts to better man'.[8] There is, however, a different way in which Bradshaw's account might be read. Irish government attempted to establish a kingdom for the first time through a series of mechanisms as set out in statute. In particular, through the act of kingly title and other bills, government sought to establish the basis for civil and functional political relationships through force of statute alone. In this respect, there was an immediate potential for events in Ireland to shape a wider English conception of civil society, because the ability of statute or prescribed solutions to bring about change came to be tested in an extreme environment; so too were the wider assumptions about man and civilized society.

By the late 1560s a definition of civil obedience had emerged, where in specifically political or civil terms it was assumed that government could only hope to hold the Irish kingdom in a basic level of external obedience, which relied on the threat of force or 'the sword'. In 1572 Lord Deputy William Fitzwilliam commented that he feared 'the state of the country will grow rather to the continuance of 15,000 or 16,000 men', in responding to Elizabeth's decision to significantly shrink the size of the army.[9] In reference to the province of Connacht, where widespread rebellion was once again a concern, it was argued that 'without force continually ... [the Irish] will never leave ... sensual barbarism to the knowledge of any civility and obedience to law'.[10] The charms of an English model of society were not so evidently true to the extent that man, corrupt by nature, would accept reform without the presence of punitive measures. Unless the queen would 'resolve ... [to] lay by her weeding hook and put in her sickle' no real change would be brought about.[11]

Here the way in which Irish civil structures came to function was very much the opposite of the original intent of commonwealth thought. The Gaelic Irish and many Old English lords came to be shut out of the political sphere and the pursuit of 'the good life', either because it was believed they would not act for the common good, or because of the open manipulation of civil structures by the English colonizer. However, I think we need to recognize that in Ireland, it is not simply the case that Elizabeth's Irish subjects were judged difficult to reform. Instead, it was the wider humanist episteme, with its optimistic assessment concerning man's capabilities and the civilizing process, which came to be challenged.[12]

The eschewing of the idea of an interlinked polity is reflected in the proliferation of martial law commissions, through the 1570s and '80s, which David Edwards identifies.[13] This entailed the rejection of English customary law, where the community, through trial by jury, should have been involved in determining the guilt of a member of that community. The role of county seneschals and provincial presidents altered quite significantly. The seneschal and provincial president should have fostered the civil and legal norms of English society. Instead, they increasingly used their executive authority to enforce martial law, where fear and force remained the operative mode.[14]

A similar departure from, or disintegration in, commonwealth values is also evident in the way in which surrender and regrant arrangements operated from the late 1550s onwards. As Christopher Maginn recently identified, a staged shift in the use of surrender and regrant can be traced. The remit of the initial policy, which was to introduce English political norms by utilizing the relationship between a lord as loyal servitor and the prince was slowly forgotten. Instead, after an initial optimistic turn, surrender and regrant was deployed in many instances as a means of formalizing aspects of the existing political *status quo*.[15] This is effectively the argument of Lord Deputy Henry Sidney's memoir of service, which was written in 1583 and gave an account of both his periods in office in the 1560s and 70s.

Acting in the midst of the first Desmond rebellion of 1568–9, for Sidney what mattered was the construction of an alternative body of crown supports who would act against oppositional forces. Thus the indentures drawn up between these lords and the prince (or deputy) paid less attention to the deconstruction of the various conditions usually perceived as limiting or preventing a more civil culture. The construction of political alliances was all that really mattered at this point.[16]

Nevertheless, government did wish to curtail bastard feudal practices, where another key motif of policy discussion was the need to end the use of coyne and livery as practised by the great noble houses and factional groups in Ireland. The great factional networks were usually identified as the Fitzgeralds or Geraldines (headed by the earls of Kildare and Desmond) and the Butlers (headed by the earl of Ormond). The basic analysis was that major lords collected their rents in kind (namely in meat and drink). This encouraged the maintenance of a large military retinue and so furthered endemic violence. However, by encouraging lords to collect fixed rents, it was suggested that the need to maintain large military forces would end, whilst the financial benefits, which would arise when lords no longer maintained large military forces, might convince Ireland's lords of the benefits of a more settled arable lifestyle.[17]

There is some ambiguity in such a position, where a sense of the self-evident quality of English civility does re-emerge. I would argue, however, that such a policy came to be thought of as operating upon the basis of self-interest as opposed to the notions of honesty, duty and fidelity. In effect, the critical factor remained the need to maintain a basic civil obedience, which would become easier if a lord's military forces had been removed; whilst the analysis relied on the lord agreeing to an alteration in current conditions because he would understand that he could not compete with crown forces. The lord would also realize he would be materially better off if he did not have to maintain a private army.[18]

A still better comparison might be the shift in how colonial projects were thought to operate. Taking Thomas More's *Utopia* as our starting point, a notion of a hoped-for unitary commonwealth provides More with the moral justification for colonial projects, because the extension of the civil and rational processes of government to colonies is seen as drawing out the better qualities of man. Access to an edifying, as opposed to a coercive, justice would be provided.[19] But in an Irish context there quickly emerged a series of stark departures from such an ideal. As the work of Nicholas Canny suggests, there is an immediate tension between such an altruistic ideal and the self-interest of the colonizer seeking to dispossess the native of land.[20]

The initial plan for a colony in the mid-lands in Ireland quickly fell short of the commonwealth model. In 1556, plans for plantation in Laois and Offaly had assumed that pockets of English civility would encourage the O'Connors and O'Mores to adopt a settled, arable and English manner of life. Like their English colonial counterparts, they should be 'freeholders' and they should 'answer the laws of the realm as the English'. In 1560, however, after the O'Connors and O'Mores had gone into rebellion, force of arms and not exemplary civility became the critical qualification for a planter, who needed to 'bring over force to defend that allowed'.[21]

A more important example is Sir Thomas Smith's own description of his proposed colonial project in Ulster in 1572, which involved the colonization of the Ards in Ulster. His promotional pamphlet *A Letter Sent by I. B. Gentleman unto his Very Friend Master R. C. Esquire* (1572) emphasizes the benefits of shire government, whereby access to English justice, and a settled arable life style, would draw man into civil conversation by eschewing a factional and militarized society based upon self-interest (and often violent) behaviour. Smith's proposal drew on an awareness of ancient Rome, and Smith's own classic view of the Elizabethan mixed polity as set out in *De Republica Anglorum* (1583). *De Republica* was originally written in 1565 and detailed the functionality of the Elizabethan polity, where the role played by the nobility, gentry and yeoman was extolled.[22] In Smith's promotional pamphlet, as Hiram Morgan has noted, explicit reference is made to More's earlier work. Smith asks, 'How say you now, have I not set forth to you another Utopia'? In particular, Smith argues that the younger sons of the gentry, due to overpopulation in England, should form the backbone of his scheme thus echoing More.[23]

Nevertheless, within the pamphlet a sense of punitive justice remains dominant, where the degeneracy of the original English colony in Ireland arises out of a latent self-interest, where English subjects 'perceiving their immunity from law and punishment' simply gave into baser desires and uncivil manners.[24] And in reality such punitive justice was understood to be the operative mode of Smith's proposal, Lord Deputy Fitzwilliam writing that 'my heart embraces the enterprise as the only means [by which government will be able] without charge ... to bridle this rebellious people who nothing but fear and force can teach duty and obedience'.[25]

Akin to this, writing in the late 1560s, Lord Deputy Sidney emphasized how problematic the Laois and Offaly project had been – that 'the conquest of Laois and Offaly is to be remembered, which I am assured hath cost the queen and this country more than would purchase so much rent no times told in England'.[26] Here the deputy was responding to a set of interrogatories Elizabeth had issued which implied that Ireland, through little more than negotiated agreements, had been brought to a reasonable level of political stability under the previous administration.[27] Sidney also had to cope with unreasonable demands made concerning the potential progress of the provincial presidency system in Munster. In setting up the presidency an inaccurate low set of costings had been submitted, which Elizabeth characteristically would not agree to alter. Sidney asked why such rapidity of reform 'should be looked for in Munster which was never had in Wales nor the north of England'?[28] Direct reference was made to the two other parts of Elizabeth's dominions that had required political reformation, where a president and council had been established in the late fifteenth and early sixteenth centuries. The council in the north had not prevented rebellion in 1536, known as 'the pilgrimage of grace', whilst little progress had been made in Wales until the appointment of Bishop Rowland Lee in the 1530s.[29] There was nothing self-evident about the English 'commonwealth' model.

Inverting Resistance Theory

The intellectual components which formed the basis of an Irish reformed protestant or Calvinist position on the failure to build the 'good life' in Ireland can be found in John Ponet's resistance treatise *A Short Treatise of Politike Power* (1556), and in Christopher Goodman's offering, *How Superior Powers Oght to be Obeyd* (1558), amongst other texts. These two treatises were originally written in order to advocate civil disobedience on the accession of Mary Tudor. Both set out a constitutionalist position, detailing the political rights of the community, and a set of conscience-based arguments in favour of active resistance against an ungodly prince. They also lamented the failure to maintain a godly order in England as established under Edward VI.[30]

Here, what tends to interest scholars is the constitutionalist position adopted by these writers, which chimes with the gradual development of a modern political sphere of various rights and liberties.[31] Both treatises adopt a mixed polity position, where sovereignty is shared throughout the community thus providing inferior magistrates, and in some cases the general populace, with the constitutional right to act against the ruler. How Goodman and Ponet speak of political relationships, however, entails not only a set of constitutional mechanisms, but a notion of grace and Christian friendship which links the polity together; and it is when these treatises are read in light of Irish policy discussion, where obedience under godly rule, as opposed to civil disobedience, was the main topic of concern, that a far wider redefinition of political relationships would appear to be in play.

In beginning with Ponet's treatise, two interconnected definitions of civil obedience can be identified. First, for Ponet, akin to the position adopted by Luther and Calvin, political authority is there to bridle the ungodly who by their nature seek out licentiousness.[32] Man might 'have reason, yet bicause through the fall of the furst man, his reason is wonderfully corrupt ... [man] is not hable by himself to rule himself, but must have a more excellent governour', the governor using 'politike power' and 'authoritie' to keep man in check.[33] But for Ponet, a notion of the 'freedom of a Christian', where man is liberated from sin, also has relevance beyond a strictly spiritual or religious arena.

Ponet follows Calvin's work where the spiritual and civil spheres are combined together in the Christian polity, the magistrate and the preacher acting together to bring the community to know God. In these terms, for Calvin, it is possible to build something of God's kingdom on earth; whilst, in contrast, for Luther, the spiritual and civil sphere are distinct, the civil sphere remaining corrupt where the Christian is simply mandated in most circumstances to obey higher powers and to look to the world to come.[34]In political communities where all 'love and feare God ... [and] in all places and countreyes wher Goddes worde hathe ben received and embraced ... all membres of the body sought the prosperitie and wealthe one of an other, for Goddes worde taught them so to doo'.[35] God's word and grace would reform and renew civil society.

It is this second position that Goodman's treatise expands upon. Goodman would spend around three years in Ireland as Lord Deputy Sidney's chaplain in the late 1560s, and his use of the term 'true obedience' would be echoed in Irish government correspondence during Sidney's first deputyship. Drawing on an emphasis placed on individual conscience, *Superior Powers* sets out a basic definition of 'true obedience', meaning obedience to God as the ultimate superior power. 'True obedience' manifests itself as civil disobedience in an ungodly context, with 'good conscience' giving each individual the ability to judge when to disobey. Goodman is more radical than Ponet, because in thinking more about a covenanted society he is naturally led to extend the discussion of individual conscience to encompass how each individual in society relates to higher powers (not simply inferior magistrates and chief citizens) thus mandating every private individual to rebel or obey depending on circumstance.

In particular, Goodman argues in the last third of his treatise that God's word will 'styrre up our hartes by ... examples, and prepare us with the grace of his holie Spirite to the like constancie and obedience'. What the stability and health of Edward VI's reign showed (in contrast to Mary's) is that 'if thou be a Ruler and covete to have the people obedient to thee in Gods freare' the people must be brought 'to truely know God by the playne and diligent preaching of his worde'.[36] That if the polity 'be well instructed [in the gospel] there is no custome so longe continued, no idlenesse so longe used, no supersticion so deeply rooted, which they will not glady ... for go at thy commandement'.[37] Again, it was God's word, through the action of God's grace, that would reform man and lead the polity to forgo bad customs, the very thing Irish government wished to achieve.

Underlying both treatises, then, is a wider redefinition of political relationships – although the more settled environment of Elizabethan England, and the set of constitutional arguments set out by both writers, would appear to have obscured such a position from view. Furthermore, if these treatises are read from a more theological perspective, two questions or problems arise concerning the potential construction of the 'good life', either in Ireland or in England. First, what exactly happens when God's word is not made available if political stability is dependent upon grace? This is especially problematic from a Calvinist perspective, where man's sinful condition means he will (in the absence of grace) seek out licentiousness and disorder. Secondly, how should we read the constitutionalist position in light of a grace based definition of civil obedience (or disobedience)? Here if discussion is extended to encompass early Elizabethan writing on the political community in England, indications of a potential breakdown in normative political relationships emerge.

In John Aylmer's *An Harborowe of Faithfull and Trewe Subjectes* (1559), like Goodman and Ponet, the functionality of political life relies on grace and conscience. In reference to the quintessential component of common law, trial by jury, it is explained how these '12 me[n]' make judgement 'upon their own co[n]science' and that this 'order as it was in it self at the first [being] without corruptio[n]: was marvellous conscionable and godly, and in my judgeme[n]t much better then the cyvill order'.[38] In considering, however, the problems that would arise if God's word were not to be preached, and the corruption of consciences not dealt with, Aylmer asks rhetorically 'wil [bad and ungodly consciences] not make this order (which was the best that could be) to be the wickedest that can be' – a thought that is not out of sync with Irish government's failure to introduce common law norms in Ireland.[39] In this manner, Aylmer's work can be viewed as a broader protestant re-reading of the nature of political relationships in the English mixed polity. The constitutionalist position, which is conducive to an active political life, is intertwined with ideas about grace and good conscience.[40] Again such a position was to find clarity and expression in Irish policy discussion; it is also to be found in Goodman's and Ponet's respective definitions of political or constitutional 'liberty'.

Here political or constitutional freedom sits on top of Christian liberty, where man is redeemed by grace and freed from sin – political liberty being the external expression of a godly order where all work to build God's kingdom. In discussing the position of inferior magistrates, Ponet argues that they are 'ordayned to see that kinges should not oppress the people'. They should 'defende and mayntene the libertie of the people' so rulers cannot rule according to 'their lustes'.[41] 'Liberty' is conceived partly in constitutional terms, where political authority is distributed throughout the community, but also in Christian terms, where the 'lust' or the unreformed desire of the ruler is at issue. This elision is more explicit in Ponet's final 'exhortation', where he argues that protestant England must rid itself of Mary Tudor's rule, where notions of 'tyranny'are both political and spiritual. The term is applied both to the Roman church, and to foreign government, which has resulted from Mary's marriage to Philip of Spain. Related to this, liberty means both self-government and the free worship of the true Christ.[42]

Similarly, Goodman shifts between both terms, calling for the 'libertie of Jesus Christe and our consciences', whereby the loss of the liberty 'assured by Gods worde' arises when a community refuses to participate in political life.[43] This leads to a number of observations important in the broader trajectory of this book. How is a notion of political liberty to be understood? For Martin van Gelderen, and more recently John Coffey, in the less primal environment of the Netherlands, or the cities of continental Europe, an emphasis on both individual conscience and a constitutionalist position came to be equated with a proto-modern call for individual liberty or freedom of conscience as a means of demarcating some room for protestants to worship freely. The right to act on the basis of conscience can be seen folding into and melding with a constitutionalist position and so quite a clear idea of individual rights and thus a taste of modernity emerges.[44]

Considered in light of 'Christian liberty', however, this suggests a very limited notion of freedom, where freedom from sin meant conformity of action not diversity of behaviour. This is something that resistance writers in England and the Netherlands confronted, arguing that too much 'liberty' provided in constitutionalist terms might actually encourage licentiousness because man retained the capacity to sin. More importantly, if a sense of negative or constitutional freedom did arise, where everyone's rights are guarded irrespective of confession, in what circumstances did a notion of political liberty detach itself from a Christian or godly model? After all, Christian freedom was only associated with those of good or proper faith and was entwined with the constitutionalist mechanisms detailed.

Interestingly, in Ireland, the language of liberty which dominated government correspondence was pejorative, where Elizabeth's Irish subjects, it was argued, sought the freedom to act on the basis of an unbridled will, the government of

Gaelic and Old English lords being labelled tyrannous in both political and religious terms.[45] In this respect, then, the narrative set out by Skinner in *Foundations*, where resistance writing is seen as contributing to the development of a more modern political sphere, where legal and constitutional form was given to various paths for political action, starts to appear more confused and contested; so too do the calls made by Elizabeth's protestant subjects for active participation in the mixed polity, if such rights are seen as being dependent on the clear presence of grace.

An Irish Preaching Ministry

Nevertheless, turning back to Ireland, it was such a position on God's word, grace and obedience that informed Irish government's emphasis on the establishment of a preaching ministry, since God's word and grace were the key elements of reform. In other words, whilst a properly ordered and structured civil sphere remained important, man had to be in receipt of grace in order to take advantage of the paths made available for his betterment. Government, however, was not to voice fully such rationale in open political debate until 1567, over a year into Lord Deputy Sidney's first term in office. In part, this reflects something about the nature of policy assumptions, where if all agreed on a set of fundamental ideas, there was no reason to critique the basis upon which certain policy decisions had been made.

For example, the operative assumptions behind attempts to introduce common law and shire government in the Irish provinces are not readily discussed in government correspondence. Scholars do, however, readily assume that the various structures of civil society were thought of as regulating conflict and as providing an example for men to follow. Akin to this, the grace-based relationships seen as linking the polity together also tended not to be scrutinized or openly discussed, because they were similarly uncontested. No one tended to explain exactly how God's word was thought to operate. Nevertheless, many scholars dismiss the evangelical motive, because it remains remote from a more present centred perspective.

Here a combination of forces would draw such underlying assumptions into open political discussion. In many ways, this is part of Ireland's importance with regard to a wider English and European discussion, where in Europe the external constitutional manifestations of those relationships came to be addressed instead, as denoted by the structure of the mixed polity. In many cases, the distribution of various political rights had a more immediate relevance when it came to arguing with a government not fully at one with your position or right to voice your view. However, because of the extent to which Ireland lacked a reformation church, and because of the level of perceived disorder, these underlying ideas would have to be openly stated.

Part of government's frustration stemmed from Elizabeth's reluctance to act as government wished and release the resources necessary for Irish church reform. Very much akin to the situation confronted by 'forward' protestants in

England, the queen was reticent in endorsing a reformative vision of society.[46] In July 1565 tentative signs of such tension can be identified in the drafting of Lord Deputy Sidney's instructions for government. The prospective lord deputy commented that he wanted 'learned pastors'; this, however, did not make it into the final draft, which simply required outward Erastian conformity. It was hoped that 'all good laws and ordinances' would be observed.[47] But Sidney remained determined and the church came first when he reflected on the implementation of such instructions a number of months later.

In April 1566 the lord deputy praised the main members of the Irish episcopacy for their diligence in preaching and 'also in the earnest calling on and looking to the other pastors and ministers within their provinces and diocese to do the like'. This was in order to pose a rhetorical question. He asked 'howbeit that for all this, it goeth slowly forward', pointing to the assumed rapidity of change God's word should have brought about.[48] The explanation given, however, pointed to the fact that farmers of appropriated benefices did not make sufficient stipends available for the employment of qualified clergy.[49] In short, God's word had not brought about change, because God's word had not been made available. This criticism was repeated by Michael Fitzwilliam, the surveyor of the queen's majesty's inheritance, in 1572, and he was more direct concerning Elizabeth's culpability since the benefices concerned were in her possession.[50] Such structural problems were critical in the government's inability to build a godly polity, because it stymied its ability to make available the word preached.

Similarly, attempts at altering episcopal leadership also reveal government's conception of the Irish church to be evangelical in character. The calls for the removal of Hugh Curwen, from the archbishopric of Dublin, whilst they addressed his suspected 'papistry', remained particularly concerned with his failure both to preach and to employ preachers.[51] In 1566 Christopher Gaffney was recommended for the bishopric of Ossory, because 'none of his country birth (that I know) are more meter than he', which alluded to the fact Gaffney was an Irish speaker.[52] At the same time Loftus had raised questions about his own suitability for the archbishopric of Armagh because it 'lieth among the Irish'; whilst James McCaghwell was recommended for the bishopric of Cashel because he was 'one of Irish birth'.[53] The archbishop of Canterbury and the bishop of Salisbury had both testified to McCaghwell's godliness.

There were certainly many expedient proposals and appointments, which included most notably Miler Magrath's succession to the see of Clogher, though he had initially sought the bishopric from the pope. Deputy Sidney also relied heavily on the diplomatic skills of the Gaelic Irish priest Terence Daniel in Ulster, though he was not known for his piousness; and Sidney had allowed himself to be received in Limerick by the suspect bishop Hugh Lacy dressed in full pontifical robes.[54] Here government was hindered by the structural and financial conditions it sought to solve.

However, pressure would continue to be exerted for church reform to be furthered by various members of Irish government; and it was as a consequence of a growing frustration with the *status quo* that various individuals would explain in detail their conception of godly reform. With such difficulties in mind, Sidney made a far bolder statement on church reform in 1576 on his reappointment as lord deputy (Sidney had left office in 1571). He outlined three 'heads' for reformation. The second and third addressed army finance and the provision of justice – two necessary components of Irish reform policy. But for the returning lord deputy the 'first [head] is the church now so spoiled, as well by ruin of the temples, as [by] the dissipation and embezzling of the patrimony', and he did not understand why government in England wished 'to begin the reformation of the politic part, and to neglect the religious'.[55] Religious reformation, then, should be government's principal concern in reforming the polity, well above 'the political' – a view very much akin to Calvin's position on the Christian polity.

There is an open note of exasperation here which is reflective of a failure to make any real progress in the 1560s. Sidney had attempted to use parliamentary statute to alter the *status quo* by forcing farmers of appropriated benefices to maintain church buildings and by establishing a university which would train preachers; but many of these bills were not passed. [56] Alongside this, in 1576 tension between a godly vision and practical reality only clarified. In a report by Bishop Hugh Brady, on the condition of the church in the diocese of Meath, the problem of appropriated benefices was raised as before, where there remained an insufficient number of qualified clergy, where 'no parson or vicar [was] resident' upon such benefices.

The lord deputy was more direct in his criticism of Elizabeth, who was the only one who possessed the legal authority to act with regard to appropriated benefices, arguing that if the problem was investigated it would most likely reveal that the benefices concerned were 'such as are of your possession'.[57] Elizabeth's continue refusal or failure to act certainly confirms, if not strengthens, assessments made by historians of England that the queen held to a conservative line in church policy. Read in the broader context of the question of civil obedience and a godly society, it may well indicate that Elizabeth held to a more Erasmian position, which put the restructuring of society first, or that she held a less inspired view that thought the *status quo* enough.[58]

No doubt in response, Sidney also felt the need to act more independently and he established a court of faculties, which gave Irish government (more specifically the judges appointed to the court by the deputy) the right to examine clerics' rights to their livings and to admit clerics to benefices that had devolved to the crown. Sidney even suggested Elizabeth 'write to the regent of Scotland [James Douglas, earl of Morton]', for men who could preach in Gaelic, 'where as I learn there are many of the reformed church that are of this language, that he would prefer to your highness'.[59] Jane Dawson's identification of a successful Gallicized Calvinism in Scotland indicates that this was far from a fanciful suggestion.[60]

Furthermore, this should inform our reading of the other sets of instructions, which were effectively programmatic statements on government's intentions.[61] Those issued by the crown to Lord Justice William Drury in 1578 restated the need for parish churches to be 're-edified' and for farmers of benefices to contribute the necessary funds for the upkeep of churches.[62] Similarly, the dissemination of God's word was put first in the 1574 articles for the Munster presidency drafted by John Perrot on his appointment as provincial president there. The new lord president looked to the 'setting forth of God's word ... [and] to the decayed churches [which needed] to be re-edified ... [where] good and meet ministers by ... their good example [would bring] the people ... to know their duty to God and perfect obedience to their prince'.[63]

Many of the letters that will be address in this book, which detail a godly view, directly connect to a continued attempt to draw government's attention in England to the unresolved structural problem of appropriated benefices. Again it was this situation that raised the question, with some urgency, over what Ireland's condition would be if God's word was not preached. And this is a motif that would be laboured in 1585 when Lord Deputy John Perrot issued instructions to Irish bishops and 'to every county' asking that farmers of appropriated benefices (and holders of benefices more generally) make sufficient provision for the repair of churches. It was further explained that laymen should be sequestered from such livings, and that 'parishioners' should be given 'instruction'.[64] A commission was even issued to laymen to enquire into the condition of the clergy in order to revive a flagging evangelical agenda.[65] On top of this, Perrot would return to the question of the establishment of a university which he pursued unsuccessfully. The revival of a scheme to found a university using the resources of St Patrick's cathedral garnered opposition from Adam Loftus, as archbishop of Dublin, thus stymieing any parliamentary bill.[66] Similarly, an attempt to pass legislation to strengthen an earlier free schools act met with clerical opposition. There seems to have been problems with the establishment and maintenance of schools (despite an act being passed in Sidney's 1569–70 parliament). Here it was proposed that the ratings of the diocesan contributions, which should have funded such schools, be revised.[67] There was also an effort to revive the forlorn attempt to produce an Irish translation of the New Testament, which was raised on the privy council in England.[68]

Potential Irish Radicalism

Remaining with the question of Irish church reform, whilst government's clear evangelism makes the subsequent emergence within government circles of an absolutist and statist position appear very much out of kilter with earlier intent, this disjuncture is more apparent when government's wider vision of the church is considered. There are indications that Irish government sought to put in place a fully reformed church model, which dispensed with the hierarchy of the medieval liturgy and episcopacy. At one level, the physical distance separating the person of the prince from the island may have suggested that in Ireland church reform could be pushed further than that allowed in England.[69] But such a view of the church should also be read within the context of government's broader programme for societal reform. For Calvin, liturgical reform was nearly as important as the preached word, since it brought man, contained still within his earthly body, as close to God as was possible whilst man remained on earth.[70] For Calvin the church, properly reformed, allowed man 'shut in the prison of his body' and who had 'not yet attained to the rank of angels ... though widely separate ... [to] draw near to [God]'.

In particular, a reformed church model mirrored the structure of the mixed polity and had a clear democratic tone because it emphasized the popular voice of the congregation and the guidance given by church elders not bishops.[71] Historians of England do recognize that such arguments had direct political implications and Peter Lake has raised the issue of a godly 'popularity'. Once again, however, scholars tend to pull back from fully engaging with the extent to which the nature of political relationships was redefined. This involved questions over the nature of man, interrelationships in the polity, and a godly mandate for all to act to build God's kingdom. Instead, scholars concentrate more on the form of government that was being advocated.[72] But in an Irish context, where the broader question of societal reform dominated, the suggestion does emerge that such godly equality denoted a wider reconception of political relationships, whilst government's subsequent absolutist turn jars quite strongly with this earlier democratic note. As before, Calvin's idea of the Christian polity emerges quite strongly.

An important figure is the resistance writer and Sidney's chaplain Christopher Goodman. The lord deputy had sought the cleric's appointment as archbishop of Dublin (in place of Curwen) in January 1567; and failing this he sought Goodman's appointment as dean of St Patrick's. Sidney wrote vociferously in support of Goodman, even writing in quite warm terms to his chaplain. Here there had actually been some attempt to persuade Goodman's fellow resistance writer, John Knox, to minister in Ireland. But Knox declined Goodman's request, because 'I more fear that your politic bishops within England should storm at our conjunction and so travail to dissever us, then I doubt that your request should suffer a repulse amongst us'.[73] And when in 1575 it seemed likely Sidney would return to Irish office, an approach was made to see if the deputy's former chaplain might return. For the radical cleric, however, without 'one year's proof to be made at Dublin of such as willingly would submit themselves to the order of that church reformed' he would not come back.[74]

Actually, Goodman had originally been appointed Sidney's chaplain in 1566 in the midst of the Vestiarian controversy, which arose in England when attempts were made to dispense with medieval liturgy and dress. Elizabeth had blocked such change, thus Sidney's clear support for Goodman was quite a marked statement of the deputy's own position and intent. The letters sent by Sidney and others to Cecil, and latterly Walsingham, also suggest that a wider reformed protestant grouping, in both kingdoms, saw each other working for the same godly agenda. Sidney told Cecil that it was 'needless' for him to outline Goodman's credentials, since Cecil knew of the cleric's 'unspotted life'. Many of the accounts of both Irish religious and political reform policy, which landed on Cecil's desk, were direct and urgent in both language and tone. Some letters sought assurance, stating that Cecil's 'zealous' action for 'God's glory' was known, and some ended by emphasizing something of a direct relationship with God. It was 'to God [that I] do leave you', where it was acknowledged that Cecil was governed 'with his holy spirit'.

Beside this, whilst the twelve Irish articles of religion published in Dublin on 20 January 1566 are known for their conservative content, we might note that they did not include the prohibition found in the thirty-nine English articles against a change in liturgy and church government. The articles also referred to the 'primitive' or biblical church model, usually used in England to suggest current ecclesiastical arrangements were non-scriptural and in need of further reform.[75]There was, then, a clear space for permissible radical reform. The other printed material available in Ireland actually fleshed out a potential reformed church liturgy for use amongst Irish speakers, again pointing to the popular element in more radical church reform. The publication in 1567 of *Foirm na nUrrnuidheadh* (book of common order) provided a translation of a book of common prayer written by the Scottish reformer John Knox. And the 1571 *Aibidil Gaoidheilge & Caiticiosma* provided a translation of the catechism from the 1559 book of common prayer, as well as prayers taken from Knox's book of common prayer and the twelve articles of religion first printed in Ireland in English.[76]

Here Elizabeth had also issued a series of clear prohibitions against any potential change in liturgy in Ireland. As before, the position of the queen is indicative of her known dislike of liturgical innovation, but it may also reflect her distance from the wider view of godly society such liturgical change expressed. For example, on Adam Loftus's appointment as archbishop of Dublin, she had sent instructions that he should be placed in his see 'by accomplishing of all directions and ceremonies as are usually to be done by any grant to proceed from us'.[77] She seems to have assumed that a reformed liturgy might be used. And in instructions to her deputy in May 1568, she explained again that he should not allow the clergy to deviate from the liturgy and order as established by law.[78]

A comment no doubt on Sidney's relationship with Goodman and the lord deputy's muted support for a fully reformed church model, the instruction may also have been a direct reference to Loftus's behaviour when Sidney had been absent in England in 1568. The archbishop had moved the communion table in St Patrick's cathedral into the centre of the cathedral, which in liturgical terms expressed the spiritual equality favoured by the church in Geneva. Startlingly, in what was supposedly a defence of his actions, Loftus demonstrated an open willingness to reinterpret the rubrics of the Book of Common Prayer. Not only was such action taken for convenience sake, since it was Easter and the cathedral was crowded, the communion table was 'placed in the body of the church, under the pulpit (as it is allowed of, by the book of common prayer)'. This quickly folded into a broader argument for the legality of his radicalism. He pointed out that, in line with the Book of Common Prayer, 'we had not the curious singing [sic] which at other times is used', whilst it was noted that Lady Sidney had taken communion indicating official endorsement of such change.[79]

This makes Loftus's relationship with Thomas Cartwright a little more noteworthy. Cartwright as Lady Margaret Professor of Divinity in Cambridge would in 1570 outline the rudiments of an English Presbyterianism in a lecture on Acts. Not only did Cartwright serve as his chaplain, Loftus suggested Cartwright be appointed archbishop of Armagh; and in October 1570, when Cartwright was under attack, Loftus defended the cleric, arguing 'that for the church of Christ's sake ... continue [your favour] towards him'.[80] In 1577, then, after Cartwright's 1575 *Second Replie* to the English parliament and *The Rest of the Second Replie* in 1577, where demands were made for the construction of a full Presbyterian church in England, Loftus had to defend himself from quite serious suspicions. Loftus was concerned that the queen 'hath been informed that I am a puritan and a favourer of Mr Cartwright and his doctrine'. He told Walsingham he was 'utterly ignorant' of such doctrine.[81]

Interestingly, Cartwright himself equated a fully reformed church with the stability and health of the wider commonwealth or mixed polity, arguing that 'the breaches of the commonwealth / have proceeded from the hurtes of the churche / and the wants of the one / from the lackes of the other. Neyther is it to be hoped for that the commonwealth shall flourishe / until the church be reformed'.[82] Grace, spiritual equality and full participation in political life were mutually conditioned. The radicalism of Cartwright's views are well attested to in English historiography, since their latent democratic qualities threaten the established order.[83] This radicalism came from a certain blending of positions concerning grace and constitutionalism found in resistance theory, as well as paralleling aspects of a discussion we will go on to trace in Ireland – the Irish context again pointing to the all-encompassing nature of this position.

Robert Weston and an Irish Definition of 'Civil Obedience'

It was, then, the continued failure to make available God's word and further church reform in general, alongside the continued question of Irish civil disorder, which eventually compelled Irish reformed protestants or Calvinists to express openly a link between God's word, the operation of grace and the island's potential long-term reform. It may even be the case that conditions in Ireland confirmed or encouraged government to think in these terms, where civil disorder sat alongside an ever growing awareness that God's word had not been made available. An initial muted expression of such a position came from the Adam Loftus in June 1566, who was at the time archbishop of Armagh. Here it was Elizabeth's continued refusal to remove Curwen from his position in Dublin, and a more general failure to answer Sidney's letters concerning appropriated benefices, which prompted Loftus to explain government's view and so to begin to outline a set of usually unspoken assumptions or presuppositions. He told Cecil he knew:

> right well that the queen's highness shall never have just obedience unless the cause of the gospel be first promoted and alas how then can that be except such sit in the chief place ecclesiastical as are of approved zeal and knowledge in god his holy law.[84]

Loftus drew a distinction between the type of obedience that would arise from the Gospel, namely 'just obedience', and the more contingent level of obedience government currently dealt with. In a second letter from the archbishop, another aspect of protestant resistance theory emerged – that of man's or the protestant community's covenant with God, which now provided government with the duty and responsibility to make available the Gospel in Ireland ensuring obedience to God and more generally political stability. Loftus asks:

> my good lords, remember also that you shall answer before the tribunal seat of Jesus Christ, if this land perish for want of faithful and learned teachers; for the keys of this realm are committed to you.[85]

But the most theologically articulate member of Irish government in the late 1560s was the new Irish chancellor Robert Weston. Weston had been appointed chancellor in 1567 and had served as part of the household of the bishop of Exeter Miles Coverdale, which had brought him in contact with a wider English protestant network.[86] Here what precipitated Weston to write was not only frustration at a failure to further religious reformation, but a concurrent disintegration in already unstable political conditions. In short, on Sidney's departure for England to finalize his Irish parliamentary programme, Ulster went into rebellion. The death of the arch traitor Shane O'Neill had provided an important opportunity to further reform in the province. Against Sidney's advice, official recognition had been given to Hugh O'Neill, who was the official claimant to the barony of Dungannon. This revealed the inadequacy of a strict application of an English model of primogeniture, as the real wielder of power there, Turlough Luineach O'Neill, rebelled in response. Alongside this, the first Desmond rebellion began in the absence of the earl of Desmond and his brother, both of whom had been called over to England, again in disregard of Sidney's assessment of the situation. James Fitzmaurice, a first cousin of Desmond, took his opportunity to defend Fitzgerald interests and undermine efforts to end coyne and livery. Such efforts threatened his position as a feudal retainer.[87] Without the need to enforce a mixture of feudal dues (which were taken in kind) the need for feudal retainers would be significantly diminished.

The explanation this elicited from Weston did not deal with the various political shortcomings of such a shift in policy – although Irish historians naturally tend to focus on such issues. Instead, the more fundamental point for the Irish chancellor was the fact that Ireland lacked knowledge of God, where in the perceived absence of God's grace, political life could only descend into corruption and disorder. The Irish were 'all universally blind through corruption of nature ... void of all knowledge of God ... with disobedience to God and their prince'. He explained that 'the blind people [were] led by ... blind guides and ... of nature given to sin'.[88] Man's condition, in the absence of God, led to civil disorder.

But Weston did not simply condemn the Irish on the basis of original sin, as the interpretative positions of Canny and Bradshaw would suggest. Instead, Weston made it clear that God's word (through grace) was the primary agent of reform. Elizabeth should 'take pity of the miserable state of this her church of Ireland', because if the Irish were 'taught Christ, and the will of God ... [in his] opinion it would work a willing and a more perfect obedience in all subjects, than any fear of the sword or punishment can do', and he stressed the need for conscience-based reform. He called for 'the reforming of their [the Irish] conscience unto the obedience of God and her majesty'.[89] In a second letter, Weston not only spoke of 'perfect obedience', but 'true obedience' akin to Goodman and Ponet. He hoped, or prayed, that 'the true knowledge of him [God] and his word may come and grow among this your poor and rude people whereby they may be framed not only to civility but their heart to the true obedience of God's will'.[90] In effect, what starts to emerge is the sheer extent to which a protestant emphasis on the preached word entailed a new reformative vision of society.

Weston's longest and most detailed statement, however, came in the midst of the failure of important parts of Sidney's parliamentary programme to gain traction, when the possibilities for furthering religious reformation under Sidney's first deputyship finally appeared hopeless. Part of the deputy's 1569–70 parliamentary programme addressed government finances and a broader proposal for tenurial reform and the end of bastard feudal practices.[91] The Commons was asked to agree to a proposed composition of various customary exactions into annual fixed payments.[92] But there were also a series of proposed statutes addressing religious reform: an 'act erecting free schools in every shire' and a bill for the re-edifying of churches, both of which were meant to provide for the dissemination of God's word. A new university bill would emerge at a later date, which it was hoped would allow for the training of an indigenous preaching ministry; so too would a bill to 'call church men to their cures'.[93]

Problems arose because of the mismanagement of negotiations, which meant that the Dublin community's representatives obstructed Sidney's general legislative programme and refused to suspend Poynings' act.[94] This required all legislation to have the prior consent of the crown in England thus limiting the progress of bills and the scope for negotiation. The Commons was concerned that any short fall resulting from new financial arrangements would end up being met by the Pale gentry (possibly through purveyance or cess - an *ad hoc* customary charge paid by the Pale community for the upkeep of the lord deputy's household). Additionally, questions were raised over the intentions behind the broader programme of reform with the arrival in Ireland of Sir Peter Carew. He had been allowed over the preceding year to pursue claims to land that the Old English *de facto* possessed. This also involved land held by the Butlers; and as a result Sir Edmund Bulter, the earl of Ormond's brother, first sided with the Dublin community, and then subsequently joined the Fitzgeralds in revolt along with his brother Edward, further exemplifying the inadequacies of a system of English land tenure and law (in the absence of grace).[95]

Here Weston reported on the progress of government's legislative programme, and he made note of various successes. Again the bills addressing directly political or civil matters have tended to draw the attention of modern scholars.[96] But crucially for the chancellor, religious reform legislation remained the most important part of the parliamentary programme. The 'reformation of Ireland must come out of them [the schools bill and the bill for re-edifying parish churches] unless good government may be without god and humanity'.[97] By 1570 when still insufficient progress had been made in terms of furthering religious reform legislation, where the university bill and the non-residency legislation had also failed, the Irish chancellor became more expansive in his comments and he set out more of the detail of the position set out by Goodman and Ponet.

First, Weston presented rebellion in Ireland as a direct consequence of the absence of God's grace. God meant 'to school us by the experience and feeling of his mercies in both realms to depend wholly of his godly wisdom and providence, and to establish our hearts in him only, and obedience of his word'.[98] The chancellor elaborated further by arguing that it was only God's word that would 'teach or move them [the Irish] to their dutiful obedience'; and he followed through with the implication, as before, that in the absence of evangelism the Irish would 'continue so still in their great disobedience' where 'only the fear of the sword' would be able to effect a basic external obedience.[99] It was here that he turned to the motif grace, looking to the 'knowledge of god grounded and in their hearts [that] would breed in them good liking and love of honesty, civility, and true obedience'.[100] The same argument was made the next year by Loftus, who pointed to 'the great want of godly preachers in this realm, for lack of whom the people continue in ignorance of God, and in disobedience'. Again political disorder and a frustrated evangelism precipitated an open expression of a protestant definition of civil order, with God's word (and grace) emerging as the primary agent of reform.[101]

Such a view was to emerge at different points throughout the next decade as government continued to face both civil disorder and a failure to evangelize. In

1576 Lord Deputy Sidney restated such a position when his reform programme still faced difficulties. Sidney explained how 'by good preaching and doctrine the people are drawn first to know their duty to god, and next their obedience to their prince, and civil order'.[102] Similarly, William Piers, an English captain in Ulster, in 1571, argued that the 'lively word of god ... would be a great help to the reducing of this country to civility'.[103] Even William Fitzwilliam, whilst serving as deputy in the period between Sidney's two appointments as governor, reflected on the 'pitiful and woeful state' of English Ireland which he thought arose from 'want of ... preaching of God and his word to them'.[104]

Alongside this, Edward Waterhouse reprised aspects of resistance theory as applied in the Irish case in a eulogy written on the death of the first earl of Essex in Ireland. He argued that government's first duty was to God and a godly ideal, not the prince and more politic causes. Waterhouse had been Sidney's private secretary, and was latterly involved in an attempted Ulster plantation under Walter Devereux. In the eulogy he had Essex lament the fact that England had forsaken God in ignoring its duty to bring the island of Ireland to know the Gospel.[105] An anonymous treatise written in 1579 even emphasized how God's grace was the 'efficient cause' that would alter civil conditions for the good; and when rebellion resurfaced in 1580, this position was voiced with greater urgency and strength, partly because revolt now began to encompass the Old English gentry community.[106] For Marmaduke Middleton, the bishop of Waterford and Lismore, writing of growing disorder in the city of Waterford,

> 'the word of God is the thing [that] teacheth all duty and obedience and is the restraint of man's wicked affections, of the want thereof occasioned such blindness, that every man, yieldeth to his own lust which is prone and ready to all disobedience and hidden in them'.[107]

This extended into a broader observation that rebellion arose because of 'the want of the knowledge and fear of God, which cannot be but where his word is planted, which cannot be planted but where there is doctrine and discipline'.[108] In 1585 a new archbishop of Armagh, John Long, would ask whether it was 'possible to look for civil peace where there is no looking for peace in conscience' because 'subjects have souls as well as bodies' making it 'grievous ... to have them [the Irish] governed in body and neglected in soul'.[109]

The Stanihursts and Some Ambiguities Concerning God's Grace

As a final comment in this chapter, we should note, however, that some ambiguity remained concerning a concept of 'grace', which is important when the later fracturing of relationships between the Old English community and reformed protestants in Ireland is considered. An ambiguity between a reformed protestant and Christian humanist conception of the presence of grace in political life allowed a level of unity to be maintained between a reformed protestant administration and the Old English community. After all, Christian humanists clearly did not discount the operation and prime importance of God's grace, they just saw it as operating in a different way. For Erasmus man's intellect searched for God and was met and perfected by grace. In contrast, for Calvin grace acted on conscience and man could not do anything in order to further his own redemption and reform.[110]

This blurred consensus would dissipate as pressure built over the next decade, because as Irish reformed protestants stressed their definition of grace, and its operation, any earlier suggestion of unity of purpose in religious and political reform could not be sustained. Nevertheless, at this stage, the Stanihurst family, both James Stanihurst, as speaker in the Irish Commons, and his more famous son Richard, were broadly supportive of Sidney's parliamentary programme – though they were of a more humanist bent and were certainly not protestant. So too was Edmund Campion, who would later have to flee Dublin, and would, along with Richard Stanihurst, become a leading exponent of an Irish and English counter-reform view. The younger Stanihurst had originally become involved with Campion during his studies at Oxford.

First, our fullest account of the 1569–70 parliament is set out in Campion's *Historie of Ireland*. Here James Stanihurst, in his closing oration to the Irish Commons, is heard describing how schools would 'breed in the rudest of our people resolute English hearts', elaborating that 'our realm is at this day an half deal more civil than it was ... babes from their cradles should be inured under learned school masters, with a pure English tongue, habit, fashion, discipline'.[111] In line with a broadly humanist bent, the effectiveness of civil education in furthering political reform is extolled, and Campion easily makes Sidney speak as though he too shared Speaker Stanihurst's position. The lord deputy's closing remarks call for the 'quickening of this godly statute' in reference to the university bill which had failed to pass. Sidney argues that the MPs should 'show yourselves forward and frank in advancing the honour, wealth, ease and credit of your countries'.[112] The ambiguity in positions is more apparent in the preamble to the schools act, where a connection is drawn between not only knowledge of 'law', but knowledge of 'holy scriptures', and obedience 'to ... princes and rulers'. In discussing how this would operate, the preamble points to civil education, 'the lack of good bringing up [of] the youth of this realm earlier in public and private schools'.[113]

In this regard, the Irish parliament did have some modicum of success, where alongside the 'act for taking away captainships' (which sought to undermine the wider noble clientage networks in Ireland) and the act of attainder of Shane O'Neill (which strengthened the crown's claims in Ulster), 'an act for the erection of free schools' was eventually passed. But Sidney's wider programme of tenurial reform, which would have seen feudal dues commuted into fixed rents, remained stymied. So too did the rest of the deputy's religious reform legislation;

and without the wider reform of the church it is hard to see how Irish government could meet the administrative task which the 'erection of free schools' entailed.[114] It was the overall failure of parliament, and pressure arising from now widespread rebellion, that caused Henry Sidney to leave Ireland in 1571 to be replaced by Lord Deputy Fitzwilliam until Sidney's return at the end of 1575.

Secondly, evidence of the initial ease with which an earlier commonwealth or humanist position could merge with a reformed protestant or Calvinist concept of grace is displayed in Richard Stanihurst's contribution to the *Chronicle of Ireland*, which formed part of the first edition of Holinshed's *Chronicles* and drew on Campion's *Historie of Ireland*. Stanihurst provided a 'Description of Ireland' and he continued Campion's narrative with an account of Irish government under Henry VIII's reign, where in the *Chronicle of Ireland* as a whole the Dublin or Pale community is presented as acting on the basis of an uncontested notion of the common good or 'weale publicke'.[115] In the 'Description' the Old English community is an exemplar of English civility and goodly political action, and the untimely death of Lord Trimlestowne is lamented, because he died 'when the weale publike had most need of his life'.[116] Similarly, Sir Christopher Barnwall is described as a 'laterne and light as well of his house, as of that part of Ireland', where his knowledge of common law is extolled alongside his godly disposition which means he managed all 'affaires with the safetie of conscience, as true as steele'.[117]

But for Stanihurst civility is not only dependent on the Old English community's continued adherence to English custom and good education, but also upon the action of grace. Irish preachers 'who reprove not in their sermons the peevishnesse' of the native Irish leave open the possibility that the island, and the Old English by implication, will degenerate and become uncivil, because they will not recognize that Irish customs can corrupt civil manners. He immediately asks that 'God with the beams of his grace clarifie the eies of that rude people, that at length they maie see their miserable estate'.[118] From this perspective, the emphasis within Old English circles on education, making available God's word and the necessity of grace does suggest some degree of unity of view with English protestants. This motif connects directly with Campion's account of Ireland's earlier history, which formed the basis of the *Chronicle of Ireland* before Henry VIII's reign and which Holinshed edited and embellished. Addressing the 'first instruction of Ireland in the christian faith and religion', the *Chronicle* notes how the early Irish church through 'learning and virtuous conversation by the speciall grace and favour of God established the faith in that rude nation'.[119]

Most importantly, for Stanihurst this combination of grace and education provides the Old English community with a right to a voice in government. In Campion's part of the *Chronicle* we find lists of the various parliaments called, which points to their crucial role in good government. In particular 'diverse parlements upon prorogations were holden in time that this earle of Ormond was governor' in 1420 and 1421, 'in which parlement it was ordained that certeine persons should be sent to the king, to sue that a reformation might be had in matters touching the state of the land'.[120]Again continuing on from the preceding narrative, in Stanihurt's account of Henry VIII's reign, of most significance is the 1539 act of attainder of the earl of Kildare, after the rebellion of Silken Thomas, and an act 'authorising the king, his heyres and successours to be supreme head of the Church of Irelande', where the community proved its loyalty and subsequently passed in 1540–1 the act of kingly title.[121] As the difference in emphasis emerged between an Old English commonwealth model, with a focus on intellect and grace, and a godly concern with grace and conscience, the community's right to a voice in government and the validity of an Irish mixed polity model, from a reform protestant/Calvinist perspective, would be undermined.

Connected to this, in the late 1570s an earlier humanist or commonwealth position on the efficacy of law and civil education did reassert itself within reformed protestant circles. William Gerrard, a new Irish chancellor, who had served with Sidney in the presidency of Wales, re-engaged with the commonwealth position. He helped destabilize the latter half of Sidney's second deputyship because he asked a very blunt question. Had English law actually been properly established, and if not could it really be suggested that an English model of reform on its own was ineffective? For Gerrard 'although they say the justices yearly have travelled circuits, yet in the county of Meath no crier to attend, no show of sheriff'.[122] He even questioned the basic implementation of crown authority, asking rhetorically 'if ten years past the governor had put a determination to subject the whole Irishry to the sword ... Ireland I suppose would be in other terms'.[123]

In a fuller discourse the Irish chancellor drew on the historical analysis of earlier commonwealth treatises, like that of Finglas's *Breviate*. For Gerrard 'records sufficiently testify that for 130 years or near about the land rested well governed under English justice', and it was 'when they [the English in Ireland] fell to be Irish and embraced the Irish orders, customs and laws ... that the decay witnessed ... first arose'.[124] Degeneracy and disobedience had taken place, not because of the nature of man (though that doubtless did not help); it was because English law and custom had stopped being properly implemented meaning the original commonwealth analysis of the Irish problem remained valid. What we see here, I think, is that ultimate tension in the reformed protestant position, where something of man's intellect has to remain intact thus leaving some ambiguity over whether civil society can somehow function in a fallen world without the ruler and the people being in direct receipt of grace. As Richard Mallette noted, the voluntaristic language of English protestant confessions of faith suggests, when man confesses his sins or professes his faith, that he can somehow contribute to his own reform, because language by its very nature expresses some sense of action.[125] This sits in tension with the theology of grace, which lies below such expressions of Christian belief; and within Irish government correspondence, the dichotomy between a coercive and a grace-based civil obedience would remain dominant.

2 THE FAILURE OF REFORMED PROTESTANT PLANS

In Irish historiography Lord Deputy Arthur Grey's uncompromising and violent response to counter-reformation inspired rebellion in Munster and in the Pale in 1580–1 is readily rehearsed. After the return from continental exile of James Fitzmaurice, who had departed Ireland after the failure of the first Desmond rebellion, the province of Munster once again rose in revolt. This quickly came to encompass part of the Pale with the abortive risings of William Nugent and Viscount Baltinglass. Ominously Fitzmaurice was accompanied by the papal legate Dr Nicholas Sanders and a combined force of Spanish and papal soldiers who landed in Smerwick, in county Kerry, in July 1579. Fitzmaurice was killed within a month of the rebellion, whilst the earl of Desmond was summarily executed in 1583 after his chance capture.[1] That, alongside the events in Ireland, a clear hardening of attitudes and policy also took place in England is well established. Such a position, however, sits uncomfortably beside the more evangelical Protestantism identified, where government throughout the 1560s and 70s remained intent on providing for the dissemination of God's word and so the operation of God's grace; and as before, this points to a need to re-examine the direct link drawn by some Irish historians between a protestant emphasis on original sin and coercive practice in Ireland.[2]

This chapter asks, then, how protestant evangelical attitudes relate to the emergence of a more coercive position. In broad terms, it examines how protestants deployed the various vocabularies of 'obedience', 'commonwealth', 'conscience' and 'grace' in an attempt to comprehend and thereby solve the problem of perpetual Irish civil disorder. Of importance here are three observations. First, the godly model emerges as severely limited. Those involved in government simply continued to restate a definition of short-term civil obedience based upon the use of external coercive threats, or a definition of a more long-term civil obedience based upon internal conscience-based reform. This informed a wider failure to accommodate diversity or divergent political behaviour, because many involved in government could only conceive of normalized political relationships in terms of fidelity and godly friendship, which severely curtailed the possibilities for meaningful negotiation; this being further conditioned by a failure to make available God's word.

Secondly, by 1580, an attempt would also be made to distinguish between two types of civil disobedience. One standard trope had been the assessment of Irish consciences as, in general, unreformed. But a growing counter-reformation threat indicated that there was a second type of civil disobedience, whereby consciences were informed by a set of different (catholic) beliefs, which led to more specific and intended acts of civil disobedience. This became categorized as 'papistry' and in acting thus government moved to externally test consciences as opposed to reforming them. The fact that the problem of 'papistry' tended to be associated with the previously obedient and 'civil' Old English community also had quite significant implications, because a notion of an English mixed polity, based upon the gentry community, now became openly acknowledged as inoperative.

Thirdly, this allows us to examine further the set of assumptions which lay below Collinson's notion of the English 'monarchical republic', which we might term a godly mixed polity. In effect, continued Irish civil disorder led individuals to speak about, explain and describe the breakdown in political relationships, where notions of lordship and a local self-governing gentry republic became highly contested; and this sat alongside the clear absence of godly reform. Here the various implications of a godly idea of 'true obedience' came to be detailed, where unreformed conscience, the question of grace and a lack of fidelity invalidated the bonds of friendship which should have held the community together. Read beside a more muted English discussion, Irish government correspondence provides a detailed commentary on the perceived nature of relationships in a godly and non-godly polity.

An Irish View of 'Civil Obedience' Restated

In general the various terminologies deployed for around a decade from 1571 to 1581 remained strained by attempts to contain the Irish problem within a godly model and so within godly vocabulary. A series of variants and a shifting of tone and meaning, within quite a rigid framework, can be traced. On Lord Deputy Sidney's departure from office in 1571 there were a series of restatements (in some shape or form) of the position so articulately voiced by Weston. Nicholas White, the Old English seneschal of Wexford (who would later gain more prominence as master of the rolls) made a direct connection between the failure of English law to operate properly in Ireland and the absence of religious reformation, very much in line with Aylmer's comment in *An Harborowe of Faithfull and Trewe Subjectes* concerning common law and the necessity of good conscience. 'For I note, by experience, that [the] correction of justice shall sooner consume away this people, than alter their manner of life, until their minds be corrected with the knowledge of God's word, whereof they are all ignorant'.[3]

This comment immediately followed an account of disorderly legal proceedings in Wexford. The town's people could not restrain themselves when faced with the due process of law, after the earl of Ormond delivered a notorious galloglass to White for trial. The galloglass had, in the midst of rebellion, spoiled a large part of Wexford. The people, in fury, sought to 'pluck me [White] from the bench'. They sought to pull the galloglass 'in pieces' because of what he had done. In other words, in the absence of God's word, civil government and the commonwealth became inoperative.[4] White's latter *volte face*, where he would become the spokesman for the Pale community against the administration, does suggest, however, that his position may have had more of an Erasmian quality to it, very much akin to James or Richard Stanihurst.[5]

Connected to this, Nicholas White also forwarded to Secretary Cecil a detailed and expansive treatise on reform, penned by his cousin Rowland White, which he (Nicholas) endorsed in a separate letter. Again aspects of a godly vocabulary emerge. Rowland White in a preface to the larger treatise draws a distinction between the duty that a subject must 'not only discharged in outward obedience', but his duty 'faithfully [to] fulfill [...] to his uttermost power ... the open setting forth of God's glory, the honour and wealth of his prince, and the common profit of the people'. The particularly godly dimension to such thinking is made clearer when the lack of Irish civility is addressed. The 'Irishry' (as opposed to the Old English) cannot be reformed, 'neither [by] the correction of one fearing another ... nor yet [by] the subjection of some procuring the rest to obedience', because they seek out 'the liberty of their uncertain civilities'; and in answering why this was the case White described how the 'Irishry' are 'so far from the fear and knowledge of God'.[6] Their wilfulness meant they sought unbridled licence which was a consequence or condition of sin.

In this manner, the treatise contrasts 'subjection' with 'liberty', where 'liberty' is undesired and equated with the unreformed will, whilst 'subjection' to God and her majesty's will is what is actually sought, thus recalling Goodman's and Ponet's conception of Christian and non-Christian freedom. The treatise argues that the foundation of civil society is 'the hearts of the people', whereby internal reform would turn 'disobedience to perfect subjection ... uncertainties to assurance, and in some vice to virtue, finally perfecting such a godly concord in the said subject toward her majesty' and so 'god's glory shall be magnified by the same'. Also akin to other godly thinkers, within the main body of the treatise, it is the action of God's word and grace on conscience that is the critical agent in bringing about such change. The 'lively word of God ... alters the conscience and also turns by grace the inward affections of all men from evil to good'.[7]

However, an ambiguity in the position taken does remain present. There are many references to 'godly reformation' and 'godly proceedings', which could very easily be read as 'goodly', suggesting Rowland White is responding to a particular 'godly' turn in the language of discussions within government circles but may not be fully committed to it.[8] The fuller detail of White's treatise departs from the covering letter by engaging with the far broader detail of commonwealth thought. He emphasizes the power of statute to change conditions in society, the operative force of law, and the benefits of commerce and industry. Akin to the Stanihursts, the ambiguity between an Erasmian and godly position emerges. The treatise and prefacing letter may be indicative of an attempt to accommodate a stricter godly position within a broader Erasmian or commonwealth view.

Thus it is striking that the more optimistic sentiment of an earlier commonwealth position is absent from other restatements and variants; though similar to the observations made by Nicholas and Rowland White, it was the continuing problem of Irish civil disorder that led other protestants involved in Ireland to address and discuss the nature of man and the condition of civil society. Here Edmund Tremayne's 'Causes Why Ireland Is Not Reformed', written at the same time as Rowland White's more lengthy view on Irish reform, presents a picture of complete dysfunction in the kingdom. Tremayne's clearer reformed protestant credentials seem to have left him with little faith in man's ability to self-fashion through his own free will. Tremayne had gone into continental exile on Mary's accession and had continued to conspire against the regime until Elizabeth ascended the throne.[9] The treatise opens with the statement that 'religion hath no place, men have no fear nor love of god', and this moves into an immediate comment on the moral condition of society, where sexual infidelity is rife 'without grudge of conscience'. The subsequent sections detail, similar to Nicholas White, the failure of the processes of English law, where 'partiality must needs be great, where judges and jurors be ... only of one shire in effect'. When turning to the ubiquitous problem of coyne and livery, it is explained that 'their unwillingness to reformation is comparable to their worst faults'.[10] Tremayne's argument is implicit and structural, but the point is well made, that sitting on top of Ireland's lack of knowledge of God and unreformed conscience is the wider dysfunctional and disorderly condition of Irish society.

In another class of documents, the reports sent from Ireland by provincial governors and administrators, it was the everyday difficulties of government, along with revolt in the provinces, which led provincial officials to address the various underlying assumptions concerning political fidelity and godly conscience. In particular, it was a breakdown in trust that drove various individuals to think about the nature of those relationships. Nicholas Malby, the president of Connacht from 1576 to 1584, deployed the same narrative model in a series of letters (sent from 1577 to around 1582) in which the queen's request for 'fair' dealing with lordly individuals was set beside their 'faithless' and 'loose' behaviour which always required an eventual reversion to force as Malby sought to stabilize the situation.[11] In others, any attempt at negotiation and accommodation, which would have followed earlier commonwealth sentiment, was shown to be inoperative because of an absence of fidelity. More importantly, it was the absence of an effective religious reform agenda that meant such conditions would remain unaltered.

Malby had been appointed to office under Lord Deputy Sidney and he was associated with the attempts made by both Thomas Smith and the first earl of Essex to colonize Ulster. He wrote concerning continued disorder, which specifically involved the sons of the earl of Clanrickard, who were members of the Gaelicized Old English family, the Clanrickard Burkes. Their rebellious activity would later merge with the second Desmond rebellion as the Desmond Fitzgeralds and their Gaelic associates rose in revolt. And in 1579 a counter-reformation outlook would combine with the resistance previously shown both towards government's attempts to end bastard feudal practices and its attempts to undermine the norms of Gaelic lordship and its clientage networks.[12]

In a report in 1577, it was acknowledged that 'her majesty's disposition [was] to bring this people to obedience by fair and courteous usage'.[13] But when writing of the Clanrickard Burkes, Malby was reluctant to follow such a course because he had 'some experience of their faithless former doings'.[14] They were presented as dissemblers who could not be trusted. Malby even suggested that if he had not 'experience[d] ... the natures and conditions of this country people, truly their simple and earnest letters might very well have entrapped me'.[15] This was because there was 'no willingness in them' to be reformed as they were 'hard hearted'.[16] In a later letter it was explained that after going into battle and taking many of 'the heads' of Clanrickard's men, Malby had sent for the earl, who on many occasions had stressed that he had not encouraged the rebellion of his sons and followers. Clanrickard's 'guilty conscience [however] made him refuse'.[17] Any earlier hope that 'god had carried their false hearts to some goodness' was now obviously misplaced; and this account of unfaithfulness was extended to include those Gaelic lords who made up part of the factional power of the Burkes.[18] O'Connor Sligo could 'not be wrought to be such a subject as he ought to be neither by good and friendly advices ... or gentle dealing ..., but what obedience he sheweth or useth is only for that he can do no other'.[19]

Read within this context the other vocabulary of Malby's letters, where he talks of the lords' 'tyrannous oppressions', takes on a wider spiritual dimension reflecting both the political and spiritual tyranny which protestant resistance writers railed against.[20] This is something Rory Rapple has observed, arguing that for military men 'blurred distinctions arose between the idea of defending the homeland and freedom against both temporal and spiritual tyranny'.[21] Such terms become littered throughout government correspondence well into the 1590s, being deployed in Sidney's memoir of service and in the second edition of Holinshed's *Chronicle of Ireland*. Interestingly, the godly dimension to Malby's position was most directly expressed by Barnaby Googe, who praised Malby's 'good government' in Connacht, where 'the people ... live in as good order as may be'. Such praise was conditioned by the observation that 'their blindness or rather senselessness in religion' meant no actual qualitative improvement in civil conditions could really be countenanced.[22] Googe's view of Ireland's condition, like the wider position taken by Irish government, was informed by the acknowledged absence of a reformation church. Googe was a client of Burghley's with a bent for poetry who served as provost marshal of Connacht in the early 1580s.[23]

Alongside this, the use of the language of 'commonwealth' thought is equally indicative of the difficulties inherent in a godly outlook in the absence of religious reform. Here the letters of Edward Fitton express a certain inability to see any aspect of civil society or the 'commonwealth' as healthy, though Fitton does flip between different positions. Fitton was Malby's predecessor, serving as president of Connacht from 1569 to 1572, and then vice treasurer of Ireland. His protestant credentials are also quite strong. Fitton had translated Luther's commentary on Ecclesiastes whilst president of Connacht.[24] He would even seek some reassurance in a notion of providence (something we will return to in the last section of this chapter). At different points Fitton reprises received commonwealth values, arguing for power to 'bridle them [the Irish]', but also the necessity of justice that will 'comfort them'. He also asked for more financial provision for the presidency in terms of a 'house' or building because 'there might grow concourse and familiarity between us and the people' (no doubt referring to the necessity of having a physical space where orderly legal proceedings could be conducted).[25] However, at other points the inverse assessment is detailed, where despite the fact English legal procedure had been made available 'no one man resorted to us'.[26]

With regard to the 'Irishry', Fitton explained how seeing 'the prince's force slack and understand[ing] her majesty and her ministers bent rather to wink at faults, then to reform them, they then are brag to do what they lust'.[27] As before, the uncontrolled and unreformed 'will', where man lusts after unbridled licence, is what undermines the processes of civil society. This sits beside a more expansive elaboration of commonwealth thought, where he stated (rhetorically) that 'I may after the common manner of Ireland say it is quiet, because we hear of no professed rebellion against the state', but if the 'universal oppression of the mean sort', 'murders, robberies and burning make an ill common weal', where there is violence, a refusal to live under the law, no revenue paid and general contempt for authority, these are clearly 'proofs of disobedience'.[28] Critically, after such a detailed statement, Fitton hints that such a view is again informed by a protestant or godly view of the world. He acknowledges that he is 'omitting to say anything at all of God or the good life', pointing to the fact that it is the absence of 'God or the good life' that (for Irish reformed protestants) is the reason civil disorder pervades.[29] In certain respects, it is the need to describe and explain current ungodly conditions (in the absence of religious reformation) that reveals something of the grace-based relationships which were thought to hold a godly community together; and again it is Irish civil disorder that draws this position into open political debate.

This folds into a more rigid deployment of the term 'commonwealth' by Nicholas Malby, and also William Drury, who served as president of Munster from 1576 to 1578 and then as lord justice and head of government from 1578 to 1579. Drury's own uncompromising Protestantism was displayed, as David Edwards notes, when he responded to the call of the bishop of Ossory, Nicholas Walsh, to enforce church attendance at Sunday services. The lord president made the gentry of Kilkenny enter bonds of 40 pounds to ensure their good behaviour.[30] Here the term 'commonwealth' now denotes simply the desire to exclude and remove corrupt lords, where a sense of negotiation is much diminished. In reference to the execution of Turlough O'Brien, the brother of the late earl of Thomond, and William Burke, both of whom were indicted for treason, it is simply described how 'the commonwealth is well ride of them'. Connected to this, with worsening conditions in 'the [Irish] commonwealth', Malby effectively asked to be returned to England because he no longer wished to be considered a citizen or member of this ungodly polity. Writing to Walsingham, he explained that since 'Ireland must decay, which now I see God hath determined, I beseech you let me not be an Irish man'.[31] The immediate context of this letter was the second Desmond rebellion, as well as growing confessional instability in the Pale. Similarly, Drury used the term to frame the removal (death) of James Fitzmaurice and other 'evil disposed' individuals as being for 'the profit of the commonwealth'.[32] Like many of his colleagues, he pointed to the sheer instability in a reformative model, where in the absence of God's word political relationships were thought dysfunctional.

Hooker, Grindal and Norton

It was from this point, around the start of the 1580s, that a more vociferous attack on the Old English gentry began. Since the 1530s the Old English had been the indigenous voice advocating commonwealth reform and the extension of English governmental norms throughout the island.[33] Similar to England, the native gentry were relied upon to govern in the localities. A growing attack on the Old English involved, at some level, the self-interest of the colonial new comer seeking to remove native office holders. But with the question of recusancy, papistry and rebellion, the original commonwealth ideal became further contested. If we consider that a view of political relationships, based on word, grace and good conscience, lay below a more general English notion of the mixed polity – Collinson's 'monarchical republic' – again what can be identified here takes on a broader English significance.

In turning back to Sidney's 1569–70 parliament, the germ of a potential disintegration in the idea of a specific Irish mixed polity (from an English perspective) can be easily identified. Somewhat ironically, the disorder of Sidney's Irish parliament inspired the writing of a quintessential English mixed polity text, John Hooker's *Order and Usage of an English Parlement.* Anne McLaren contextualizes Hooker's work as responding to the problem of female rule in England – although she does suggest that Hooker's description of the distribution of sovereignty between the Commons, the Lords and the prince was understood as a manifestation of the external constitutional mechanisms or structures that rise out of grace-based political relationships. It gave constitutional form to a godly equality of participation.[34] Nevertheless, it should be kept in mind that the immediate context inspiring Hooker to write was his experience as an MP in Ireland, and Hooker was connected to Robert Weston, the Irish chancellor. Both were natives of Exeter and both served in the 1569 Irish parliament. It was also Hooker who, acting on behalf of the bishop of Exeter, Miles Coverdale, sought out Weston for service in the bishop's household under Edward's reign.[35]

When Hooker asks in the *Order and Usage,* 'What is become of the prudent government of the Ephoros in Sparta [?]', and thus draws upon Calvin and more importantly Ponet's discussion of civil government and the mixed polity, it could be argued that it is Irish disorder that causes Hooker to engage with resistance theory and broader ideas concerning the nature and structure of civil society (something chapters 1 and 2 have continued to emphasize).[36] The example of Spartan ephori, the magistrates appointed annually by popular election in ancient Sparta, and who exercised a controlling power over the kings, was used by Calvin and Ponet to argue that it was permissible for inferior magistrates to bridle and even act against the prince. Again this constitutional position can be seen blurring with notions of grace, conscience and a godly right to intervene; and it is the wider godly discussion in Ireland that really draws our attention to the elision between both positions. Hooker produced two editions of his work, one for an Irish audience published in 1572 which he dedicated to Sidney's successor Lord Deputy Fitzwilliam, and one for an English audience published in 1575 which was dedicated to the chief citizens of his native city of Exeter.

The potential problem with such a model emerges in the preface to the English edition. Echoing a recurrent theme of Irish political discussion, Hooker raises the question of degeneracy and a concern that men may forget their customs and laws – something that from an English perspective had clearly taken place in Ireland. It is possible that in the Irish version Hooker wished to avoid offending the audience he wished to reach, thus he pulled back from making such an observation. In the English edition a comparison is made between the different consultative assemblies in Israel, between Solomon's 'wise and ancie[n]t senators' and the 'rash and yung cou[n]cellers of Rohoboha[m]'. Hooker asks if those who:

> feared God, and hated covetousnes, did direct the people in judgement and govern the[m] in justice: what shall children, yungmen, and such as neither fear god nor hate iniquitie, which are of no experience or knowledge: sit in Senate of the wise, and give judgeme[n]t emong the grave and learned?[37]

If read against events in Ireland from 1579 to 1583, in many ways the counter-reformation-inspired rebellion of both Old English lords and the Old English gentry negates the vision of the mixed polity which had emerged in the Irish parliament, since they had become the equivalent of Rohoboham's councillors. Hooker's own (partly surprising) support for Peter Carew in his pursuit of hidden land claims in Ireland, at the expense of the native population, may reflect the beginnings of such a position, where ungodliness negates indigenous rights. Hooker's later translation of the *Expugnatio Hibernica* by Gerald of Wales for the second edition of Holinshed's *Chronicles* only reinforced the impression that no civil society, and a lack of civil norms, were pervasive in the kingdom of Ireland.

The implications of this position can be seen in the combination of Lord Deputy Arthur Grey's actions and statements. As is well rehearsed in Irish historiography, in response to the Pale revolts Grey executed some twenty members of the Pale community before Elizabeth stayed his hand, whilst he summarily executed the Spanish and papal garrison which had landed at Smerwick in county Kerry in aid of the second Desmond rebellion. His actions can be explained by a number of ideological factors: apocalypticism, a fear of papistry and a growing statism.[38] There remains a pressing need, however, to reconcile such behaviour with the norms of the English mixed polity and Irish government's evangelism – though such an outlook has tended to be ignored by Irish historians.

Lord Deputy Grey effectively argued that a clear refusal by Elizabeth, and others in government in England, to support a widespread effort to further religious reformation in Ireland, had left the Irish administration with no other option but punitive force. This was the only factor that would bridle an unreformed and corrupted will. After all, Grey had ceased 'to marvel of the disordered life of this nation, because of the most part the people either never hear of God, or seldom, or never, have his word truly preached amongst them saving in this place [Dublin], and a few other parts of the Pale'. In a second letter, he openly acknowledged that no effort had been made to further religious reformation, very much akin to Sidney's 1576 letter.[39] The deputy pointed out that of 'the many challenges and instructions that I have received for the civil and politic government and care taking to the husbandry of worldly treasure, where is there one article that concerns the looking to God's due service' which might have seen God's 'church fed with true food'.[40] It was this that undermined the community's rights in Ireland (though by no fault of their own), Grey arguing in a third report that it was 'the small care had of true religion and settling of God's word [that] hath been the only destruction of this government, which trial enforceth me to say that only the sword will solve'.[41] The comments made by Marmaduke Middleton concerning the city of Waterford, where the city's inhabitants had fallen from obedience, expressed the same doubts over the viability of civic or civil society in the absence of a reformation church.[42]

But the dual English/Irish context of Hooker's work also indicates that the impending crisis in the normative values of Elizabethan government in Ireland would continue to have implications for a wider English discussion. Whilst events in Ireland remain more extreme, a parallel and equivalent set of problems can be traced in the English kingdom. The silencing of the religious reform agenda under Sidney's second deputyship in 1576 coincides with a dispute that took place between Edmund Grindal, the archbishop of Canterbury, and the queen over prophesying – the combined lay and clerical gatherings where scripture was discussed. Here Lord Deputy Sidney was actually told in quite explicit terms by Lord Burghley to back away from such an agenda due to a change of atmosphere in England.[43] Later contemporaneous reflections by both Malby, and the bishop of Ossory, Nicholas Walsh, acknowledge such a clear shift in agenda, where even Walsingham, it was observed, began 'to give over your hope of reformation in Ireland and ... [was] very sorry ... [he had] spent so much time ... in that behalf'.[44]

For Patrick Collinson the prophesying dispute marks a significant watershed in the eventual demise of the earlier phase and hope of the Elizabethan puritan movement.[45] This is indicated by Elizabeth's decision to sequester the archbishop of Canterbury because he had refused to follow her instructions and end the prophesying movement. Nevertheless, the extent to which such a dispute encompassed two fundamentally different ideas about the nature of the political community remains downplayed. Of course, the fact that Grindal was asserting the need for godly reform is readily acknowledged. So too is the fact that Grindal was asserting the constitutional right of protestant Englishmen to counsel the prince (in particular, because they spoke on behalf of God and sought more godly reform). Actually Peter Lake makes the point that the prophesying dispute was so controversial, because the particular assumption concerning a protestant right to participate in political life, and advise the prince, came to be stated bluntly and thus came to be negated.[46]

But there remains a strained distinction here between 'the religious' and 'the political', where religious motivation impels individuals to find a political voice but it does not fundamentally alter how they conceive of relationships in the polity. Read against events and discussions in Ireland, however, the extent to which this dispute involved a protestant view of the nature of man, grace and obedience becomes more apparent. As suggested, it would appear that more settled conditions in England meant such an operative redefinition of notions of political obedience and godly relationships were not voiced as regularly or as openly, because the same stresses and strains did not exist to force these assumptions into open political debate. Thus it is the wider Irish context that gives the language used by Grindal and others import and meaning.

Here the exchange of views between queen and archbishop strongly parallels the dichotomy of positions found in Ireland. For Elizabeth such a godly free-for-all actually encouraged disorder and disobedience. It would lead to 'inconveniences to the disturbance of our peacable government'; it was a 'breach of common order and to the offence of all our other quiet subjects'.[47] In contrast, for the archbishop it was through God's word and grace that a level of internal reform would be effected in Elizabeth's subjects, where a notion of 'true obedience' as found in Irish government correspondence and resistance theory resurfaced.

Grindal explained that 'by preaching ... due obedience proceedeth of conscience, conscience is grounded upon the word of god, the word of god worketh this effect by preaching, so as generally where preaching wanteth, obedience faileth'.[48] Building on this, Grindal drew on current political conditions to illustrate his view of political obedience, again paralleling aspects of Irish policy discussion. He pointed to the Northern rebellion in England of 1569 which had arisen when the earls of Northumberland and Westmoreland had raised revolt partially in defence of a medieval and 'papist' religious heritage:

> If your majesty come to your city of London never so oft, what gratulation [sic] ... and other manifest significations of inward and unfeigned love, joined with most humble and hearty obedience are there to be heard. Whereof cometh this Madam? But of the continual preaching of god's word in the city ... On the contrary what bred the rebellion in the North? Was it not papistry and ignorance of God's word, through want of often preaching, and in time of that rebellion were not all men of all states that made profession of the gospel most ready to offer their lives for your defence.[49]

When wider signs of such language are sought within English political and religious discourse, such a position appears more pervasive – though more mute in comparison to its Irish counterpart. After all, Grindal elaborated upon an earlier English parliamentary discussion. In a 1576 petition concerning pluralities and other abuses, such as non-residence in the Church of England, the same connection was made between 'the preaching of the word' and 'true obedience to your majesty and the magistrates'. It was stressed that the dissemination of God's word was the 'only good means' by which stable and long-term political obedience would be fostered.[50] In fact, it was acknowledged in the 1576 and 1581 parliaments that within England, akin to Ireland, there was an insufficient number of preachers, and this suggests that a definition of 'true obedience' had, at least in the medium term, been rendered inoperative. As Patrick Collinson, Christopher Haigh and Michael Braddick have all noted, a problem of appropriated benefices, under finance and a lack of sufficient university graduates was readily acknowledged by many in government in England.[51]

Similarly, Thomas Norton, the English translator of Calvin's *Institutes*, had argued in a pamphlet in 1569, entitled *To the Quenes Majesties Poore Deceived Subjects of the North Countrey*, that the Northern Rebellion had arisen in the absence of God's grace. Like Lord Deputy Sidney, Norton was an associated of the earl of Leicester's reformed protestant grouping in England.[52] He described how in the absence of a functional preaching ministry, the two northern earls had been able to persuade the populace to rise in rebellion, warning that in general there was a 'known want of sufficient preachyng... as well as a want of grace to receive the truth of God preached'.[53] In the midst of the 1581 English parliament this view of civil society and obedience was reprised by Norton. In an extended document, written at the request of Secretary Walsingham, he detailed the need for free schools and more preachers so God's word could be properly disseminated to the population at large. He added that such a course was 'the foundation of true obedience', echoing, like his Irish and English associates, the terminology of earlier resistance theory. He argued that it was in London, where many reformed protestant preachers were active, that one would find 'a strong knot of true subjects to their sovereigns ... [both] God and her majesty', thus pointing to grace-based relationships thought absent in Ireland, and which were difficult to sustain in England.[54] This further suggests that shifting notions of commonwealth, godly community, and the institutional state, which this study examines, are reflective of a wider shift in English thinking. As before, it also raises questions over how we should read discussions of God's word and evangelism. Do references to God's word denote an educational enterprise or a grace-based model for the political community?

'Papistry' and Penal Legislation

The failure to establish a reformation church, however, had another darker consequence, because it impelled government to seek to test and classify conscience, as opposed to reforming Elizabeth's subjects. The concurrent emergence around the 1580s of the language of 'papistry' reflects such an alteration in attitude and outlook, where it denotes the need to separate and categorize. It is also indicative of a new definition of civil disobedience. This was applied to those whose conscience was wedded to an opposing set of religious values or beliefs. This gave their disobedience a more ominous intent. In many ways, the terms 'papist' and 'papistry' are the religious partner of a broader statist and institutional discussion, which also sought to externally regulate and reorganize the political community.

The initial use of such vocabulary occurred, quite naturally, in the letters of Arthur Grey, Marmaduke Middleton and others, since they confronted counter-reformation-inspired rebellion more directly than their predecessors in office. Interestingly, at this early stage the term still lacked a certain level of critical intent. It acted as a factual observation concerning the events or actions that had taken place, and what might happen when the space, which should be filled with God's word, was left empty. However, the process of categorization which the term implied gradually took over, partly due to the diminution in a clear evangelical agenda. This points to a lack of intent in the development of a more rigid or coercive policy, where it was in the assumed absence of the reformative agents of word and grace that government grappled for alternatives.

Signs of such tension can be identified in a 1579 anonymous treatise, which continued to emphasize the reformative power of God's word. It was described how it was in the absence of 'knowledge of God, proceeding through lack of his sacred word, which [led to] ignorance and blindness [which] bringeth idolatry, superstition, vain worshiping and papistry'. But this folded into the warning that 'papists' would actively seek to overturn the current institutional *status quo*. 'The advancement of papists as officers unto her majesty ... by natural inclination and profession cannot choose but ... the overthrow of Christ his church'.[55] It was further observed that the counter-reformation campaign in Ireland was now better organized, because the Irish youth are permitted to go to the catholic universities of Louvain, Padua and Rome 'where they learn not only idolatry and papistry themselves but procure the seducing of all the country practising with foreign powers'.[56] The bonds of kinship also made this more problematic. As Malby noted 'the best of the Irish being in company with us cannot be made to do anything against the rebellious papists'.[57]

Turning to the subsequent lord deputyship of John Perrot, to which we will return in later discussions, further incremental shifts in the notion of 'papistry' can be identified. Here government's awareness that the behaviour of the Old English gentry possessed an intent that was more seditious than before seems to have strengthened. Perrot was appointed lord deputy in 1584, having previously served as lord president of Munster. His reformed protestant or Calvinist credentials, like Sidney and his associates, were strong, with Perrot sheltering compatriots during Mary's reign.[58] For the new lord deputy writing in 1585, 'this country people ... are generally addicted to these three dangerous humours, papistry, change of government, and licentious liberty'. The unsettling consequence was that such a 'party' now sought to take advantage of specific opportunities in order to further its agenda, such as exploiting factional rivalry within government.[59] Similarly, by 1586, Robert Rosyer, the New English attorney general in Munster, associated 'papistry' with other specific acts of rebellion and disloyalty, where the Irish 'convey out of Ireland unto Spain all such papists as fly out of England unto them'.[60]

A deepening sense of distrust reflects the extent to which an idea of 'papistry' sat outside a notion of Christian friendship, such terminology and categorization helping government rationalize a new problem. Later discussion will address in more detail how this language helped condition an emerging emphasis on the limits of office holding.[61] In fact, a notion of confessional disobedience was unknown and untested, since beforehand the problem had simply involved the consequences of a failure to preach, thus government had no model upon which to base its response. The fullest expression of such sentiment can be found in the letters of Andrew Trollope and in a series of documents written by the now bishop of Cashel, Miler Magrath, both of whom are slightly unusual characters. Miler Magrath's Gaelic credentials, and the fact his ecclesiastical career began in

Ireland as a papal appointee, makes him a rare example of a high profile protestant convert.[62] On the other hand, Trollope, as a particularly recent New English arrival, had few connections within the New English community. Here Trollope engaged in a series of cack-handed attempts to gain influence through wide-scale criticism of his associates. Their sense of difference seems to have encouraged both Magrath and Trollope to be more vocal.

In the case of Trollope, papistry provided him with an easy and direct way of undermining colleagues. Writing in 1587 he suggested that 'papistry' made those associated with the Irish untrustworthy, where he described a factional interest that aimed at overturning the norms of English government. He made reference to 'Captain St Leger [who] professeth himself to be an earnest protestant ... yet being married to an Irishwoman, overmuch favoureth her countrymen, being papists'. Critically, St Leger had supposedly spoken in favour of 'a rude Irish kerne' in opposition to an 'ancient English gentleman', St Leger's proximity to 'papistry' thus undermining the normative processes of gentry society.[63] In Magrath's case, either the zeal of a convert or the need to distance himself from his past, seems to have led him to focus on the issue. In a series of long letters or discourses in the early 1590s, Magrath identified more directly the political implications of a specific 'papist' civil disobedience as found among the Old English of the Pale. He pointed out that 'recusant papists are made of the jury to inquire for her majesty, who return or present in session, nothing but white paper, especially of any statute against the usurped power of the pope, or touching any abuse or contempt of the new established religion'.[64] 'Papistry', as civil disobedience, more so than Trollope's comment, involves the inversion of the normal operation of English law in the supposedly civilized parts of Ireland. There also arose the spectre that legitimate paths existed by which 'papists' could attack the godly community, Irish protestants appearing before juries and judges who refused to take the oath of supremacy.[65]

By the 1590s such individuals are even described as 'hollow-hearted' – the implication being that the consciences of such individuals are inured against any hope of reform or moral dictum.[66] As the bishop of Cork, William Lyon, remarked, any attempt at evangelism was now being blocked by a 'papist' faction who were 'charged not to reason with any Christian minister'.[67] This reinforced a sense of panic, since God's word, even if made available, would now be irrelevant, thus further invalidating the godly model. Furthermore, the identification of 'papisty' was mutually conditioned by an emerging institutional process, whereby consciences were externally tested and categorized – this later folding into a statist reframing and re-conceptualization of political relationships (in the conscious absence of good conscience).

In England, this took shape with the new 1581 penal act 'to retain the queen's majesty's subjects in due obedience', which now directly addressed not only active disobedience, but the external signals of a catholic or 'papist' conscience.[68] The act made it a felony to attend mass, whilst making it treason to seek to convert subjects or to be reconciled to Rome. This reflected an attempt to construct a different (external and institutional) definition of obedience, which might be more operative, and this sat alongside an upsurge in the activity of high commission.[69] But how should these policies be understood? Within English historiography, Elizabeth's apocryphal comment, that government should not make 'windows into men's souls' has tended to determine how such a policy has been interpreted.[70] For government in England, it is argued, the question of sovereignty and a secular definition of political obedience were the main points of contention, and so it was the papacy's temporal jurisdiction alone that was at issue. However, this interpretation only really remains valid if the preceding view of godly or Christian political relationships is ignored. In fact, such policy took shape in a climate where godly reformation, as we have discussed, had not actually taken place to the degree protestant policy makers would have liked. Such a shift in policy therefore is not simply about a Jesuit threat, though that clearly played a part; as before it involves an attempt to rethink relationships in the absence of unity of conscience.

An attempt, therefore, to set out a more secular definition of authority in the 1581 statute represents a first half-formed distinction, which remains caught by a preceding conscience-based definition of political relationships. Thomas Norton's authorship of Burghley's treatise the *Execution of Justice in England for the Maintenaunce of Publique and Christian Peace* (1583) demonstrates this quite clearly, since Norton had articulated beforehand a protestant definition of 'true obedience' positioning him firmly within the strained debate over how civil obedience should be defined. At one level the treatise seeks to demarcate some level of institutional allegiance in order to argue that the actions of Jesuits and 'papists' in England are unacceptable, not on the grounds of 'religion', but because they are treasonous. Norton writes of the regime's objections to 'the Popes' claims to 'absolute authoritie', straining to suggest this is simply an issue of temporal jurisdiction.[71] The treatise was commissioned by Burghley after the execution of the Jesuit priests Edmund Campion and Alexander Briant, along with another priest, Ralph Sherwin. These individuals were 'lawfully executed by the auncient laws temporall of the Realm', and interestingly, Stephen Alford takes Norton's assertions at face value.[72]

But despite his own protestations, Norton is led to acknowledge throughout the pamphlet that the real problem is 'conscience', where the bonds of Christian unity in the polity are dissolved, despite his outward protests to the contrary. For Norton the catholic mission to England claimed it only intended 'to informe or reforme mans consciences from errors in some points of religio[n]', when in reality it sought to bring over papal bulls whereby 'her subjects are discharged of their othes and obedience'.[73] The issue is that 'in their hearts and consciences [they were] secret traitors'. Norton continues, that at least radical protestants know that in conscience they are mandated to obey the prince.[74] The Irish context also loams large, events and actions in England being set beside the second Desmond rebellion and the activity of Dr Sanders (as well as that of Edmund Campion in England).[75] Here Michael Questier has observed a move away from a discussion of 'heresy' in England towards a religious 'policy' as 'the state' sought to enforce a level of outward conformity – and I think what Questier hints at here should be understood as part of a more fundamental shift in thought, which entailed the need to conceptualize the state in light of the fracturing of the earlier model.[76] Again, it represented an attempt to find an alternative definition of civil obedience now that a conscience-based definition of 'true obedience' could not be applied.

Following suit, in Ireland the activity of the ecclesiastical commission intensified in enforcing church attendance, or at least in indentifying recusants and issuing fines.[77] Lord Deputy Perrot sought to introduce penal legislation into an Irish parliament in line with the English acts.[78] This was preceded by an attempt to administer the oath of supremacy more widely than allowed in the statute. Perrot sought to administer the oath to the entire population of the Pale, whilst the statute only made provision for the oath to be administered to those taking office in church or state.[79] This sat beside a continued diminution in the frequency with which the evangelical agenda was reprised, although John Long, the archbishop of Armagh, was one of the few to directly articulate the reformed protestant view linking God's word, grace and conscience. What is interesting in this regard (as will become apparent in later chapters) is that Long rejected government's insistence on testing consciences and the *raison d'etre* of an emphasis on 'papistry'. Possibly because he remained more committed to an original evangelical view, persecution and exclusion of the community in Dublin sat uneasily with him; and despite everything, here Perrot did attempt to revive the godly model. Within the 1585 Irish parliament, the lord deputy, like his predecessor Sidney, hoped to legislate for a university. More generally, he sought to further church reform and make available God's word.[80]

Confessionalization and Statism

It seems appropriate at this juncture, then, to turn to consider some of the historiography relating to religious change and in particular the wider paradigm of confessionalization which tends to dominate Germany history writing of the period and which some scholars have attempted to extend to the study of Elizabethan Ireland.[81] The distinction we have made involving the intellectual or theological assumptions which lay below decisions to preach and evangelize, I think, should alter how we read the process of confessionalization and 'statism'. There is a tendency to identify three general stages in the process of confessionalization, beginning with the 'popular' or 'communal' reformation, then the 'magisterial' reformation and finally the 'territorial' reformation. At one level this involved a move away from simple evangelism towards an attempt to catechize and school individuals in specific doctrinal positions. The confessionalization model, as outlined by Heinz Schilling in his study of Lutheran and Calvinist principalities in Germany, suggests that a general need to discipline and order fragmented communities fed into the modernization of society and the state.

But for Schilling the particular confession was incidental, it was the wider problem of social disorder, a general drive for religious renewal and the need for princes to consolidate and reorder their territories that was paramount.[82] In other words, a particular confession does not define the precise nature of the state, where an idea of the state tends to be treated as axiomatic. Here, therefore, a Calvinist government can be seen adopting an absolutist position, because the need of the ruler to exert authority against an unruly aristocracy required such a move. Akin to this, if a constitutionalist position is adopted, it might arise because the prince needs to repudiate the wider jurisdictional claims of a superior.[83] Calvinism then does not necessarily equate with more democratic structures.

However, in recognizing the linguistic shift which took place with the emergence of the term 'the state', and also in recognizing a more dramatic shift in interpersonal relationships, the emergence of a protestant absolutism, which did develop in Elizabethan Ireland, seems far from incidental. It might be suggested that this was not only about the implementation of religious and confessional change, but, as will become clear in the next part of this study, it concerned a shift in the way in which the bonds that join us together were thought to operate. 'Popular reform', with its optimism, expressed a belief that God's word would quickly perfect interpersonal relationships in the polity. A move towards institutionalization, therefore, was about an altered conception of political relationships, which is less assured and instead looks to institutions and the state (not word and grace) to regulate and stabilize interpersonal relationships.

In particular, such a position helps make sense of an idea of double confessionalization in Ireland as applied by Ute Lotz-Heumann, where the wider Catholicism of the Irish sits in stark contrast to the construction of a strong protestant governing establishment. Here Heumann is attempting to reconcile the Irish exception to Schilling's model, which suggested that state and confession should be effectively one. Instead, she argues that two separate protestant and catholic processes are at work. One reflects the broader process of catholic confessionalization, where the Universalist claims to authority made by the papacy are not necessarily associated with regional state structures. The other is a more state-centred Protestantism.[84] It could be suggested that such a process reflects two different views on the nature of political relationships. In more precise terms, perhaps catholic Ireland saw itself as united in the bonds of Christian catholic friendship, in opposition to a state which would be physically and intellectually constructed by protestants who sought to exclude (temporarily) those not thought to be in receipt of grace from political life.[85]

This can also be extended into a possible re-reading of the reformation of manners. If the operative assumptions concerning the nature of man are thought to be different then by implication the process of social discipline and education also looks different. A notion of Calvinist discipline should not be directly equated with a modern idea of social discipline. In fact an idea of Calvinist discipline, following Calvin's idea of a Christian polity, rests on an elision between the spiritual and civil spheres, where both magistrate and preacher work together to construct a godly polity. The magistrate addresses outward behaviour, the reform of which is (somehow) mutually conditioned by grace-based internal reform. This is not simply about instilling correct external behaviour, but about an attempt to construct a society bound together in grace. If, however, the mechanism by which grace would be made available is thought absent, because God's word is not widely preached, how then should a reformation of manners be understood? In such a context educating people to behave well, and eradicating social habits which are thought bad, becomes less about edification and instead glosses over man and his unaltered sinful condition.[86]

The Evangelical Difficulties of Derricke and Others

Finally, within the various material published by a group of slightly disparate individuals in Ireland, John Derricke, Thomas Churchyard and Barnaby Rich, broader evidence can found of the difficulties protestants faced in attempts to construct an operative and more long-term model based on an external and coercive civil obedience (as opposed to 'true obedience'). Possibly clarity was added to the way these individuals thought, because of their desire to construct broader narrative accounts, which sought to make sense of what had or had not happened, as well as the distance between this group and Irish government. A later shift in discussion is also anticipated, whereby God and the common good would be replaced by 'the state' and the need to uphold its political authority where the room left for dissent and disobedience narrowed.

Within Derricke's *Image of Irelande* these two concurrent processes can be easily identified. Derricke had clear protestant credentials and he had been a minor figure in Ireland during Henry Sidney's second deputyship. *The Image of Irelande* was published in 1581, and the work was dedicated to Henry's son Philip, the dedication being dated 16 June 1578, which coincides with Elizabeth's decision to recall Sidney. The work may have been intended to further Philip's prospects of being appointed to the lord deputyship after his father's departure from office.[87] Derricke sets out a strong defence of Henry Sidney's service in the Irish kingdom, and it is in constructing a defence that Derricke departs from an evangelical position.

Quite simply, in order to defend Sidney, Derricke sought to remove any doubt that the English, as opposed to the Irish, might be responsible for the failure to reform the island. *The Image* ignores the fact that no provision had been made for the dissemination of God's word. Instead, it starts with Ireland's early history and the ministry of St Patrick. In doing so, Derricke sidesteps government's failure in the 1560s and 70s to provide for a functional preaching ministry. In a marginal note he asserts that 'Sainct Patrickes preachynges, could never bring Woodkarne to holly perfection of life'. Preaching had been tried and failed, meaning the Irish were beyond God's aid.[88]

> 'No strength maie prevaile whom God doeth withstande, no phisicke can cure, whome God in is ire striketh, showing that God hath given up Woodkarne to a repobrate sence infectyng them also with an incurable botch'.[89]

A hint of a predestinarian theology emerges, which, as Alan Ford notes, would be used under James I and VI to explain the continued failure of the church in Ireland to further religious reformation. Nevertheless, there remains a certain awkwardness here because, as Ford again points out, such a presdestinarian view is theological speaking quite crude. In Calvin's *Institutes* the argument that God had foreknowledge of events, because he was omnipotent, was simply an observation concerning the nature of God's existence and was not meant to imply that man's condition and man's possibility of salvation was pre-determined.[90] A predestinarian position immediately jars with a notion of universal redemption (and the sense of the power of grace). This is something Derricke would actually appear to acknowledge. In *The Image* he quickly drew back from this view when he asked 'God tourne them to a better life: / reforming whattes a misse, / For man maie not comprice the same, / tis not in hands of his'.[91] This may explain the growing polemical nature of such a critique, whereby those individuals involved in setting out such a position sought to drown out the more obvious and dominant evangelical note in Protestantism, because this made their position more difficult to sustain.

Saying all this, *The Image* also points towards an alternative definition or way of thinking about obedience and the community, which becomes more important when we consider that *The Image* was dedicated to Philip Sidney. (Philip would be important in articulating an alternative set of statist values and language.)[92] A series of twelve detailed woodcuts were produced which depicted, for instance, Sidney setting out from Dublin castle for a progress through Ireland; Sidney successfully defeating the Irish in battle; the misery of Rory Oge O'More; Sidney taking submission from Turlough O'Neill and other Ulster lords; and the lord deputy returning in triumph to the lord mayor and aldermen of Dublin. At one level the images present civil obedience in a strictly political frame, where it is the strength of the authority exerted by Sidney that narrows the potential avenues and space for rebellion that is important.

Considered alongside the statist debate, which would emerge in the late 1570s / early 1580s, *The Image* hints at such a position (even if it does so somewhat unconsciously), where upholding state institutions and sovereign authority became an alternative basis for political action. In two of the woodcuts involving Sidney, on his return to Dublin in triumph after military service in Ireland (Figure 2.1), and in the submission taken from the Ulster lords (Figure 2.2), the sword of state features prominently, representing the full authority of the English/Irish crown as delegated to the lord deputy. Sidney, in taking submission from Turlough and others, is also ensconced in full vice-regal regalia in a monarchical pose.[93] Pictorially the physical and symbolic manifestation of the sovereign authority is shown. Quentin Skinner's suggestion that Hobbes, in writing *Leviathan*, and in thinking about the community and its organization, drew on images presented in popular *emblemata* books, further suggests that the images in Derricke's work helped clarify and encourage the development of new ideas and a more abstract conception of institutional authority.[94]

Figure 2.1: Sir Henry Sidney returns in triumph to Dublin Castle and is received by the Lord Mayor and Aldermen in John Derricke, *The Image of Irelande, with a Discoverie of Woodkarne* (London: [J. Kingston for] Jhon Daie, 1581). Image © Edinburgh University Library.

Figure 2.2: Turlough Lynagh O'Neale and the other kerne kneel to Sidney in submission in John Derricke, *The Image of Irelande, with a Discoverie of Woodkarne,* (London: [J. Kingston for] Jhon Daie, 1581). Image © Edinburgh University Library.

On the other hand, in the work of Thomas Churchyard, we see again two interconnected languages at work – one concerning political authority and the other the unreformed nature of man. Churchyard was a soldier and a somewhat prolific writer. In *A Generall Rehearsal of Warres* (1579), a notion of fortune or mutability is brought to the fore for the first time. Terror becomes the *modus vivendi* in such an environment as the only force that will motivate unreformed man (something which remained implicit in most Irish government correspondence). Such terror is associated with authority as delegated to provincial figures, the officers of 'the state', where such officers act as permanent instruments of coercion. Some hint or suggestion of a notion of 'state' and institutional sovereignty is also to be found in the text.

Churchyard refers to 'this crooked age, where no one thing is streight and upright but a noble mynde, that neither stoupes to the mutabilitie of fortune, nor boweth doune to the wickednesse of this waiward worlde'.[95] In fact the references to military involvement in Ireland form part of a larger narrative description of England's involvement in continental wars, including the Netherlands, which suggests that Ireland is viewed as simply a symptom of a European wide fracturing of the church, religious unity and proper obedience to God. This departs from the optimism of Edward Fitton's comment in August 1573, where he had strained to see a providential plan within Ireland's disordered and unstable conditioned – that:

> he that sees not mutability of all things, depending either upon time or man's judgement, or that determines not as well to bear the sour as enjoy the sweet, is unskilful of this world's care, and most unmeet for action especially in government; and though night be but shadows yet the light under a shadow appears more perfect to him that hath [godly] judgement.[96]

It is Churchyard's account of Humphrey Gilbert's actions in Ireland that most vividly displays the combination of delegated authority, as held by the local or regional office holder, and the subsequent use of 'terror' or fear to hold the population in obedience. This section of his *Rehearsal of Warres* begins with an:

> abstracte of the aucthoritie, and entertainemente, that was given and committed by the honourable sir Henry Sidney Knight, Lorde Deputie of Irelande: to sir Humfrey Gilbert knight ... Written to showe how that severe and straight handely of rebellious people, reformes them sooner to obedience, then any courteous dealing ... with extremitie of Justice, and stoute behaviour.[97]

Gilbert had served as a colonel in Ireland under Lord Deputy Sidney in the midst of the first Desmond rebellion in 1569. He was also involved in various plantation projects in Ireland and North America.[98] Churchyard recounts the captain's quite infamous actions in his uncompromising use of violence. 'Manne, woman, and childe' all submitted because of Gilbert's 'resolute and irremoveable determination towarde them, [which had] bredde suche an universall feare and terrour as that thereby verie many yeelded without blowes, bloodshed, or losse'.[99] The treatise tells how Gilbert would place the heads of those killed on 'the waie leadying into his owne Tente: so that none could come into his Tente for any cause, but commonly he muste passe through a lane of heddes, which he used *ad terrorem*'.[100] Again, when Churchyard discusses the passing of 'the Sworde' or political authority to William Drury as lord justice in 1578, he suggests that it is 'majesty' and authority properly used and displayed that causes unreformed man, through fear and awe, to obey – that 'the hartes of rebelles trembleth, where the Princes power is presented, and the wittes and purposes of savage people, goes a Wolle gatheryng: when the civill Soldiour is certainly grounded in a manly determination'.[101] In this manner Churchyard comes close to articulating a level of medium, if not long-term, coercive civil obedience, which is effected by the continual fear or terror as manifest in the institutions of government and their agents.

Finally, in two pamphlets or treatises written by Barnaby Rich, *Allarme to England* (1578) and *A Short Survey of Ireland* (1609), we return to more familiar territory, where the absence of a godly polity is fully acknowledged – though what Rich has in common with both Derricke and Churchyard is his assumption that the unreformed condition of the island will not change, which again encourages a more external definition of civil obedience.[102] As before there is at many levels a crude and confused attempt to find away of thinking about the

Irish problem. First, in the *Allarme to England* it is argued that 'martiall' discipline is required because of the absence of a godly polity (though here normal tropes concerning the need for discipline to preserve and maintain an active citizenry, coming for Italian republican thought, are also repeated). Rich starts with a moral problem, that 'first to speak of warre ... I knowe there be many whose consciences be so scrupulous, that they thinke no warres may be lawfully attempted, allowed of by Gods worde, or agreeing with true christianitie, for the number of outrages which by it are committed'.[103]He argues, however, that in the absence of a Christian polity (which read in the light of the last two chapters might suggest in the absence of 'true obedience' and Christian political relationships) something needs to stabilize the commonwealth, which becomes external brute force. For Rich if 'the state of the commonwealth can not be established ... it must needs be stayde, and as it were propped up with the strength and force of armes ... he that taketh away the knowledge of feates of armes, worketh the overthrowe of the commonwealth'.[104]

This slides into a restatement of Ireland's condition in the absence of God's word. The normal programme of reform is repeated, where it is acknowledged that a university, schools or preachers have not been provided. Though, as before, what is important for Rich is that this produces a situation where under Sidney 'there is no hope of their promise, no holde of their worde, no credite in their oathe, nor no trueth in their dealings towardes him'.[105] Reflecting a shift in Irish government correspondence, by 1609, when Rich pens his *Short Survey of Ireland*, the observation that religious reformation has not been furthered, has been replaced by the assertion that 'papisty' and 'anti-Christ' are rife, making any attempt at reforming consciences now impossible. He describes how the Irish have been 'daily seduced, infected and perverted by Jesuites' and how they have 'blinded the zeale of many good people which otherwise without all question would bee more confirmable in the knowledge and love of God, and in their obedience and dutie towards their Prince: but so many seducing spirits are planted in all parts of that Realme, that if there be one that wil stand for the King, there is twentie for that one to maintaine the Pope'.[106] It is also later remarked how 'Anitchrist' 'bringeth the consciences of people under him through superstitious feare'.[107]

There emerged then a slow shift in Irish government correspondence, away from a blunt dichotomy between a coercive civil obedience and 'true obedience', towards a strained attempt to articulate a notion of a more institutional coercive obedience in the absence of God's word and grace. The various pressures arising because of perceived civil disorder and rebellion, which took place in the acknowledged absence of a reformation church, also drew out into open political debate various English views concerning the condition of godly and non-godly political relationships. This meant there was a need to redefine a more basic coercive obedience so a more operative model might be found, and there followed a more specific classification of civil disobedience as 'papistry', which entailed categorizing conscience, as opposed to reforming it. There was also an initial attempt to articulate an institutionalized notion of terror or fear as a means of employing force in order to hold Elizabeth's Irish subjects in abeyance. It is this fraught attempt to think in terms of external political relationships, not internal reform, that conditioned and formed part of an attempt to conceptualize a 'state', in contrast to thinking in terms of commonwealth or godly polity. It is the character of this 'state' that the subsequent chapters of this study address.

3 IRISH CONSTITUTIONAL PECULIARITY

In 1578 there gradually emerged within Irish government correspondence a proto-modern use of the term 'state'. The term had of course been used to refer to the condition or state of the island. Sidney, for example, wrote on 12 September 1577, of 'the state of the North' and about 'the state of the realm'.[1] The term, however, began to be used to denote the authority of crown government. No doubt the administration's constant need to report on the condition or state of the country encouraged such a linguistic shift. In February 1578 Sidney wrote of the earl of Desmond, somewhat optimistically, 'that he [Desmond] meant no harm to the state nor would [he] be author of any disorder'.[2] Lord Justice William Drury also used the term to draw a distinction between Elizabeth in England and the authority possessed by government in Ireland. In November 1578, Drury described how Walter Gall, a citizen of Kilkenny, who had submitted to the Irish Council, had 'disobediently behaved himself towards' not only 'her majesty' but 'the state'.[3] In December Drury also addressed the behaviour of Hugh O'Neill, the baron of Dungannon in Ulster. 'The baron [was] the metest of any other [lord in Ulster] to be countenanced by the state'.[4]

Not only was this in advance of a similar linguistic shift in England, the term as deployed in Ireland was also conceptually advanced. In England 'the state' expressed simply the idea of a sovereign territorial unit. John Guy argues that it was 'by the 1590s [that] they [government in England] began to conceptualize "the state", whilst beforehand 'politicians had spoken only of "county", "people", "kingdom", and "realm"'.[5] Wallace MacCaffrey also notes that around the same period the privy council in England began to write 'of the queen and the state' to refer to the wider English political community.[6] In Ireland, however, 'the state' denoted a more abstract and institutional sense of sovereign authority. No doubt Elizabeth's physical presence in England prevented government there, that is the English privy council, from making use of the term to draw such a clear distinction between its authority and the person of the prince.

As this chapter will discuss, such a linguistic shift reflects at one level Irish constitutional peculiarity. First, Ireland's distance from the person of the prince in Elizabeth, who was physically located in England, not Ireland, meant that Ireland's lord deputies had to act in many respects independently of the crown, because in many circumstances it was not possible to discuss events and political happenings with the prince. The prince's distance from the island meant any sense of *lèse majesté* was significantly diminished, because it was the deputy's and council's authority, not the prince's, that was being discussed or exercised, giving room for more radical thinking to emerge.[7] Secondly, if Irish government was led to conceive of its authority as somehow distinct or independent from the person of the prince, it was never going to root that authority with the wider political community, which it thought corrupt. This encouraged government to adopt an absolutist position which saw sovereign authority as being neither limited by custom or law.

Irish government clearly took its cue at some level from the French political philosopher Jean Bodin and the absolutist position detailed in his *Six Books of the Commonwealth* (1576). The presence of Philip Sidney in Ireland, along with Geoffrey Fenton who was appointed secretary of state in 1580, and Lodowick Bryskett who served as clerk to the council until 1582, brought successive Irish administrations in contact with a large body of contemporaneous political philosophy.[8] But Irish constitutional peculiarity also placed a significant twist on Bodin's definition of sovereignty, in which absolute authority had been located with a particular estate in society, such as the prince, the nobility or the populace at large.

As Julian Franklin notes, Bodin's 'celebrated principle that sovereignty is indivisible ... meant that the high powers of government could not be shared by separate agents or distributed among them, but that all of them had to be entirely concentrated in a single individual or group'.[9] But as briefly detailed, in Ireland sovereignty could not be positioned with any of these groups, because the prince was absent and the polity was thought corrupt. Sovereignty had to be located within the high offices of state, namely the institutions of government.

This, in part, is what the shifting use of the term state attempted to express; and whilst developments in the Irish kingdom clearly remained at least one step behind Hobbes's *Leviathan*, tentative form was given to the two principal assumptions Quentin Skinner identifies as embodying a modern abstract notion of the state.[10] Sovereign authority was conceived of as absolute and so distinct from the wider political community, and as somehow distinct from the person of the prince and so inherent in state institutions. What concerns us here is the way in which Ireland's constitutional peculiarity allowed a discussion to emerge, which encouraged the free and advanced application of absolutist ideas and state theory more generally. This primed Irish political debate so that these ideas were near at hand, which provided government with the needed language and ideas for a statist alternative to a godly model of reform now in crisis.

Henry Sidney and the Levying of Cess

What has been important, but unstated, so far, is the extent to which lord deputies interpreted the powers delegated to them quite widely, in negotiating with Ireland's lords, in attempting to further church reform, in punishing perceived rebellion, or in renegotiating taxation arrangements. Whilst an extensive set of powers had been delegated to Elizabeth's deputies, there remained a significant degree of ambiguity over what exactly that meant. The lord deputy had the right to appoint many of his officials, grant pardons and issue various commissions, but he could not make appointments to higher offices in church and state, all of which remained the preserve of the prince. He was also required to consult with the council in Ireland in the exercise of his duties.[11]

Of critical importance is the manner in which crown prerogative powers were used by lord deputies, which gradually encouraged a shift away from an absolutist definition of specific prerogative rights towards a more general absolutist statement on the nature of sovereignty. The way in which various deputies, and to begin with Henry Sidney, interpreted their powers came under scrutiny because of the expansion of crown government in Ireland. Various attempts to push forward with political and religious reform, meant some of the independent use of sovereign authority by the deputy directly impinged upon the life of the gentry community of the Pale.

In England, within the work of John Aylmer and Thomas Smith a mixed polity view was detailed, but critically the idea of limited monarchy or mixed government was not always boldly articulated in everyday exchanges. Obviously in England parliament met, and the privy council had a dominant if not controlling voice in policy, but there was a reluctance to openly assert a mixed polity position when the advice of the council or parliament was dismissed.[12] In Ireland, the fact that the Pale community was beginning to lose its voice in government, with the appointment of New English governors, meant that unlike the gentry and lordly community in England, the indigenous Irish gentry community had little to lose in voicing loudly its opposition to executive actions.[13]

What initially precipitated the open application of a limited monarchy or mixed polity model was Sidney's decision in 1575–6 to levy cess – a prerogative right of the crown and an *ad hoc* customary charge levied for the maintenance of the lord deputy's household. There are certain immediate factors surrounding the cess dispute. Cess, which was known as purveyance in England, had already been extended beyond the boundaries of simply maintaining the deputy's household and was actually used to fund the entire military establishment. As Ciaran Brady notes the lord deputy inflated what he initially proposed to levy, because he wished to persuade the Pale community to agree to commute cess into an annual fixed payment and so free Irish government from the erratic financial assistance provided by Elizabeth and the *ad hoc* charge. The community concluded that the deputy had come to take the country to farm, because the surrounding area was suffering from plague, so Sidney had to lower immediately what he proposed to levy before he broached the commutation of the charge. This revealed the charge to be needlessly high.[14]

Here the community with some confidence applied the limits of custom and law with respect to Sidney's use of this specific prerogative right. In response three representatives or agents were sent to the English court, Barnaby Scurlocke, Richard Netterville and Henry Burnell, to object to Sidney's behaviour. The agents suggested that the use of the prerogative was limited by the wider community, whose general consent had to be sought, and that aspects of the application of the prerogative were also governed and limited by statute. As William Gerrard, the Irish chancellor, reported, they argued 'that without parliament or grand council there could be no imposition laid upon the subject; that by the statute of 27 H: 8, grants of freedom had continuance'.[15] Their position was also bolstered by the Old English councillor Nicholas White, the master of the rolls; as a judge in chancery, an equity court of the crown, he should have favoured an interpretation of prerogative powers that benefited the prince and the deputy. White would appear, however, to have supported the community's position, as later complaints by Lord Deputy Sidney suggest.[16] A document dated January 1579 and calendared as a 'Collection of the matters of cess and victualling in Ireland in White's hand' details the counter offer put by the Pale community where they proposed to supplement the pay of 1,000 soldiers by 1d per day and to undertake the contract to victual the army themselves in order to avoid Sidney's proposed levy.[17]

The radicalism of the Old English community is further exemplified by the fact that in England, when the issue of purveyance was addressed, any discussion of the nature of the prerogative was scrupulously avoided. In an equivalent debate in England it was the behaviour of the purveyor that was discussed in the 1559 and 1563 parliaments. Similarly, when Robert Bell MP raised questions over purveyance in the English parliament of 1571, he too avoided the question of the crown's right to the charge and stuck to the behaviour of purveyors who held royal licences.[18] Such was the sensitivity surrounding the prerogative that Elizabeth's response to Bell and others was that parliament had no right to call 'her majesty's grant and prerogative ... into question', although the individuals involved had been conscious of avoiding the topic in the first place.[19]

Again Elizabeth's physical distance from Ireland was important, in that the prince's use of the charge was not examined in the Irish kingdom; it was the deputy's use of purveyance or cess that was at issue. Additionally, there are also suggestions that the way in which the Old English viewed the political community may have been different from their English counterparts – and as later chapters will discuss, an awareness of the constitutional norms of the Irish kingdom would consciously inform Pale opposition to the perceived arbitrary actions of Irish lord deputies.[20] It had, after all, only been in 1541 that Ireland had been raised from a lordship to a kingdom through 'the act of kingly title'. At one level the act was understood as granting rights already inherent in the English crown.[21]

But another reading of the act is that sovereignty had clearly passed from the polity at large to the prince through the fact Henry VIII had become king of Ireland by virtue of parliamentary statute. Part of the act reads that it should be 'enacted, ordained, and established by authority of the present parliament, that the king's highness, his heirs and successors, kings of England, be always kings of this land of Ireland'.[22] This is noteworthy considering various contemporaneous political philosophers (involved in resistance theory) went searching for ancient precedent concerning the initial transfer of sovereignty from people to prince, whilst in Ireland there was a contemporary example of such a process.

In turn, the confidence and boldness of the Pale community elicited from Sidney a similarly advanced and controversial statement on the crown's prerogative powers. In May 1577 Elizabeth complained that she found the lord deputy 'and the rest of our council there did very much fail in your duties in suffering our royal prerogative so to be impugned ... tending to so notorious a contempt of us and our authority'. Here the deputy described how some members of the Pale community sought to 'make the people discontent'; but Sidney also took a more contemporary and radical line arguing that 'it were good they [the Pale community] were taught that her majesty's prerogative is not limited by *Magna Carta* nor Littleton's Tenures, nor written in their year books'.[23] He rejected the urtexts of the common law/mixed polity view and asserted that the prerogative was unlimited by law. At one level this reflected the fact that Sidney could not allow his right to cess to be challenged, since he needed to maintain his administration on a decent financial footing. There are also suggestions that he did not see a popular sovereignty argument or a mixed polity position as appropriate in Ireland, where there were doubts about the health and loyalty of the political community.

Nevertheless, there remained a degree of cautiousness surrounding such a view. For instance, Rory Rapple recounts how when the chancellor William Gerrard 'defended Sidney's right as viceroy to exact cess and its commutation without consent from a "grand council", he did so by virtue of legal precedents from the reign of Henry III to the deputyship of Edward Bellingham, not by virtue of the viceregal office *per se*'.[24] An absolutist position was controversial, because as with the position taken by the Pale community, it involved directly addressing the nature of sovereign authority and thus the person of the prince. The lord deputy's reformed protestant colleagues in England, moreover, were reluctant to engage in absolutist thought. Protestants in England could not adopt an absolutist position, because to advance such a view would have been to deny themselves a voice in government. As Ann McLaren points out, Aylmer and other commonwealth thinkers advanced mixed polity and popular sovereignty arguments in order to insist on their right to participate in government.[25] This was conditioned, in part, by Elizabeth's religious conservatism and a reformed protestant desire to further reform beyond what Elizabeth on her own might allow.[26] In contrast, for Sidney, an absolutist position would only increase the deputy's ability to act independently of the prince, as well as his ability to act independently of the wider Irish political community.

The deputy's view was given greater clarity by his son Philip, who, in a 'Discourse on Ireland', written in 1577, defended his father's use of cess at the English court. Philip raised not simply the issue of the prerogative, but sovereignty more generally.[27] His time in France in the early 1570s, along with time spent in Venice, Padua, Genoa and Florence, all suggest that he was *au fait* with contemporary developments in European political philosophy. Philip framed the dispute over cess by asking where exactly sovereignty lay in Ireland. He explained that the right to cess directly touched upon Elizabeth's authority, arguing that if government was not allowed cess and could not fund a garrison then that was the equivalent of the respective community in Dublin saying they wanted 'her [Elizabeth's] authority out of the country'. He even went on to point out that in general 'skarsely she [Elizabeth] hath the acknowledgement of sovereignty'.[28] Intentionally or not, Philip, in tackling the question of sovereignty in Ireland, in conjunction with defending his father's actions as lord deputy, an inferior magistrate, mixed ideas about the rights of inferior magistrates with ideas about the absolute authority of the prince. Here the beginnings of a significant twist on Bodin's definition of sovereign authority can be identified. As Bodin put it 'inferior magistrates', such as Elizabeth's Irish lord deputy, could not possess any degree of independent political authority, but for Philip his father exercised such authority.[29] The location of sovereignty with the office of deputy is further hinted at in Philip's decision to style himself on his European travels as son of the *pro Rex* of Ireland.[30]

Beside this Lord Deputy Sidney engaged in a direct attack on Nicholas White. This brought the executive authority in Ireland in direct confrontation with the judiciary and so foreshadowed a later Jacobean confrontation between James I & VI and the attorney general Edward Coke over the independence of the judiciary from the crown.[31] From the lord deputy's perspective there 'is not a worse man of this country birth than Nicholas White [who] ... craftily and seditiously impugneth the queen's prerogative', and so the lord deputy sought alternative legal advice.[32] He wanted a new master of the rolls, but since White was a client of Burghley's, and since chancellor William Gerrard was not fully comfortable with Sidney's absolutist position, White remained in place. Sidney, nevertheless, had the attorney general John Bathe replaced by the English reformed protestant Thomas Snagge and the result was a direct attack by Snagge on White who was charged with misfeasance in office and suspended from his position. The locks on White's desk were broken and the rolls in his desk removed so they could be inventoried. This was because the master of the rolls had been charged with failure to certify writs, patents and licences.[33] Considering the type of material White had gathered it would also appear that Sidney was seeking literally to remove the written legal checks on his own authority.

It should also be noted that as with Henry Sidney, the Protestantism of Philip Sidney and Thomas Snagge raises more directly the question of why reformed protestants in Ireland rejected a mixed polity view and embraced absolutism. Snagge's brother Robert would come to outline a view similar to the agents of the Pale community when discussing the common law in England. As Alan Cromartie has shown, Robert Snagge argued in 1581 as a common lawyer that the authority of monarchy was not absolute because it was an aspect of English customary law – that 'if the law of the land made the king, there was none before it; but kings we find by all stories to be of great antiquity here in this land and so by consequence the law must [be]'.[34] Philip Sidney's friendship with the Huguenots Philippe Du Plessis Mornay and Hubert Languet, who both set out arguments in favour of popular sovereignty or a mixed polity view, in opposition to Bodinian absolutism, is more striking in this regard. I will return to this in chapter 4, where it will be argued that popular sovereignty was seen as synonymous with a godly community – something Ireland was deemed not to be. Suffice to say Sidney's dispute with the Pale community came to an end when the deputy's right to levy cess was upheld, though it was agreed that the proposed commutation of the charge would cost the community too much and so an alternative proposal was accepted.[35] This prerogative right would remain an unresolved issue in Ireland throughout the 1580s.

The Erection of a Court of Faculties

If a discussion over the prerogative right of cess elicited the first open articulation of an absolutist position in Ireland, a more extended and detailed discussion of the nature of prerogative rights, and more broadly speaking the nature of delegated authority, followed Henry Sidney's use of the ecclesiastical prerogative when he erected a court of faculties in Ireland in March 1577. This reflected, more so than the cess dispute, the need for the lord deputy to act upon the assumption that the ability to make use of prerogative rights was inherent in the office of lord deputy. Sidney's decision to erect the court, as mentioned, arose out of Elizabeth's reluctance to support religious reform and appoint preachers to the Irish church.[36] The court had the authority to sequester clergy and to grant dispensations. It also had the authority to examine clerics' rights to their livings and to give admission to benefices that had devolved to the crown. Alongside this the court undercut the existing visitatorial jurisdiction of the archbishop of Dublin, and previous provision made in English and Irish statute law.

What remained critical here was the island's distance from the person of the prince, which diminished significantly any sense of *lèse majesté*, as it was the deputy's use of the prerogative that would be examined. It was the archbishop of Dublin, Adam Loftus, who raised the issue, although Loftus had largely supported Sidney's religious reform programme. On the deputy's departure from office the archbishop clearly wanted to take the opportunity to re-establish his authority within the Irish church. Sidney had erected a new ecclesiastical commission on the same basis – although the fact that this seems to have been accepted procedure, and that a key member of the previous commission, Dr Robert Weston, had died, meant that Sidney's use of the prerogative in this respect was more inured from open attack. In the dispute which developed, two critical assumptions made by the deputy were drawn out into open political debate.[37] The deputy's actions implied that the ecclesiastical prerogative was absolute, and secondly, that as governor he had full use of that prerogative right. This began to move discussion over the state and sovereign authority in Ireland further along and shift focus onto a more direct discussion of the nature and extent of delegated authority.

The detail of what Loftus argued is recorded in a document in the Irish State Papers dated 20 December 1578 and the archbishop examined the source of crown authority over the church in Ireland. First, he adopted a mixed polity position and he argued that the ecclesiastical prerogative had been defined and limited by parliament. For Loftus:

> they [Dr George Acworth and Robert Garvey, who had been appointed judges in the court] have authority to grant all manner such licences, dispensations, compositions, faculties, grants ... and instruments as may be given and granted by act of parliament holden at Dublin, the 10th day of May, in the 28th year of the reign of King Henry the eighth, entitled act of faculties.[38]

For Loftus this meant that only the monarch could set up such a court in Ireland and make appointments to it because authority had been given to the monarch and no one else:

> It is thought that this commission granted by the lord deputy of Ireland, is not warranted by law, for that such commissions are specially reserved to her majesty, her heirs and successors by the words of the statute of faculties in Ireland.[39]

Loftus suggested that the ecclesiastical prerogative was governed and limited by parliamentary statute and was by implication not absolute. He also argued that Sidney had held 'his authority *durante bene placito* [during the pleasure of the crown]', which meant he 'could not grant a commission for life'.[40] He suggested that if authority was delegated to the lord deputy then he did not receive that authority in full, thus such authority could not be further delegated to lesser office holders.

As a result certain definition began to be given to the various constitutional assumptions Sidney had made. This was only reinforced when Robert Garvey, one of the judges Sidney had appointed to the court, responded to Loftus's argument in order to defend his own position, thus Sidney's assumptions came to be further critiqued. In particular, Sidney's second assumption, that crown authority could be exercised in full by crown officers, gained more clarity, because Garvey showed how bishops, who received their authority from the prince, could and had delegated that authority in full to their subordinates. He explained that:

> the bishops by their commission do give the jurisdictions ecclesiastical, that to themselves in right of their own dignities do properly belong, to their chancellors, professors of laws as men of better skill ... by means whereof the archbishop of Canterbury's chancellor, the archbishop of York's and Dublin's chancellors have authority over all bishops, and suffragans within their provinces, and over all other in laws ecclesiastical that are to be corrected and reformed by the said archbishop's authority.

Garvey also referred to Thomas Cromwell's vicegerency in ecclesiastical affairs under Henry VIII.[41] This was a particularly significant example since it had been under Henry VIII that the idea of an imperial monarchy had first been voiced: the idea that the English crown had absolute authority, or *imperium*, in both temporal and spiritual matters. Henry VIII's authority over the church had been exercised in full by Thomas Cromwell with dramatic consequences.[42]

Furthermore, in a second exchange between Garvey and Loftus, which was again conducted openly at the English court, the prerogative and delegated authority was scrutinized more thoroughly. The archbishop responded that 'Cromwell's commission was not otherwise than *durante bene placito*'.[43] He suggested that there had been clear limits on what Cromwell could do, and Loftus returned to consider the limitations placed on crown authority by statute. As before, he argued that because statute law had only made provision for the prince to exercise such authority over the church and issue commissions, the prince could not further delegate his or her authority because the statute had not made provision for the prince to do so. The statute read that:

> faculties should be granted by the archbishop of Canterbury and by such as the king his heirs and successors should authorize by their commission and not otherwise [or] the statute should contain a manifest repugnance and derogate in general terms, from that which the intent of the parliament was in the statute.[44]

The archbishop came close to suggesting that *imperium* rested in parliament and not with the prince. It is not clear whether Loftus knew the full implications of his argument. Garvey was also more explicit and direct, arguing in response on 7 January that 'the prince's power cannot be restrained by act of parliament, especially in bestowing the offices that appertain to her gift'.[45] He responded that *imperium*, namely the prerogative, was not limited by statute and that it could be delegated in full to officers of the crown. Significantly, what Garvey argued was accepted and the validity of the court was upheld. Loftus accepted this because he was appointed to the court in place of Dr George Acworth in 1579, so in political terms the archbishop's objective had been met.[46]

It is also possible to read the dispute over the use of the ecclesiastical prerogative as foreshadowing and providing precedent for a wider shift in English thinking. In the late 1580s, as John Guy notes, a new archbishop of Canterbury, John Whitgift, made similar assumptions about the ecclesiastical prerogative. Here Whitgift used the prerogative court of high commission to remove nonconformist protestant clergy who refused to accept the ecclesiastical *status quo*. The general use of high commission in this way was not novel, but the court, as John Guy notes, proceeded on the basis of *ex officio mero*, in other words by virtue of the judge's office alone, with defendants being compelled to answer interrogatories under oath.[47] In some respects, similar to the court of faculties in Ireland, the judges acted on the basis that as crown appointees the ecclesiastical prerogative had been delegated to them in full. It is ironic that Sidney may have set out in Ireland part of the constitutional basis upon which Whitgift would proceed against Sidney's English protestant associates.

Martial Law Commissions

The two cases so far examined, then, concern the detachment of prerogative rights from the prince, and their location with the deputyship, as well as the gradual emergence of an absolutist definition of those rights. There is, nevertheless, a level of conservatism with both these cases, in that the prerogative, whilst being defined as absolute, is viewed as a set of specific rights or executive actions that the prince or the lord deputy can take. This is reflective of an early Elizabethan definition of the prerogative as found in Thomas Smith's *De Republica Anglorum*, where Smith referred to 'diverse other rights and preeminences the prince hath which be called prerogatives royalles, or the prerogative of the king, which be declared particularly in the books of the common lawes of England'.[48] Turning to examine the increasing use of martial law commissions, however, a notion of absolute authority, which was associated with a particular prerogative right, also began to naturally expand to cover the authority of the state and sovereignty more generally.

Sidney's decision to erect the court of faculties in Ireland may have resulted in a direct examination of the deputy's use of the ecclesiastical prerogative; the issuing of martial law commissions by Sidney and his predecessor Sussex, however, represents a more radical view of the nature of delegated authority. First, similar to Sidney's use of the ecclesiastical prerogative, the letters patent issued to governors did not exactly specify whether or not martial law commissions could be issued to the deputy's subordinates. The lord deputy was simply authorized 'to punish all persons invading or intending to plunder or lay waste to the kingdom'.[49] More significantly, martial law commissions, by their very nature, denoted a far broader absolutist position, because they allowed an individual to step outside the normal limits of custom and law. Letters patent even followed a standard rhetorical formula and so referred to the 'King's Majesty' as opposed to the queen.[50] This is suggestive of the way in which the patents issued helped separate sovereignty from the person of the prince, since the language of the patents did not change even though a female monarch was on the throne. Smith in *De Republica* again associated such use of absolute power (namely martial law) solely with the person of the prince and he also treated its use as an exception:

> In warre time, & in the field the prince hath also absolute power, so that his worde is a law, he may put to death, or to other bodily punishment, whom he shall thinke so deserve, without process of lawe or forme of judgement ... This hath beene sometime used within the Realme [of England] before any open warre in sodden insurrections and rebellions, but that not allowed of wise and grave men.[51]

Secondly, when the question of state authority is directly considered, the issuing of such commissions undermined the Bodinian singularity of sovereignty itself. For Bodin absolute authority lay with a particular estate in society, and preferably the prince, but the number of martial commissions issued meant that the authority to act outside the law was not simply located within the upper echelons of the state, but shared out amongst the various office holders in the Irish kingdom. Rory Rapple has observed the way in which the language of the various lord presidents reflected a desire to maintain the integrity of the crown's *imperium*, as well as the growing assumption that *imperium* was not necessarily held only by the prince but also positioned in the offices held. Rapple points to Perrot's reference to *precarii imperii*, as president of Munster, as well as references to *imperium precarium* by provincial presidents Fitton and Malby, which Rapple describes as 'a pejorative term for crown government characterized by careful deference to seigneurial interest'.[52] For Rapple this represents the application of the language of the Roman digest, and a play on the established phrase *merum imperium*, *imperium precarium* implying that the 'conferral of all the people's command and power to the prince had been merely conditional rather than perpetual'.[53] If we add to this the appointment of sheriffs throughout the island, their use of martial law, and the later reframing of various actions as being on behalf or for the state, a sense of a broadening and expanding notion of institutional sovereignty well into the 1580s and '90s only strengthens.

The discussion and critique of martial law and its use, as with cess and the court of faculties, also helped make normative such extralegal procedures, when for Thomas Smith in England this aspect of sovereign authority was clearly exceptional. The two most notorious cases relating to the use of martial law in Ireland are Arthur Grey's actions at Smerwick, and the execution of the Roman catholic priest Dermot O'Hurley in 1584. At Smerwick, Grey faced the invasion of a combined Spanish and papal force in support of the second Desmond rebellion. The deputy saw little need for restraint and put the entire garrison to death. Grey's decision received little contemporaneous scrutiny since it was directed against an invading foreign force – although modern historians feel very differently about Grey's actions.[54] On the other hand, the awkwardness surrounding O'Hurley's eventual execution by martial law, points to one occasion when some of the rationale behind the use of such procedure was actually detailed. Here the use of extralegal measures was argued to be appropriate because of the perceived corrupt or suspect nature of the wider political community, which might not allow recourse to normal legal procedures. Martial law sits as part of the wider trend which chapter 4 will continue to chart, whereby Irish government rejected notions of popular sovereignty and located authority solely with the executive and the state.

It was explained by Lords Justices Wallop and Loftus that one Dermot O'Hurley, in light of the 1580 Pale revolts, had been 'instructed from Rome to poison the hearts of the people'.[55] In interrogating O'Hurley they had felt it necessary to torture the priest, that 'not finding that easy manner of examination to do any good, we made commissions to Mr Waterhouse and Mr Secretary Fenton, to put him to torture, such as your honour advised us, which was to toast his feet against the fire with hot boots'. Irish government actually seems not to have wanted to torture O'Hurley.[56] The Irish council complained that they did not have a rack in an attempt to pass the problem over to the privy council in England. Torturing O'Hurley, however, raised two other problems. First, since O'Hurley refused to admit anything, it was felt that a common law jury would not convict him, that 'if he should be reformed to a public trial, his impudent and clamorous denial might do great harm to the ill affected here'.[57] Secondly, what O'Hurley was charged with, either bringing in papal bulls or attempting to convert Elizabeth's Irish subjects to Catholicism, was not technically illegal in Ireland. With the infrequency of Irish parliaments, and their often obstinate behaviour, government seems not to have realized that the critical pieces of penal legislation, which had been passed in England, had not been placed on the statute book in Ireland.[58] It was further noted that:

> having had conference with some of the best lawyers in that land, we find that his treasons were committed in foreign parts, the statute in that behalf not being here as it is in England. And therefore we think it not amiss (if it be allowed there) to have him executed by martial law, against which he can have no just challenge, for that he hath neither lands nor goods.[59]

Martial law was applied quite explicitly in circumstances where the wider polity was thought untrustworthy and where insufficient provision had been made in statute law, thus martial law expressed or denoted the separation of state and sovereignty from the wider political community.

The 'Monarchical Republic' and the Irish Lord Justiceship

Saying all this, however, the significance of the issuing of martial law commissions becomes clearer when Collinson's seminal essay on the Elizabethan 'monarchical republic' is again raised. An essential aspect of Collinson's 'monarchical republic' is the local self-governing English polity, which he identified in the town of Swallowfield and in other 'gentry republics'.[60] Clearly, from an Old English perspective, such a local self-governing republic existed in Ireland, as described by Campion and Stanihurst in Holinshed. From an English protestant perspective, the rights of such a self-governing community were, however, negated by the corruption of that community. In turn, according to Rapple's account of the actions of those English gentlemen employed as provincial presidents and sheriffs, their authority could not be based on their position within the wider community. After all, they were outsiders so their authority had to come from the office they held. Thus a notion of popular sovereignty, so integral to government in the English localities, remains absent, further encouraging Irish government to think of sovereignty in more institutional terms thus separating state from polity.

A second strand of Collinson's argument is his identification of a later draft English bill drawn up by Lord Burghley around 1585, 'the bill for the queen's majesty's safety'.[61] Burghley's bill was a response to a specific problem, the possibility that Elizabeth might die without an heir, which would mean the succession might pass to Mary Queen of Scots. The bill made provision for the privy council to retain its authority in the event of Elizabeth's death. The bill read that 'the government of the realm shall continue in all respects'. This was quite a radical departure since crown officers lost their positions on the death of the prince, because their positions were directly dependent on his or her person. A parliament was also to be summoned so an acceptable successor could be elected. Here, whilst Collinson notes that the bill remained in draft form, once again this bill was foreshadowed in Ireland by an Irish statute – 'an act for the election of the lord justice' passed in 1541.

This Irish act gave the Irish council the authority in cases of emergency to choose a lord justice to head government, as an interim arrangement, without first consulting the person of the prince. It is important to note that though the council could act without consulting Elizabeth, it did so by virtue of a statute which the crown had approved for emergencies. Also such an appointment would be either confirmed or revoked by the prince at a later date. Nevertheless, the statute in many respects separated sovereign authority in practical terms from the person of the prince. It took the right to elect a head of government, which in normal circumstances was the preserve of the prince, and placed it within the higher offices of state, namely the Irish council. The statute allowed:

> that immediately upon the avoidance of every the king's lieutenants, deputy or justice of this realm, by death, surrender of their letters patent of office, departure out of this realm, or for any other cause, the king's chancellor of this realm [shall] ... call and assemble together ... [the] king's councillors ... which of them so assembled, shall by authority virtue of this act to elect and choose one such person, as shall be an Englishman, and born within the realm of England, being no spiritual person, to be justice and governor of this realm of Ireland during the king's highness pleasure.[62]

In particular, in 1579 such an emergency situation occurred when Lord Justice William Drury died in the midst of the Munster rebellion. Drury had been appointed to head government immediately on Sidney's departure from office. The Irish council, therefore, by virtue of the act, elected William Pelham lord justice and head of government. As Geoffrey Fenton's brother Edward Fenton explained in a letter to Walsingham, with 'the death of the late queen's justice (the same being known unto you already) ... the lords and others of her majesty's council here, have (as well in regard of the necessity of this troublesome time) as by virtue of a statute' chosen another.[63]

Beside this, the constitutional ambiguity of the position of lord justice only encouraged those in Ireland to more consciously examine the nature and extent of the authority inherent in state offices. This is because it was unclear whether or not a lord justice possessed the same authority as the lord deputy, thus raising the problem of multiple points of sovereign authority in the Irish kingdom. Connected to this, the term 'absolute' now became more commonplace in government parlance. Such a discussion emerged in 1583 because a mistake had been made in the letters patent issued to Lords Justices Henry Wallop and Adam Loftus, who had been appointed as interim joint heads of government on Grey's departure from office. It was explained in August 1583 to the English privy council that the letters patent contained the words '*in absentia deputati nostri*, which divers here skilful in the law do think doth extinguish [their authority] with the discharging of the governor'. In other words, their authority had been dependent on Grey departing for England and remaining lord deputy, and now he was no longer deputy their authority had lapsed. It was further pointed out that 'by custom here the patents of the justices have been always altered when their authorities were made absolute and confirmed by her majesty as in Sir William Drury's time and Sir William Pelham's, each of them having had two several patents'.[64]

As before, the fact that 'absolute' authority had to be exercised by the officers of state in Ireland, at a distance from the prince, meant the extent and nature of the type of authority delegated to Irish officers of state came to be scrutinized. And by September the lords justices faced another problem. The continued appointment of the earl of Ormond as lord general of the queen's forces in Munster complicated further any attempt to establish to what extent sovereignty or absolute authority had passed to Loftus and Wallop. Ormond would appear to have acted with full independence from government in Dublin, and this raised the question as to whether or not the lords justices and council, or the earl, possessed and exercised full authority. A letter from Wallop and Loftus reads:

> We hold it a most assured rule in government (which your lords well alloweth) that the credit of a governor shall be thoroughly maintained, and by the same rule if any superiority were ... [to] hold the sword, we ought not to have been made so meet strangers ... [because] either there is in his lord [the earl of Ormond] an absolute authority above us, or else [there is] such weakness in us as we are thought unmeet to give council in such an action.[65]

Nicholas Malby, the president of Connacht, also noted the ambiguity in the location of absolute political authority under the combined lord justiceship, referring to the gap between lord deputies as 'this *interregnum* when the government is not established'.[66] Malby clearly did not mean that this was a period when Ireland did not have a reigning monarch. Instead, it seems he was searching for the right word to express the peculiar nature of the authority, which tended to be held by lord deputies, and a gap in the exercise of that authority. Elizabeth and the privy council did try to resolve the situation and in September they instructed Wallop and Loftus to have a new letters patent drawn up following those issued to Drury and Pelham, instructing them 'that your authority be made absolute and equal with any other justices'.[67]

Perrot's Absolutism and Trial for Treason

It was with Perrot's appointment as lord deputy in 1584 that the notion of absolute authority finally broadened out and was no longer simply associated with a set of prerogative rights. It should be kept in mind that this continued to be conditioned by increased confessional division and a need for an alternative model for the regulation of political relationships. Nevertheless, what concerns us here is the way in which the absence of the prince, and competition on the Irish council for advancement, meant that the various assumptions made did not go unspoken or unexamined. In particular, Perrot's dictatorial behaviour, and the growing animosity of members of the council, meant that a broadening absolutist conception of the deputy's authority, as before, was openly debated. As J. G. Crawford notes, there was by this stage general consensus amongst the high officers of state in Ireland, namely the Irish council, that full sovereignty had been delegated to Irish government.[68]

In the first instance, Elizabeth was concerned with Perrot's immediate intervention in Ulster in 1584. The presence of an increasing number of Scots under Sorley Boy MacDonald had required an increase in military resources, which the deputy had raised on the basis of the authority inherent in the governorship. Unsurprisingly, Elizabeth's main concern was the cost of military action in Ulster, the 'extraordinary increase of charges'. But she went further and explained that the Irish council should have acted as a check on Perrot's behaviour, that

Irish lord deputies did not have 'absolute authority to determine and proceed in matters of weight' – though clearly Perrot thought they did.[69] What followed was the identification, by various members of the Irish council, that Perrot had in general acted on the assumption that the deputy's authority was in actual fact unlimited by law or any other check, and again the term 'absolute' was deployed with an increased level of intent. Adam Loftus, in his position as Irish chancellor, not as archbishop of Dublin, pinpointed something quite extraordinary, that the lord deputy, on the basis of his authority, was willing to override the ordinary courts of justice in Ireland. With regard to Perrot:

> it is an usual thing with my lord to remove such cases as are begun in chancery out of that court and to call the same before himself, to be ordered by him and his favourites of this council. And in case any person by me, the chancellor, be in court committed, either for disobedience and contempt, or upon an execution after judgement, his lordship at his pleasure releaseth the parties by his authority, which he supposeth is absolute, and neither can nor ought to be limited.[70]

Loftus went on to note that this behaviour extended beyond chancery and that 'like dealings are used by his lordship in the other courts, which his lordship overruleth in the same manner, especially in the king's bench, to the great discouragement of the chief justice there'.[71] And whilst the appointment of minor officeholders was under the proviso of the Irish council, with 'the choice of sheriffs in the several counties ... [belonging] to the nomination of me, the chancellor, the treasurer, the two chief justices and the chief baron of the exchequer', which critically had been established 'by custom and statutes', Perrot tended to intervene and appoint whomsoever he wished to such positions without any discussion or regard for due precedent. This even extended to the appointment of the local law officers, the justices of the peace and the justices of the assize.[72]

Again it might be surmised or suggested here that Perrot's decision to make himself effectively chief judge, bypass the normal court system and take control of the appointment of sheriffs and justices was informed by a continuing concern over the unreformed nature of the polity and the fact that many of the Old English were thought suspect in conscience. The state as such had to act and ensure those holding office were of right conscience, which government attempted to do by focusing on the institutional limits and conditions of office holding.

This critique of Perrot's behaviour was repeated by both Geoffrey Fenton and Chief Justice Gardiner. Fenton raised the point that Perrot was 'in every cause of weight, to take the advice of the council or the more part of them, with other cautions tending to concord and conformity'. Perrot, however, saw this 'as a curb to bridle the absolute authority he pretendeth whereby both my consultations are passed over with lameness and defects, and my good efforts of service put off'. Fenton even linked this with the idea of the state, that if this was not prevented, and the council not allowed to participate in decision making, this would do damage to the 'honour of the state'.[73] On the other hand, Gardiner explained that his office gave him particular competences, which Perrot would not recognize – that his letters patent of office gave him 'special regard to her majesty's exchequer causes, with care of her grace's revenues, and collections thereof'. He was 'not to admit any decay without just ground' and 'for confirmation whereof my patent authorizes me to have superintendence and oversight, with some mean of reformation of abuses', whereby he was 'named one of the six commissioners touching the acceptance of surrenders and granting of leases, the lord deputy only of the quorum'.[74] Governmental authority was split between each chief officer on the Irish council, the general upper echelon of the administration possessing the full authority to govern. As before, Perrot questioned the 'plain words in my patent ... it often pleased his lordship to make question of my authority, affirming he will use his sole absolute and arbitrable power not yet restrained'.[75] And this was further clarified with Perrot's trial for treason in 1590–1, which brought the Irish notion of absolute authority more firmly within the domain of English political discourse.

As Hiram Morgan has examined, Perrot's successor, Lord Deputy William Fitzwilliam, set out a series of accusations to undermine Perrot in England. Morgan has traced in detail the various cloak-and-dagger aspects of the trial, Fitzwilliam priming an Irish priest Sir Dennis O'Roughan, who was a prisoner in Dublin castle, to allege that the quite obviously protestant Perrot had heard mass, received the sacrament in Dublin castle and even offered to help Philip II conquer both Ireland and England in return for an hereditary grant of Wales.[76] What precipitated Fitzwilliam's animosity was the fact his administration was particularly corrupt, and Perrot as a former deputy was a focal point in England for complaints emanating from Ireland. Perrot easily deconstructed all of these charges whilst on trial. Why then was Perrot convicted of treason?

Here Perrot's absolutist behaviour, his assumption that as lord deputy and chief officer of state he held full sovereignty, is important. Philip Williams, who had been Perrot's private secretary, and was now Fitzwilliam's, gave evidence to the effect that when Perrot received a rebuke from the queen or received countermanding orders, he would exclaim that 'she shall not curb me, she shall not rule me now' referring to her as 'a base bastard piss kitchen woman'.[77] These charges were repeated by Marshal Bagenal, who further recounted how 'her majesty sending him letters ... to certify [to] him that she had given the office of clerk of the cheke' to a particular individual, Perrot answered 'that she had done more than she could do and so afterwards he gave the said office to one Sir Thomas William a kinsman of this said Sir John Perrot'.[78]

It might be asked whether Perrot really did say or do these precise things and whether he actually uttered these words. The former lord deputy was certainly known for his violent temper and very impolitic behaviour. What is important for our present discussion is that these charges gained traction. This was because they reflected some form of reality, where the idea of absolute sovereign authority had broadened to such a degree in the Irish kingdom, and sufficiently detached itself from the person of the prince in its association with the deputyship and Irish council, that it was really very plausible that Perrot could have dismissed Elizabeth's authority as it was suggested he had done. However, it seems that it was a growing sense of *lèse majesté* that helped in Perrot's conviction for treason, despite the clear untruth of the main charges presented. What was critical was that once the deputy's behaviour was not solely read within an Irish context, where a sense of *lèse majesté* remained much diminished, but was associated with a former deputy who was now a privy councillor in England, the atmosphere, tone and implications dramatically shifted.

Perrot's trial also provides some suggestion that the deputy's absolutism in Ireland was informed by contemporaneous political philosophy and an awareness of theoretical models. Regarding the various accusations made concerning his treatment of the council and absolutist behaviour, Perrot commented in response that if he were 'king of Utopia I would banish or hang all those which would make me thus to work for their private displeasure against my servants'. Here it seems that the fact that 'Utopia [was thought] to be a heathen kingdom and governed by a heathen prince' caused offence. Also the suggestion that he was actually advocating a very different form of government in England or Ireland, the implication being that he was dismissing or attacking Elizabeth's sovereign authority, also caused a problem, in that it only confirmed the accusations being levelled against him.[79]

Perrot replied that those present 'must know my meaning and the etymology of the word, for the same being a Greek word ... showeth what it signifieth and it being indeed but a device of a wished commonwealth framed by Sir Thomas More'. Critically, for Perrot, the idea of Utopia was fictional, so it was not loaded with meaning. He elaborated that 'every comparison is between persons or things by comparing one person or thing one against another in the positive, the comparative, or the superlative degree, but the words before cannot be drawn to any of those degrees', because Utopia was not a real kingdom and so no real comparison could be made. He added, obviously realizing that this point was strained, because a comparison quite clearly could be made, that 'Utopian government is set forth only for an example ... and not alleged to be better than another or to be the best'.[80] Perrot's reference to the etymology of Utopia indicates that those involved in government also understood the need for new terminology when discussing and describing new ideas. The next chapter will chart this shift in the use of terminology in Irish government correspondence, where the term state was deployed in an attempt to make sense of, and move beyond, a collapse in a godly model of Irish reform. Despite Fitzwilliam's attack on Perrot, he too was to draw on a statist critique and apply absolutist thought when facing England's Irish problem in the later 1580s.

4 THE END OF AN IRISH MIXED POLITY

By 1580 statist vocabulary in Ireland was deployed in conjunction with a clear description of the political community as corrupt and unreformed, and what is particularly interesting about the Irish example is the way in which it inverts a European norm. It has already been raised, briefly, how the mixed polity position tended to form part of the armoury of European protestants arguing in defence of their customary rights and religious freedoms. It also tended to be catholic political authorities who then adopted an absolutist position in order to undermine a protestant constitutionalist position.[1] The opposite, however, was the case in Ireland, where the catholic community of the Pale held to a mixed polity position and was opposed by the absolutist pretensions of a reformed protestant administration. As both Ciaran Brady and James Murray have noted, the Dublin community was to combine a defence of its customary rights with a defence of the community's medieval religious practices.[2]

Here an Irish absolutist position broadened and solidified, because government sought to shut down the avenues by which constitutional and custom-based opposition to the state could be expressed in order to maintain public order and the integrity of sovereign authority. The state gradually emerged as an increasingly abstract entity distinct from the wider and unreformed political community. Turning more generally to European historiography, it might be suggested that the Irish case further reveals the extent to which unity of conscience and the presence of grace was thought critical in the mixed polity model for protestants, where in the perceived absence of these factors an absolutist position was adopted. As mentioned, for Skinner, whilst religious reformation and confessional division is clearly considered an important context influencing the way in which we should read the various constitutionalist arguments developed by different European protestant groups, the reformation context is incidental. It drives or precipitates a re-engagement in constitutionalist thought as individuals sought the constitutional right to act against the ruler.[3]

What becomes apparent in Ireland, however, due to the inversion of standard protestant political language, where proto-absolutism, not constitutionalism, was the norm, is the centrality of the collapse in friendly relations in the Christian polity to a statist discussion. The state, sovereignty and various institutional regulations were aimed at finding at least a medium-term solution to the absence of the Christian body politic and all which that entailed. Here the state was not about providing for political freedom *per se*, whereby state institutions acted as a minimum negative check on man's actions, thus allowing man to act however he wished or desired.[4] The state in Ireland remained conditioned by a notion of Christian freedom, where all in a Christian community, if free from sin, should act in the same way – the state and its agencies seeking to enforce externally how a Christian/protestant community should behave.

Furthermore, this chapter traces a progressive shift in statist language and ideas. Initially, under Grey's deputyship (1580–2), and under the combined lord justiceship of Wallop and Loftus (1582–4), the term 'broken state' was deployed in order to denote a contingent political situation, whereby Irish government sought to stabilize current unreformed and disorderly political relationships, as opposed to furthering long-term reform. There is a sense of a tentative shift in conceptions of the political community as described by J. G. A. Pocock in his study of Italian republican thought, where in the absence of a clear providential plan Italian republican writers began thinking about how current political arrangements or the institutional *status quo* could be maintained, as opposed to looking towards a more eternal model for the community as offered by a Christian idea of redemption and reform. For Pocock, a sense of historical linear causation, of secondary causes (as opposed to a focus on providence or God as the first cause), encouraged political thinkers to turn to the question of state institutions and their maintenance in a context where the unchanging constant of the redeemed polity became remote.[5] Political action was about balancing unknowable contingent forces that might undermine state institutions, as opposed to reforming the community in line with knowledge of the greater good.

Philip Sidney, John Stubbs and Anjou

It is Philip Sidney's involvement in the cess dispute, concerning his father and the community in Dublin, which initially raises the question as to why a set of reformed protestants in Ireland turned to absolutist thought. Philip Sidney, after all, was connected to a wider protestant and European intellectual network and was on close terms with French resistance theorists such as Du Plessis Mornay and Languet. Mornay and Languet both took the position that sovereignty rested with the political community at large and that inferior magistrates, as representatives of the community, possessed the legal and constitutional right to act against the ruler in order to defend the customs and rights of a given community. As Skinner notes it was in response to such a position that the catholic Jean Bodin wrote his *Six Books of the Commonwealth* (1576), in which sovereignty is defined as an 'absolute and perpetual power'. Bodin argued that sovereignty, as an indivisible quality, could not be shared throughout the political community, contrary to Languet's and Mornay's argument.[6]

Philip Sidney's decision to support his father's absolutist interpretation of crown prerogative powers in Ireland, in the midst of the cess dispute with the Pale community, raises the question as to why Philip adopted a position he knew to be antithetical to his reformed protestant contemporaries in Europe. Part of the answer would appear to lie in the fact that a mixed polity was seen as being synonymous with a godly polity, and the community of the Pale was not thought to be godly from the perspective of Philip and his father. Even within French resistance tracts there is a clear suggestion that the notion of popular sovereignty was something protestants strictly associated with godly communities. As Ann McLaren has pointed out, a godly language, as opposed to that of classical republican thought, tends to dominate the classic French tract *Vindiciae Contra Tyrannos*.[7]

In *Vindiciae* it was argued at one level that the people had entered into a contract with the king and so passed sovereignty to that office – the king losing such authority if he broke the terms of the contract and acted in a way that was disadvantageous to the community, such as overriding its customary rights. A second argument was also made, and it was explained that the community had also entered into a contract with God. This contract or covenant mandated that if the king were to act in an ungodly way, not only does he break his contract with the people, but also the people were directed by their covenant with God to act against the ruler and maintain godly standards. Clearly, at one level, the two positions set out in *Vindiciae* can be seen as an elaboration of an argument in favour of popular sovereignty, whereby the king has responsibilities to the community and the community more broadly speaking guards its rights and liberties.[8]

The idea of a covenant as opposed to a contract, however, suggests something more (or less depending on your perspective), because it immediately involves the notion of grace and God's first covenant with Israel, where the promises given to Abraham had been sealed through the act of circumcision. This was by no means a simple contractual arrangement. This also points to the grace-laden second covenant, as set out in the New Testament, in the promise of redemption for all offered by Christ's sacrifice on the cross. In this light the theological or religious dimension to a theory of popular sovereignty becomes critical, not incidental, and without a covenanted community an argument for popular sovereignty cannot be made.

This suggests that the position Sidney adopted in Ireland was by no means out of sync with his French contemporaries. The godly dimension to Philip's thinking in his 1577 'Discourse on Ireland' is, nevertheless, far from apparent. Philip stuck rigidly to the question of the crown's sovereign authority and he argued that without the payment of cess, or taxation, to fund an armed force in Ireland, the Pale community was effectively saying that it did not support

Elizabeth's claims to sovereignty over the Irish kingdom.[9] It is in Philip's contribution to discussions in England over Elizabeth's proposed marriage to the catholic Anjou in 1579, two years after the cess dispute, that a godly aspect to his use of statist thought becomes more apparent. This draws our attention not only to a parallel English discussion, but to a more tentative and general deployment of the term 'state' by protestants to cope with emerging chinks in the ideal of a godly polity, although it was in Ireland that form and definition was to be added through the practical application of statist ideas and language.

Working from the position that a shift in focus onto the question of sovereignty and the state was a response to a failure to build a godly community in Ireland, made good by grace, it is noteworthy that Philip's open letter to Elizabeth in 1580, protesting against the proposed French match, deploys the language of the state. As Blair Worden has argued, Philip's aim was, in part, to preserve the protestant mixed polity. For Worden this is how Philip's *Arcadia* should be read, where the consequences of Elizabeth's failure to listen to the good counsel offered by her loyal godly subjects, it was argued, would result in civil war and the collapse of the kingdom of Arcadia.[10] The state Philip wished to maintain in England was not absolutist in character – the point, however, is that Philip used the general idea of the state, its institutions, sovereignty and the prince's position as head of the political community, to make sense of policy and political action in a community divided along confessional lines. He needed to chart a political path for England that addressed or took into account the problem of divisions in conscience.

Philip's 1580 letter raises the issue of alteration and change, which would arise from tampering with the present *status quo*, and which entailed marrying a foreign prince. For Philip making alterations 'in this body politic, whereof you are the only head, it is so much the more dangerous, as there are more humours to receive a hurtful impression'. This points to the problem of conscience and Christian friendship, and Philip adds that there are actually two communities, since England is split 'into [two] mighty factions [catholic and protestant] (and factions bound on the never-dying knot of religion)'.[11] It is in making sense of this religiously divided community that the term 'state' is deployed. Philip explains to Elizabeth that 'your state is so entrapped' that it rests upon the protestant party 'as it were impossible for you, without excessive trouble, to pull yourself out of the party so long maintained'.[12] He elaborates further and argues that 'because of the pope's excommunication' that the catholic community in conscience is actually mandated to overthrow the queen, again adding that because 'the affairs of state have not lain on them' they have great riches and are large in number.[13] Most critically, it is explained that the marriage would provide an avenue by which the catholic community could undermine the present 'state' by finding a head for its own alternative 'state'.[14]

Here a set of more clearly political arguments is also detailed. Anjou, Elizabeth is told, may try and 'enlarge the bounds of France upon this state' and that any children which might arise from that marriage might be used to topple her. Philip concludes that since 'it is dangerous for your state' because of 'inward weakness (principally caused by division)', Elizabeth should not marry – especially considering she does not wish to marry.[15] In talking about 'the state', conscience-based division is recast as an institutional problem.

This transitional use of the term 'state' is more readily apparent in John Stubbs's printed treatise against the French match *A Gaping Gulf* (1579). There has been some discussion about whether or not Stubbs, in writing his treatise, was acting on the direction of members of the privy council in England, such as the earl of Leicester, who opposed the French match, and therefore whether or not Stubbs was giving voice to general public opinion, or was employed to set out a more popular version of Philip Sidney's 1580 letter.[16] For our purposes, what is important is simply the broader view it gives of the initial development of statist language and ideas in England in line with Philip's thinking.

Stubbs opens his treatise by exclaiming, 'Oh the strange Christianity of some men in our age, who in their state consultations have not so much respect to Pietie'. He then makes direct reference to the political or 'politique' arguments advanced in favour of the French match, such as the need to secure an heir to avoid civil conflict and the need to secure French support to prevent Spanish hegemony in the Netherlands.[17] In the first instance what emerges is a particularly pejorative use of the language of the state. What Stubbs argues, like Philip, is that many figures advising the queen to marry are in fact not fully reformed in conscience, and that their decision to think in 'politique' terms and discuss how state sovereignty can be maintained is flawed. This is because they do not take into account the true basis of a healthy political community which is based on Christian or godly unity. He argues that these 'halfe taught Christians ... pretending hereby eyther against their own conscience of some other humor ... to bring greate advancement to religion and advantage to the state' are in reality very much mistaken.[18]

He further clarifies his position by expressing exasperation that 'these Politiques' think 'anye counsaile wholesome to the state' and that they will 'use the word of God with as little conscience as they doe Machiavel'. Stubbs even stresses the motif of 'circumcision', drawing attention to the covenant that the community of England, like Israel, has made with God, although a focus on the maintenance of 'the state' has led some Englishmen to forget all about this covenant.[19]

But if the first part of Stubbs's treatise rejects a statist model in favour of godly reform, the second half begins, like Philip's letter, to show how the language of the state could provide an alternative non-godly way of thinking about political action. This arises because Stubbs aims to convince 'politique' thinkers of why the marriage is not a good idea and so he frames his oppositional argument in terms of the need to maintain the Elizabethan 'state'. He suggests that the English will not like or tolerate the rule of a Frenchman, that it 'is naturall to all men to abhor forreigne rule as a burden of Egypt ... [and that] it agreeth not with thys state or frame of government', namely current institutional arrangements, 'to deliver ... government to an alien'.[20] What Stubbs is concerned about is present political conditions, the contingent condition of the state, where Englishmen are used to their own rule.

Alongside this, like Machiavelli, who Stubbs acknowledges, and in line with Bodin's *Six Books*, the emerging problem of plurality of confessions is treated from a strictly political perspective. Stubbs argues that allowing for competing confessions will mean competing interests and objectives which will similarly undermine institutional stability as different opposing factions fight it out. For Stubbs freedom of worship for Anjou will mean that the duke will be:

> a most daungerous guest to ... [the] quiet of the state ... to the griefe of the greatest part and chiefe strength of the lande, [he] requires open exercise of a contrary religion, for him selfe and hys, giving great hope therby to others of obteyning some indifferent Interim. Now to prove that any alteration in religion or expectation to have religion altered, is a politique bile enflaming the peace of a set[t]led and even state: I might have sufficient authority, to some men, out of macciavel.[21]

Stubbs also turns to the question of finance, giving a very modern angle to the question of 'state' authority, where control of the community's financial resources is a key attribute of sovereignty. He argues that Anjou will drain the English exchequer for his foreign wars, thus undermining the authority of the English state since 'treasure is a principall sinew of any state'.[22] He adds that there is the possibility that any child from the French marriage may end up inheriting the French throne leaving the realm to be ruled by a governor, which would fully undermine the integrity of the state. Here Stubbs's deployment of statist vocabulary demonstrates the fine line between the use of the term state to denote Elizabeth's personal sovereignty, her position or *status* and the institutional state. He concludes that the French will 'governe her [Elizabeth] and her state', and that those in favour of the French match never loved 'hir majesties person, they never shewed themselves lovers to the quiet of thys state: they account not themselves any way beholden to prince or state'.[23] If we consider that at this point the state remained conditioned by a Christian ideal, it is nevertheless possible to identify two points or aspects that would allow the state to separate from a Christian body-political model – both the idea of the contingent political situation, and the need to maintain the state and its institutions (as opposed to action being directed towards God and the community's redemption).

Geoffrey Fenton and French and Italian Political Thought

Whilst the marriage debate in England provides an initial sense of transitional English thinking regarding state and polity, it is the translation work of Geoffrey Fenton, who was appointed secretary to the Irish council in 1580, and the intellectual background of Lodowick Bryskett, who served as clerk to the Irish council until 1582, which provides a more immediate source for the shift in Irish policy discussion. In their respective positions as secretary and clerk, Fenton and Bryskett penned much Irish government correspondence and took ample opportunity to frame policy discussion using the vocabulary of state theory throughout the lord deputyship of Arthur Grey. Fenton would continue to pen government correspondence under the lord justiceship of Adam Loftus and Henry Wallop and the lord deputyship of John Perrot.[24] This further suggests that the deployment of statist vocabulary in Irish government correspondence from the 1580s onwards represented a conscious decision to apply a statist model and critique in response to the failure to further religious reformation.

The translation work undertaken by Fenton in the 1560s and '70s, prior to his appointment to office in Ireland, strongly indicates that he understood a statist model as responding at some level to the collapse in the unity of the Christian or godly polity. Fenton's treatises or translations can be divided into three broad groups.[25] First, there are the more optimistic texts about Christian action, virtue and the political community, which lay out an image of a Christian body politic united at the level of conscience and drawn into union through the action of God's grace – the very community government sought to construct in Ireland. There is, however, even in these more optimistic or positive treatises a clear sign of tension and weakness in such a model, in that it is immediately clear that functional political communities, where everyone or the majority work towards the good, is something only applicable to a protestant or reformed community. More specifically, it is clear, as events in Ireland had confirmed for Sidney, Grey and others, that in the absence of grace subjects and citizens would not act with the wider good in mind.

In Fenton's 1569 translation of a treatise entitled *An Epistle or Godlie Admonition*, it is explained in the frontispiece that 'the christian Reader [will] lerne to know what is the true participatio[n] of the body of Christ, and what is the lawful use of the holy supper'.[26] The treatise had originally been written by Antonio del Corro, a Spanish monk who had converted to Protestantism and was a noted Calvinist. There is also an opening prayer 'to Jesus Christ, for peace and unitie in the Church' – though this should be read as an exclusively protestant church. But Fenton also makes reference to man's fallen nature, pointing to qualities such as 'infidelitie' and 'distruste', which are not conducive to healthy political relationships. Reference is made to the 'poore children of Adam, lost by their infidelitie, distruste, and perverse opinion against their Creator'.[27] It is with this in mind that the prayer asks Christ to 'reconcile our hartes, knitte oure wils, and sende thy spirit of truth amongst us, to the ende, that we all concurring in one judgement and opinion, may remember that we are called to bee members of one body', and to 'reduce us at last to the obedience of thy holy and only worde: reveale unto us thy holy spirite with this privilege of grace, that by hys vertue he may drawe us all into one coporation and bodye'.[28]

What Fenton's opening prayer assumes is that without the bonds of Christian unity and grace, man will not be bound together in brotherly unity. Fenton reiterates this point, about the centrality of grace in instilling virtue in man, in his preface to his 1575 translation of the work of the Spanish Franciscan and court preacher Antonio de Guevara, entitled *Golden Epistles Conteyning Varietie of Discourse, Both Morall, Philosophicall, and Divine*. He tells the reader that a man who 'is possessed with a spirite of virtue, in the same man is truly expressed the similitude and action of beatitude'. This virtue 'is originally administred by divine influence and grace', and although moral and political philosophy do serve to perfect virtue the implication is that true political virtue is not possible in the absence of grace.[29]

The second group of Fenton's translations deal with the breakdown in Christian unity and the consequences of confessional division, alongside the absence of God's word and grace as reforming agents in society. First, the treatise *Actes of Conference in Religion, Holden at Paris*, published in 1571, is a translation of a French account of a dispute which took place between two French Huguenot ministers, one of whom was Sureau Du Rosier, of the church of Orleans, and two doctors of divinity from Paris. This disputation took place in the duke de Nevers's house and was instigated by the Duke Montpensier who wished to win his Huguenot daughter, the duchess of Bouillon, back to Catholicism.[30]

As with the first group of translations, it is the link between grace and good or godly action that tends to be stressed. The prime place allotted to grace in the account given of attempts to reconvert the duchess to Catholicism is immediately apparent. The reader is told 'that neither by private persuasions, nor other publike meanes' could the Duke Montpensir 'stoppe the course of Gods grace working in her'.[31] The reader is also told how the protestant ministers demanded that they be allowed time to pray before entering into any disputation, 'to the ende that by the helpe of Gods grace ... they ... might be made cleane from all passions'.[32] Fenton even informs the dedicatee of the treatise, Lady Holby, that it should help us settle 'our conscience' and that whilst we look to 'Histories to discerne pollicies of times ... [and] other Artes and Sciences', it is 'by the knowledge of the Scriptures [that] the ma[n] of God is made perfect, and redily prepared for al good works'.[33] A clear distinction is drawn between knowledge of secondary causation, namely history, and a more primary focus on virtuous life, namely God.

What is also to the fore in Fenton's translation, because it involves his first foray into the French Wars of Religion, is the problem of confessional division which had undermined the unity and stability of the French political community – something vividly displayed in the attempt by the catholic and Huguenot parties to openly convert the duchess. It is Fenton's 1570 translation, *A Discourse of the Civile Warres and Late Troubles in Fraunce*, originally written by the Huguenot Jean de Serres, however, which directly confronts the consequences of the breakdown in unity in the political community. The work is dedicated to

'Sir Henry Sidney ... governour in her [Elizabeth's] realm of Ireland', giving the first indication that Fenton sees a clear resonance between his translation work and the situation Irish government was confronting.[34]

The fractured nature of the French body politic is immediately raised when we are told how the leader of the Huguenots, the prince of Conde, had 'absolutely disarmed the governors of the provinces (which be all of the Romish religion) [and] seased upon all the towns, ports, passages and fortresses in Fra[n]ce'.[35] This is because the Catholic party had 'attempted uppon the naked Protestants many actual and violent wrongs', and as the treatise gives an account of events in France from 1568 to 1569 a dichotomy emerges between the protestants, who are loyal and faithful because they are sound in conscience, and the catholic league in France who cannot keep faith or the bonds of friendship.[36]

The treatise recounts how 'the sayd [members of the protestant] religion should not [have] be[en] in any sort cyfted or searched in their consciences, albeit both after and notwithstanding the saide Edict [of peace], they have been oppressed more than afore, and that with such violence as divers have revolted'.[37] The queen of Navarre, another major figure of the Huguenot party in France, had appealed 'to the cardinal of Bourbon her brother', who headed the catholic league, to abide by the peace promulgated by Charles IX and leave the prince of Navarre and the Huguenot community to practise their religion. She had made an appeal to the cardinal, 'notwithstanding the separation of Religion', to consider 'the proper office of friendship and dutie of nature and bloud concurring togyther, to consider their [the catholic leagues] present pursute against the Prince his brother'.[38] It is later argued how the cardinal and his associates, in breaking the peace, had 'convert[ed] the said fidelitie of his [the king's] people to a lamentable warre', whilst the Huguenots only wanted 'to entertaine a charitable quiete in their conscience'.[39] These themes are reiterated throughout, the queen of Navarre calling for the king to 'quenche or qualifie this unnatural fire so burning daily with in your realme', and arguing that the Huguenots were being 'unjustly assailed and pursued in their consciences'; those of right conscience, however, were the individuals who still maintained their 'naturall bonde and affection to your Majestie'.[40] There is even an appeal to 'God (by his special grace)' to restore the unity of the Christian polity in France:

> '[Will] God (by his special grace) ... not unseele the eyes of your Majestie, and to gyve you speedie and true light into the hartes and willes of youre Subjects, [whereby your realm will be] reconiled and knitte with an indissoluble bonde, and your Realme returne[d] into his firste estate [?]'[41]

Beside this, some hint of a possible statist solution is also provided, where obedience to the state and its institutions is presented (akin to Stubbs and Philip Sidney) as a possible way of regulating political relationships in the absence of unity of conscience. In his preface, Fenton suggests that the content of the treatise is relevant for 'all states and policies, as also conducible to religion' thus drawing a distinction between questions of religion and questions of government.[42] In the main body of the treatise, the queen of Navarre, when first addressing the need for freedom of conscience, argues that the Huguenots are willing to do 'service to the soverayntie of the king, and with mayne lyfe and goodes to help that edict of pacification to be obeyed'. This is further clarified when the actions of the catholic league are framed, not only as being against their protestant brothers, but against 'the soveraigne majestie of the king', since they will not abide by the edicts.[43] Their actions are 'contrary to the will and meanyng of his Majestie avouched by so many general edictes' and so they are 'commo[n] troublers of the publike state of this Realme'.[44] The Huguenots are presented as working for the 'preservation of your Crowne and Realme', as well as the 'true advancement of your [the king's] greatnesse and royall estate'.[45]

In Fenton's other foray into French political and religious writing, his 1574 translation of *A Forme of Christian Pollicie*, he allows himself more of a critical voice. He identifies directly the absence of religious reformation and the failure to provide for the dissemination of God's word and the operation of grace as the crucial factors involved in the disintegration of the French political community. The treatise was originally written by a French catholic polemicist, Jean Talpin, who was granted authorial privilege in France to engage in a polemical exchange on the subject of religious controversy – something generally prohibited in order to try and maintain the 'publike state of this Realme'.[46] For those in the know concerning the original author of the treatise, Fenton engaged in what might be termed an inter-textual joke. Talpin argues that only with religious unity and the maintenance of the church would the polity be stabilized and subjects brought to know they should be obedient to the prince. The point Fenton would appear to be making, given the emphasis he places on God's word and grace throughout his translation of the treatise, is that he agreed with Talpin's basic position. The critical implication is that Talpin does not know what the true church is since he is a catholic polemicist, and what Fenton is saying in the act of translating the treatise is that the French body politic remains fractured and dysfunctional, because of the attempt by catholics to build and unify a community that is not in fact godly.

The treatise is split into seven books and the first half concentrates on the need for God's word to be preached, and the relationship between grace, conscience and the behaviour of the members of the polity. It is argued in book one that a sound political community could only be founded on 'the word of God, which cannot be preached in any place without some fruite'.[47] There is a clear echo of reform discussion in Ireland, and it is further explained that the force of God's word could not be resisted by sinful man, 'that there is no man what vice or inquity so ever ... [who] by the force of this [God's] word' or because of 'feare of the judgements of God' would not be brought to behave well.[48] The position of the preacher in the political community is similarly emphasized. It is argued that 'Religion and the Lawe, the Priest and the Prince, the Preacher and the Magistrate, can not bee disjoygned without perrill of disorder', and in book two the sense of God's 'special grace' as the reforming force was brought forward.[49] It is explained that 'if the doctrine of god were rigthly preached and understood, how could there bee any assault or acte of murder, when even to bee angry, hate, or speake evil of your neighbor, brings with it the paine of eternal damnation'.[50]

Quite strikingly, a notion of *fortuna* and civil disorder is also encountered, which in his preface to the treatise Fenton sees as arising in a context where grace and good conscience, and therefore the permanency of God's eternal plan, are not present. For Fenton, whilst a 'common weale' is never 'more happy' when it is:

> disposed in conversation of justice and pietie: which, yet if they bee not joyned with true Religion, can holde no long continuance, for that chaunging according to the perplexities of tymes hap[pe]ning daily in Realms and Countreis [sic], they suffer alteration by little and little, and in the end slyde into vices and imperfections, which breede the revolucions and ruines of all estates.[51]

This brings us to Fenton's other translation work, that of Guicciardini's *Storia d'Italia* which was published in 1579 as *The Historie of Guiccardin*. Critically, *The Historie*, unlike Fenton's other translations, assumes that grace and providence are most definitely not present in civil life. Instead, Guicciardini's work assumes that the abnormal or unwanted situation Fenton referred to in his preface to *A Forme of Christian Policie* would be the norm. Fenton explains that *The Histoire* will provide an example of how to act in a world governed by fortune. It offers the reader:

> many wholesome instructions aswell to all men generally, as to every one in particular, considering that by the trial, consent and demonstration of so many examples, all princes, people, and patrimonies may see ... to what inconstancie humane things are ordeined, and how harmefull are the ill measured counsel of princes.[52]

The question of sovereignty and the state, as Pocock suggests in *The Machiavellian Moment*, emerges as the only way of making sense of political action and the community if God's grace and a clear providential plan are no longer present in political thinking. In *The Historie* the decline of Italy's city states is understood in terms of each state's ability to maintain its sovereign authority and historical events are separated from any notion of an eternal plan and are read in light of what man can know of those events. Lodowick Sforza, the uncle of the duke of Milan, because of the duke's idiocy, had 'reduced by lit[t]le and lit[t]le into his power the strong holdes, men of warre ... and all other the groundes and foundacions of the state of Myllan, persevering in the government not as a tutor and regent, but (except the onely title of Duke) with all demonstrations and actions of an absolute prince'.[53]

The treatise also provides a clear sense of the problem facing Italy's city states, where in order to maintain peace between each other, each state has to ensure its neighbour possesses the same degree of military strength so that things 'should not waigh more on the one side then of the other'.[54] It presents political life as a temporary balance between different factional forces, where for Fenton the work is a 'discourse of state and government', not a treatise about the construction of a Christian polity.[55] Interestingly, Maurizio Viroli has suggested that it is Guicciardini who should really be viewed as the first 'reason of state' theorist, because for Guicciardini 'the political' is about military and political power regardless of morality and 'the good life', whilst for Machiavelli the good life remains a normative point of reference from which Machiavelli openly departs. Thus Guicciardini has, from a reformed protestant perspective, a certain applicability in Ireland where 'the good life' was thought near wholly absent.[56]

Beside this, the background of Fenton's colleague, Lodowick Bryskett, the clerk to the council, should be noted, along with Bryskett's later translation work, which further reinforced the Italian republican trend in Irish government thinking. Bryskett was of Italian descent and his father Antonio Bruschetto, a native of Genoa, had taken up residence in England in 1523. Lodowick was also a close associate of Philip Sidney having travelled with him on his tour of Europe, and Lodowick's *Discourse of Civill Life* (1606), which chapter 5 will address, demonstrates not only a clear and intimate awareness of Italian republican writing, but the beginnings of a direct application and re-reading of those ideas in an Irish context.[57]

Arthur Grey's Proto-absolutism and the Irish Mixed Polity

Alongside, then, Irish constitutional peculiarity, statist thought found practical application in the heated and unstable Irish political and religious environment. For Stubbs and Philip the notion of 'the state' is still very much linked to the godly polity. Elizabeth's *status*, or the security of her sovereign authority, rests upon the maintenance of a godly community. On the other hand, Fenton's translation of Guicciardini tends to use statist language to refer to territorial units, such as 'the state of Milan', and whilst the question of sovereignty, and the maintenance of such authority, is clearly an ever present question in Guicciardini, the use of the term 'state' remains ambiguous. Does it simply denote a kingdom, principality or city state, or does it denote the political authority inherent in governmental and institutional structures?

In contrast, however, the problem Irish government faced was an extreme and ever present version of the problem dealt with by Philip Sidney and Stubbs. Irish government confronted not only its failure to further religious reformation, but an ever growing counter-reformation threat. This encouraged (even drove) government to separate and draw a distinction between the wider polity and the state, where the counter-reformation threat, unlike in England, involved the political community at large, not a minority section of that community. This reinforced and encouraged a reformed protestant absolutism, in line with Bodin's *Six Books*, because a notion of a mixed polity had become highly problematic in the absence of a significant godly grouping within the community.

Thus beside the godly (and confessional) view of civil disorder or disobedience, this chapter now considers the way in which Lord Deputy Grey and his associates understood the second Desmond rebellion, and the Nugent and Baltinglass risings, in terms of sovereignty and the integrity of government's authority.[58] Here Lord Deputy Sidney's concern with protecting Elizabeth's prerogative right to cess began to morph into a more general attempt to uphold absolute authority and shut down the legitimate avenues of custom and law by which the religiously suspect Pale community could voice public protest and discontent. This also sat beside a gradual increase in the frequency of references to 'the state' in government correspondence.

The 'interrogatories' drawn up by government, which were to be used in questioning those arrested in response to the risings, speak of a rigid and uncompromising approach to civil disobedience. For example, the earl of Kildare and the baron of Delvin were arrested, not because they were suspected of direct involvement in the risings, but because they had been accused of having had some foreknowledge of what Baltinglass had planned. Viscount Baltinglass, in response to the counter-reformation overtones of James Fitzmaurice and his associates, and as a result of his own commitment to Catholicism, gathered some of the Pale gentry, along with the Gaelic lords of Leinster, such as Feagh McHugh O'Bryne, and led them in insurrection.[59] Adam Loftus, the archbishop of Dublin, had reported that the earl of Kildare had told him he had known something of Baltinglass's intentions. Kildare was asked, therefore, 'did the viscount Baltinglass at any time deliver a book'; 'did you ever tell the said archbishop [Adam Loftus] that such a book was delivered to you'; and 'did you ever affirm to the said archbishop you were so sworn [to secrecy] and what moved you so to say'.[60] Kildare was not asked – did you act with the rebels?

Similarly, in his response to William Nugent's conspiracy, Grey arrested many members of the Pale community even though they were only vaguely connected to the conspiracy. William was the baron of Delvin's son and had risen in support of Baltinglass. If there was any common denominator in the arrests it was the Pale's previous opposition, in the late 1570s, to the cess levied by Sidney. The 'schedule of those who are accused for the conspiracy of William Nugent', drawn up in October 1581, included 'Robert Scurlock, Christopher Barnwell ... John Scurlock ... Richard Barnwell ... John Plunkett ... the brother of the lord of Howth ... James Nugent, [and] Christopher Nugent'.[61] These men were relatives of the Pale's spokesmen and others, who had objected to the cess on the basis of a mixed polity/limited monarchy view. There had been a Barnaby Scurlock amongst the agents sent to the English court in 1577, whilst Lord Howth had led opposition in Ireland. Howth's first wife Elizabeth was the daughter of Sir John Plunkett, and Howth's son would later go on to marry into the Barnwells.[62]

When one Patrick Bermingham, another representative of the Pale community, complained about the abuses of the commissioners employed to collect cess, now that a larger army needed to be maintained in response to rebellion, the whole matter was framed as an issue concerning 'the state'. Bermingham's complaints fed into an examination of the limits that might be placed on the authority of various minor office holders and even the lord deputy. For Grey it was not only about 'the private injury he hath done me', since there was the suggestion that Grey's government was corrupt, it was the fact that 'others of his disposition might thereby be admonished to be better advised how they shall abuse the state or governor hereafter'.[63] Allowing another avenue of constitutional protest to open up, which could undermine the integrity of the authority invested in the offices of state, was the point of concern. The Irish council even described how they had told Bermingham that his charges against the commissioners 'should be heard presently ... before the state here'.[64] By the time the privy council in England was discussing Perrot's appointment as deputy in 1584, the prospective Deputy Perrot expressed concern that he might not be allowed cess; and here Perrot referred to cess, not as an attribute of the prince's authority, but as 'the said prerogative of cess incident to the state'.[65]

There are clear indications that Grey understood his proto-absolutism to be a conscious departure from the norms of a mixed polity or Christian body politic model. This emerges most clearly in Grey's account of the execution of Nicholas Nugent, the chief justice of the common pleas in April 1582. Nicholas Nugent had been arrested because William Nugent, who had headed one of the Pale conspiracies, was his nephew, although Nicholas, like his brother Lord Delvin (William's father), had not been involved in the conspiracy. He had simply had some foreknowledge of William's plans. Elizabeth, however, had issued a 'proclamation of general pardon' at the end of 1581/beginning of 1582, which made it clear that Grey was to proceed with leniency. She took the view:

> [that many] that joined in this action [in rebellion] was not altogether of will and desire, but in some sort and in some persons compulsory for want of timely defence against the violent insurrections and incursions of those traitors, as being otherwise to preserve their lives and estates.[66]

Elizabeth thought many of the Pale gentry had been forced to support the rebels. She added that 'our mercy doth not decline with the fall of our subjects'.[67] A sense of flexibility inherent in a mixed polity becomes apparent, where the lord or subject had a form of personal relationship with the prince, where a sense of presumed leniency or mercy was present. We might also associate this with the idea of a Christian body politic where amity and love were meant to be the norm.

Grey, however, in his initial response, demonstrated a reluctance to respond to these instructions. In June 1581 he had written to Walsingham concerning an earlier draft proclamation, that 'I received a packet from you being in camp then in Byrne's country ... I could neither answer you nor as yet execute the direction for the proclamations'.[68] More importantly, Elizabeth explained that foreknowledge should not be defined as sedition. She drew a specific distinction between those who had concealed 'the conspiracy being made privy to it', no doubt thinking of Delvin and Kildare, and those who had 'concealed the same and given their consent to it'. She was 'content to extend our gracious general pardon to all offences committed against our state'.[69]

This meant that Nicholas Nugent's trial and execution should not have gone ahead, because Nicholas had been 'made privy' to William's conspiracy but he had not given his 'consent to it'. In this case Grey was forced to set out his proto-absolutist rationale, and the lord deputy explained his position with reference to John Cusack – a man who was on trial with Nugent. Cusack had been pardoned in line with what Elizabeth had ordered because Cusack had agreed to be 'received to a better estate and course of life and to do to her majesty some acceptable service to repair this his offence'.[70] Nugent, on the other hand, could not be pardoned because he had supported the Pale's opposition in the 1570s to the cess – 'his wanted disposition to repine and impugn her majesty's prerogative many years past'.[71] A document entitled 'Touching Nicholas Nugent' also describes how the chief justice had 'about four years past when the matter of cess and other things touching her majesty's prerogative came into question ... did not only resist [the matter] ... but also persuaded others to do the like'.[72] In short, the integrity of the state's prerogative rights, its sovereignty, was more important than mercy and conciliation.

Furthermore, how the Old English community responded to Grey's actions indicates that within the community there was also an awareness of the extent to which Grey's actions departed from the norms of the mixed polity. It was Nicholas White, the master of the rolls, and one of the most articulate of the remaining Old English councillors, who identified the main points at issue. In December 1581 he wrote to Burghley reminding him of what he saw as the correct constitutional nature of the Irish kingdom. White described how Elizabeth's 'ancient kingdom, [was] subjected to her by God's ordinance, and confirmed by consent of the nation'.[73] He referred to the 'act of kingly title', which had turned Henry VIII from lord into king of Ireland; and his reference to 'consent' points to European resistance theory, in tone at least, whereby sovereign authority is passed from the community as a whole to the prince, the prince having a responsibility to govern well and respect the customs and laws of the wider political community.

White explained, however, that Grey had departed from such a model and now looked to root out the 'ancient houses' such as Kildare, Ormond and Desmond.[74]

Similar to Elizabeth, White also pointed to the bonds of amity and friendship, which he thought had been forgotten. He argued, 'neither is it good (in mine opinion) that her majesty extend the uttermost of her correction against this people; and if any want of duty hath here [been] found in any great ones of this estate (whose cases I know not) I hold it for more surety ever to ... remit it'. He reminded Burghley that Elizabeth had 'showed herself so far from desire of blood as she hath measured punishment far under the quality of men's offences by which she hath gotten the unfeigned love of her people'.[75] In line with this the earl of Kildare deployed an earlier language of fidelity and loyalty in an attempt to avoid Grey's uncompromising attitude to the gentry and noble community. He explained in his defence how 'in mine own conscience as I protested yesterday before your lords, I stand clear in my loyalty and fidelity to her majesty'.[76] Kildare and Delvin were called over to England by Elizabeth, no doubt to protect them from Grey's narrowed position on rebellious behaviour.[77]

It is interesting, then, that Grey had excluded the master of the rolls from the council board when the decision to arrest the earl of Kildare was being taken. White explained to Burghley, in February 1581, two months after the earl's arrest in December 1580, that he had not been present – that he had come 'but suddenly to the signing of the letter containing the causes of Kildare's commitment, whereof I never understood anything'.[78] Did Grey understand that White was looking to a very different model for the political community? Here, in line with the notion of a free-state or republic, White grasped the implications of sovereignty being vested with the institutions of the state, and not with the political community as a whole.

There is a certain complexity here concerning how we might define the notion of liberty White comes to articulate. Skinner argues that in classical republicanism a notion of negative liberty entailed not only a series of negative customary or constitutional checks on the actions of the ruler, where freedom was freedom from coercion, but that popular sovereignty and the potential ability to act in political life had to exist in principle for political liberty to exist. After all, it was through active participation in political life that customs and rights were preserved.[79] Obviously, White's frustration at his exclusion from discussions, and the wider exclusion of the Old English gentry from political life, informed his various complaints. But alongside this, the position taken by White and others does echo the specific constitutional critique of the resistance writers Ponet and Goodman – that magistrates should not be allowed to govern according to their unbridled will. The fact that the Old English could not invoke the conscience- and grace-based elements usually associated with this position, because they were catholics demanding inclusion or rights in a protestant state, seems to have allowed a more straightforward notion of negative liberty to emerge. For White 'all law were ended' and Elizabeth was 'not to suffer the particular government of her country here, to be committed to such as cannot govern themselves ... [where] their own wills to be holden for laws'.[80]

There followed a more detailed discussion by Lord Delvin, concerning the types of checks which could be placed on the authority of the various officers of state in Ireland, elaborating on White's position. He argued that there was 'too absolute authority in the governor' and that on top of this the provincial governors 'many times live more absolute than the governor himself'. The solution, he suggested, was that laws and statutes be strictly observed and that none be put to death by martial law.[81] Again Delvin's experience of Grey's government, where he had come under suspicion, no doubt spurred him to detail what would effectively be a series of negative checks or limitations on what the governor could do.

But such a demand for customary rights to be recognized quickly became confessional. It was further noted in 1583 that, with a growing threat posed by Spain, the catholic inhabitants of the Pale had actually begun to look to the king of Spain to uphold their customary rights. That the community of Dublin believed, considering the example of Portugal, which had just come under the Spanish crown, that:

> what prerogatives they [the Portuguese] have above the Spaniards that it is like he [the king of Spain] will deal so with any nation that subject themselves to his government and that he expecteth no gain of his subjects but union in the Roman religion.[82]

Clearly this was not the case in the Netherlands, where for Calvinist resistance theorists it was the traditional rights and privileges of the Dutch states that were being attacked by a tyrannous catholic Spanish monarch. Does this further suggest that rights and privileges within the community are thought to be somehow synonymous with Christian unity – different confessions thinking the other corrupt and therefore forfeiting their right to full participation in the political community?

With all this in mind, conditions in Ireland were unique in forcing Grey, White and others to explain the intellectual or philosophical reasons behind their respective positions and why they opposed the actions of various officers of state. As Michael Braddick has noted in *State Formation in Early Modern England*, the 'real difficulty ... lies in the attempt to recover the motives of an individual from a study of their actions, a problem made even more difficult since they themselves may not have been clear about their motives'.[83] Here the expansion of Tudor government through physical institutional structures is discussed. This more physical process is important as a background context to the various intellectual developments charted in the second half of this study. Braddick traces the growth of the institutional state, as local government relied less on the gentry and more on the institutions and minor offices of state. He does not, however, trace any concurrent shift in statist language or in political thought because, it would appear, the minor office holders in England tended not to have to explain why they had acted in a particular way beyond the received and static norms of provincial English society. But in Ireland the rapidity of change forced individuals to speak, search for, and repackage ideas in a new vocabulary in order to make sense of what was happening.

From 'Broken State' to Abstract 'State'

Returning to the deployment of statist vocabulary, at one level the term 'state', following its initial use under Sidney, was deployed in order to make reference to government's relationship with Ireland's lords. In September 1581, when Fenton wrote concerning the surrender of Feagh McHugh O'Byrne, a Leinster lord who was in confederacy with Baltinglass, he used 'the state' to denote the relationship between McHugh and the crown. For Fenton, 'if at his coming in he [McHugh] had put himself into the hands and possession of the state ... [then] his reconciliation to the state ... [would have] been void of suspicion and holden more firm and assured'.[84] There is a clear sense here of a double distinction between the prince's authority and the state in Ireland, and between the wider lordly community and the authority of the Irish state. Similarly, Fenton wrote a month later about Shane O'Reilly, an Ulster lord. O'Reilly had executed two of Shane O'Neill's sons because, it would appear, he thought Grey's government would agree with what he had done. Fenton reprimanded O'Reilly because he had been instructed to place O'Neill's sons 'into the hands and possession of the state'.[85] In April 1581 the term 'state' was used by Bryskett when discussing the problem of victualing the army. He referred to the problems confronted by 'this state or government'.[86] As will be discussed further in chapter 5, the idea of the state came to dominate government's relationship with Ireland's various Old English and Gaelic Irish lords.

The phrase 'broken state', however, also came to be deployed in a manner that indicated Irish government was seeking to understand how to respond to temporal political circumstances, where different interest groups and political or sovereign authority appeared to be distributed in a way that was destabilizing current institutional arrangements. Here Irish government would appear to have been searching for new vocabulary in order to express or describe its attempts to cope with the politically contingent event. Lord Deputy Grey, in January 1581, made reference to 'this disordered and broken state', and the same month Warham St Leger, a prospective candidate for the presidency of Munster, deployed the term when arguing against the appointment of the earl of Ormond as lord general of the army in Munster.[87] There was no doubt a note of self-interest in St Leger's comment, in that St Leger wanted to undermine a rival; but he also explained that the matter needed to be 'looked into, as things greatly disliked in all politic government that I have seen or read, chiefly where a broken state is'.[88] His reference to 'politic government' and things he had 'seen or read' suggests that St Leger was *au fait* with contemporaneous politic philosophy. It seems he was suggesting that allowing a powerful lord like Ormond to remain in control of a large armed force threatened to unbalance 'a broken state' even more.

Similarly, Fenton, in a letter to Burghley in May 1582, deployed other vocabulary associated with the writing of Machiavelli and Guicciardini to denote and make sense of a set of events in a strictly temporal or contingent sphere, writing of 'alteration', 'mutation' and 'innovation'. On a positive note he described how 'touching the state and present government here, there is no alteration happened since my last [letter]'. But he continued and made reference to the possibility of mutation or change, explaining that:

> Munster retaineth still the former suspicions of a further mutation and ruin: the earl of Desmond finding no forces to control him, taketh what liberty he will ... where he doth not a little encourage the hollow and unsound subject to shake off obedience.[89]

For Fenton the solution was either the deployment of a large army or an 'absolute pardon' for Desmond. The earl either had to be fully bridled or allowed to retain his previous position. Similarly, in a letter touching the reform of the earl of Clanrickard a number of months later, whilst Fenton discussed Clanrickard's willingness to reform his lands and rents in line with English custom, how the success of such a project was understood departed further from earlier commonwealth thought. As before the need to undermine the retention of a large private army by the earl was critical, but this was explained in language akin to that of Italian republican writing. For Fenton 'I doubt not though at the first it may be thought an innovation', but the result of such a process would be that Connacht might 'not be so easily drawn again into alteration'.[90] The point was that conditions would settle down if these new arrangements were enforced for long enough – they would become a new *status quo*.

Fenton also pinpointed, when praising the actions of Nicholas White, the master of the rolls, whose close association with Burghley meant he was once again rehabilitated, that White's ability 'in civil and martial government ... [was] very fruitful in this tottering time' – that in a context where mutability seemed to be to the fore a particular type of political action was required.[91] White himself, as Nicholas Canny notes, even deployed the language of innovation and change in opposition to his New English colleagues. He suggested that it was the new arrivals who held government posts who actually sought 'to better [their] state by change', adding that 'innovations hath been in all ages accounted dangerous, and the busiest men that way be not the profitablest ministers'.[92]

In June 1582 Lord Justice Wallop also talked of the 'brokenness of the state', whilst making reference to the second Desmond rebellion and the Baltinglass revolt.[93] In a letter in December Wallop and Loftus even made reference to the wider breakdown of order and institutional stability in the Netherlands and France, which had arisen out of confessional division. They pointed to:

> affects (as we find before and your lord gravely considereth) which wars do bring forth in all countries having any continuance, whereof France and Flanders might yield us many and notable testimonies.[94]

And within a contingent political setting the maintenance of sovereign authority was identified as a clear focus for political action, which would help shut the avenues left open for dissent and protest. In April 1583, the Lords Justices Wallop and Loftus, in the midst of a dispute over whether they actually possessed the full authority usually given to the deputy, asked for 'the establishing of the state here under some settled governor'. They explained that in 'this slippery time', the rumour or expectation of a new governor is 'very dangerous to the state ... [because] the people ... expecteth change', and therefore 'a settled governor' is needed immediately 'before any further enterprise be made to trouble the state'.[95] In another letter they further stressed their point asking 'to whom we may resign the government being persuaded that this universal quiet cannot long last, but under an absolute governor', and again in another letter they asked for a 'settled governor which may reduce this broken and uncertain state'.[96]

This established itself as a verbal tag in Irish government parlance. In 1588 the new Lord Deputy Fitzwilliam examined 'the public state of this realm' with regard to 'this dangerous and broken season'.[97] It was further explained by other figures in government how those involved in the first plantation of Munster were 'discouraged in the action with the sight of this rude, tottering and uncertain state' (the plantation taking place after the attainder of the earl of Desmond and his associates following the second Desmond rebellion).[98] And in 1594, William Russell, on taking office and facing widespread rebellion under the earl of Tyrone, again turned to the topic of 'this broken state'.[99]

Furthermore, from 1583 onwards, in many of the letters written by Fenton, 'the state' also began to be presented as arising out of, or in opposition to, the unreformed or corrupt polity. Fenton's comments can be read at some level as a response to White's and even Elizabeth's reassertion of the earlier mixed polity model. From Fenton's reformed protestant perspective, after all, the bonds of friendship and amity had been eroded or collapsed as a result of divisions in conscience. There is also a clear sense in which his comments were informed by his translations of both theological and statist treatises, where two models for understanding the political community were detailed.

First, in a letter in early 1583, Fenton directly tackled the question of how exactly the bonds of loyalty in the community would be re-established, considering the mercy shown by Elizabeth, which Lord Deputy Grey had opposed. He considered how lessening the financial burden placed on the Pale community would bring 'the country to flourish and spring again ... [and would] do much to regain firmly the hearts of the people'. Implicit in Fenton's comment, however, is the assumption that rebuilding these bonds is unlikely, as he does not dwell on this point at all, but instead quickly moves to discuss the issue of state sovereignty. For Fenton, the mercy Elizabeth has shown, or any possibility that she might remove or abolish cess, threatens instead the very integrity of 'the state'. He argues that the queen:

> shall open a dangerous gap to the diminution of her prerogative, which is a mark that many [of] the impugners of her majesty's government here have long shot at, so as in yielding to suppress the cess which being handled with moderate and uncorrupted ministers is nothing so hurtful ... her majesty shall give way to have in time some of her other regalities shaken, for that it is well discerned here that the people do loath all other prerogatives ... [such as] answering of their rents and their ordinary services and tenures due upon their lands.[100]

Writing in April 1583 he suggested that the discontent of the community of the Pale arose, not only out of their internal disposition, 'an argument of their minds', but also because the mercy shown by the crown continued to suggest that available avenues of protest were open, which as a consequence encouraged further expressions of discontent:

> 'For besides the discontentment in the most part of the better sort even of the Pale which many ways showeth itself, yet the universal disdaining of the government and public authority daily seen and observed, is not only an argument of their minds, not thoroughly recovered to soundness and obedience, but also that they have an expectation of some great matter from the former [the queen]'.[101]

Fenton continues that mercy and liberality might be thought 'by reason the strongest bond to assure and bind them to her highness, and the only way to seal in them and their posterity a sound conscience towards her government here, yet I see not but that pity hath wrought in them impressions of greater insolence and that they make this inference upon her majesty's liberality'.[102] Quite bluntly, in the absence of 'sound conscience' legitimate avenues of customary protest needed to be shut, whereby institutional avenues and structures, in conceptual terms, replaced the bonds of brotherly love.

The replacement of the language of godly reform and good conscience by the vocabulary of the state can even be found in the final letters sent by the now ageing bishop of Meath, Hugh Brady. In 1582 Brady had expressed his intention of reporting on the condition of the church in Ireland. He hoped to follow up on his 1576 examination of the Irish church, which he had completed for Sidney.[103] But despite his longer-term intention, the bishop's immediate concern remained the threat posed by the Spanish to 'the security of this state' and he pointed to the men 'amongst those factious nations, a company of desperate and roving Machiavellians' who looked to 'disturb and disquiet our poor state'.[104] Whilst as late as 1592, with regard to Connacht, Fenton returned to theme of brotherly love, arguing that:

> If ... the hearts of the people [were] won from revolting and stirs, her majesty might say that the realm of Ireland were in an universal quietness in all parts therof, but until there be a better liking and trust between the people of Connacht and their governor [Bingham], it cannot be denied but still a gap will be kept open to greater alterations.[105]

The lack of the bonds of friendship allowed for innovation and change.

The distinction or contrast between the state and the previous bonds of conscience and Christian love, moreover, further clarified under Perrot's deputyship as a consequence of government's failure to gain consent to its parliamentary programme through 1585 into 1586. In particular, the attempt to place English penal legislation on the Irish statute book, alongside an attempt to enforce the oath of supremacy quite widely, exacerbated quite significantly religious strife in the Old English community.[106] This added clarity to government's awareness of the sheer extent of the collapse in the norms of Christian friendship. Here John Long, the archbishop of Armagh, asked how the community in Dublin could 'be true hearted unto her majesty when in conscience they are severed from her'. He also addressed the problem of forcing individual consciences.[107] Long explained that if those in government should consider how they resisted 'injuries offered us in external things, how much more do we wish to be freed from them and to be able to overmatch them which we think offer us oppression in spiritual things'.[108] Thus any residual optimism coming for an earlier commonwealth or godly position, which can be found in Perrot's initial disposition as deputy, dissipated, and this encouraged a further separation of the state and its institutions from the wider polity.[109]

In his dealings with the Irish parliament, the new Lord Deputy Perrot commented that if 'their [the Commons] contemptuous manner of dealing go unpunished, I may bid farewell to any reputation that either Irish or English will give to the state'.[110] Similarly, Perrot described how 'some [members of the Pale community] cannot abide that the state should have any leisure to look more narrowly into their doings, and to that end serve [*sic*] the factious instruments of the Pale to oppose themselves under good pretences against the state'. It was the 'good of the state' and the 'blemish of ... public injury', not necessarily the common good, that the deputy was concerned with. He even explained how Elizabeth's usual policy of temporizing with her subjects in Ireland helped feed the problem, whereby 'these kind of people by the mild dealing of that state [England] have ever found favour there than hath been for the good of this state [Ireland]'.[111] What is quite striking is the extent to which Perrot seems to be asserting that England and Ireland represent two distinct and independent institutional structures, as well as the sense of the state as a distinct political being overseeing the Pale community or the Commons. He also pointed out, with regard to wider Gaelic Ireland, that:

> forasmuch as the Irishry here are naturally unconstant and desirous of change, as your lordships well know ... the good opportunities and means of late devised to retain them in duty are now overpast.[112]

Constructing a loyal political community was no longer an option. Perrot even drew a distinction between 'this state and the people', whilst the deployment of such terminology was more consciously absolutist than it had been under Grey.[113] For example, the Commons had opposed various financial reform proposals, and it had also refused to pass the bill suspending Poynings' law, similar to the 1569–70 parliament, in order to block the progress of the deputy's parliamentary programme. At one level this reignited a simmering debate over the nature of prerogative rights. The financial reform proposals touched upon the prerogative right to cess thus raising the question as to whether or not the crown's ability to act in this regard was limited by custom and the community at large. For Perrot, as for Sidney and Grey before him, the Commons wanted to 'close up her majesty's prerogative right' to cess. But this now combined with an awareness that the attack on the prerogative had a confessional dimension, since the Commons sought to resist the placement of penal legislation on the Irish statute book.[114] Although the Commons would pass an act attainting the earl of Desmond and his followers.

Perrot broke parliamentary privilege, which did not allow the lord deputy to curtail free speech in the Commons or to threaten arrest, and he summoned the leaders of the opposition to the council board and attempted to extract under oath their motivations in opposing the legislation. Once again such an act would not nor could not have happened in England where the sensitivity surrounding parliamentary privilege and crown authority was intense. He 'found therein some more malicious and undutiful dealings by practise and combination against the proceedings of the state out of parliament than ever would be suffered in England'.[115] He also directly questioned the Commons's use of Poynings' law. Perrot acknowledged that the act had originally been designed to take away from 'deputies or governors all power to call a parliament' and to 'restrain the power of the deputies' when 'the natives of this land', such as the earl of Kildare, had held the office of governor. This was because Irish lord deputies had tended to use parliament for their own personal gain.[116] Perrot thought, however, in the context of growing religious division, that the sovereign authority of the Irish state, as exercised by the lord deputy, needed to be upheld.

Interestingly, the lord deputy actually justified his attempt to curtail the political freedoms of the Old English with the statement that 'the good [Roman] emperor Trajan speaking of the Sicilians upon his return from his conquest of Asia ... [thought] that servitude did conserveth citizens and liberty did destroy them'.[117] If Perrot's comment is placed within the wider context of protestant resistance theory, it is startling how he openly rejects a notion of political 'liberty' which was so important in protestant continental thought.

In this respect, the protestant elision of an idea of Christian liberty with political liberty becomes important, where in the absence of good conscience such liberty could only be licentiousness. This position would be more directly articulated by Edmund Spenser in a *View*, as well as by Richard Beacon in *Solon his Follie*, which will be discussed in the final chapter of this book; and such pejorative references to liberty had been made throughout the 1570s where different letters talk of 'libertines' or equate 'liberty' with 'lust' and an unbridled will seeking out mutation and change.[118] Catherine Ballériaux notes how, in the New World, Christian Missions deployed similar terminology to refer to the behaviour of the native populations there.[119] This continues to draw attention to the lack of modernity surrounding certain aspects of a protestant conception of the state, where its institutions are not there to provide for liberty in terms of freedom of action, but instead enforce a level of external conformity thought lacking when true Christian freedom and conformity were absent.

The Language of 'the State' and the Possibility of Toleration

The appropriation of the language of the state by the Old English community in 1585–6, however, was very different from Irish government's use of statist vocabulary. Here it was suggested that state institutions, especially those of a mixed state, as opposed to an absolutist state, might allow the wider community to participate in government and political life irrespective of conscience. An idea of negative freedom re-emerges, where it was proposed that the state and its institutions act, not to foster a particular type of behaviour, but in order to protect a variety of individual liberties.

Clearly, this model was not to gain significant traction within government circles, but its importance rests in further revealing the breadth of the statist discussion. It suggests, as did White's brief reference to negative liberty, that the link between modernity and the state was dependent on the diminution in the dominance of particular Christian values. Catholics within the Pale community, after all, represented a suppressed religious majority, and because they sought to act out of sync with the values and behaviour which Irish government sought to impose on the community, the community had to conceive of freedom and the state in a different way.

An initial parallel with both Dutch and French protestant writing can be found in the way in which the catholic community in Dublin, through the Irish Commons in 1585–6, had deployed pre-existing customary checks in an attempt to protect or preserve its religious freedom and stop the passage of English penal legislation. It has been rehearsed how the Irish Commons used Poynings' law, following precedent set in the 1569–70 parliament, as well as its ostensible opposition to the lord deputy's financial reform proposals, to block such legislation. As Perrot himself commented, the Old English wanted 'to make void the parliament itself, that none of the good laws that do there establish her majesty's safety or supreme authority, or that shall touch their corrupt customs or religion may take place'. A member of the Irish Commons 'in open parliament' even spoke of how 'things did prosper in Henry V and former kings' times when mass was up'.[120]

Alongside this a compromise position was voiced by Nicholas White, who had previously championed the Old English constitutional and mixed polity position. In fact White suggested at the Irish council board, sometime in 1586, that it might be a good idea if some form of religious toleration was offered in order to quell parliamentary dissent. The fact that we know this is in itself significant, since topics discussed at the council board should not really have had a full public airing. As with many aspects of the Irish historical record, where distance from the person of the prince led to a level of free discussion not found in England, this particular Irish case may be indicative of a far wider discussion that went unrecorded. Sensitive topics tended to be discussed behind closed doors and *sole voce*. Interestingly, Elizabeth instructed her deputy to temper his actions and to stop pursuing conformity in religion. Secretary Walsingham took the view that 'matters of conscience' should be dealt with by 'instruction' not 'compulsion', whilst Elizabeth questioned why Perrot should have attempted to enforce the oath of supremacy more strictly and widely than in England where 'more teaching and preaching there is'.[121]

Again, the whole idea of toleration remained conditioned by the possibility of shifting focus onto the general idea of the state and its authority. This can be seen in the political row which erupted and revealed what White had said in camera at the council board. Thomas Jones, the bishop of Meath, condemned White publicly in open pulpit for making such a suggestion at the council board. In acting in this way Jones broke protocol. A number of days later one Mr Powell responded to Jones in another sermon arguing 'that princes might tolerate with idolaters for the strength of the realm' as long as idolaters 'were not permitted publicly to commit idolatry [and] not [to] infect others'.[122] Powell attempted to phrase the problem of plurality of confessions as one simply concerning public order, which he defined in terms of external behaviour. In response, some days later, Jones entered the pulpit to rebut what had been said.[123]

The above events were recorded in a letter from John Long, the archbishop of Armagh, to White; and in response to such a discussion over religious or confessional difference a statist position further clarified. Long identified that religious division, or difference in opinion, was a problem when it specifically touched upon the authority of 'the state'. Long thought Jones had been wrong to attack White because 'the foundation was laid at the council board, and there ought the rest of the building to be finished, and not to make a matter of state ... table-talk through the whole land'. More generally, the dispute was problematic, because it might 'bring our own name in controversy, and lay our imperfections and nakedness too open, the people being very prone to misjudge us, making mountains of molehills, and opening every scar in us to find out wounds, albeit they were sufficiently healed before'.[124]

It is with the closing oration to the Irish Commons given by its speaker Nicholas Walsh in May 1586, however, that a real sense emerges of how the state might provide for toleration. This involves the mixed state and the possible participation of a catholic gentry community in Irish protestant political life. Walsh had found favour with Perrot and had been the government's candidate for speaker in the Irish Commons. There are also indications that he was a protestant. But Walsh was from the Old English community, his father having been mayor of Waterford, and as a result he sympathized with the Pale community and the position it found itself in.[125]

In his oration Walsh took a more traditional mixed polity or commonwealth position, which saw sovereign authority as being distributed throughout the political community. From the outset he makes it clear he is drawing on a wider debate on the nature of sovereignty. He refers to 'Plato, Aristotle, and the later philosophers ... [who] divide all civil and allowable governments unto three', that is monarchy, aristocracy and democracy. He then explains that whilst monarchy was clearly the soundest form of government, he thought a mixture of all three forms was not only best, but was how the Irish state had been constructed. Walsh adopts the view of the ancient philosopher Polybius, and he argues that whilst 'her majesty's laws, do not only confirm that [Ireland is a] monarchy ... [they also] draweth thereunto the best parts of the other two [aristocracy and democracy] (in a most happy harmony) to the universal comfort of all estates'.[126] Walsh even suggests that sovereign authority is actually located with all three estates, explaining that in 'this most high court of parliament are in meet proportion annexed the sovereign majesty of the prince, the honourable assembly of peers ... and lastly a brotherly society of commons'.[127] Walsh therefore rejects Bodin's position on sovereignty, and so he immediately distances himself from, even rebuts, the increasing absolutism of Lord Deputy Perrot in his dealings with the community in Dublin and the Commons. Bodin argued that the Polybian position was by definition false, because it divided up sovereignty which was an indivisible power.[128]

It is the question of individual conscience, however, that really interests us. In support of his position that Ireland was a mixed state, Walsh drew on the urtexts of the English common law or mixed polity position, such as Fortescue's *De Laudibus Legum Anglia* and Bracton *On the Laws and Customs of England*, which had informed the earlier oppositional stance of the Pale. But Walsh also referred to the Athenian judge Licurgus and the example of Spartan ephors. Walsh explains that a mixed polity did not 'impair the majesty of the monarch but rather doth (as Licurgus said) when he ordained magistrates called ephori to assist his kings of Sparta that the state of kings was made thereby more durable'.[129] Walsh points to the position taken by Calvin, Beza and Huguenot resistance theorists, who had used the example of ephors to argue that inferior magistrates could resist the actions of an ungodly ruler when consciences were touched. There is a clear sense of irony here, in that Walsh uses an example from protestant resistance theory to begin to build an argument that will suggest the catholic Pale should also be allowed some form of political liberty. The example of the Spartan ephors had also been referenced in Hooker's *Order and Usage* and Ponet's *Politike Power*.[130]

From this position Walsh engages in a second attack on the absolutist view taken by Perrot. He argues that 'as laws were first ordained to bridle men's affections who [are] accustomed to rule by their wills, I hold those laws most commendable that leave least to the will of the magistrate'.[131] He suggests that the benefit of a mixed state was that it did not allow the magistrate to act as he wished and impose his will on the polity, thus echoing White and Delvin but now in a more obviously confessional context. More critically, Walsh shifts the argument in order to tackle the godly model of reform, which lay behind Perrot's concern over the question of conscience – the view that without the dissemination of God's word man could not be brought to know what was good and the polity established on a sound foundation.

Walsh echoes the position taken by Dutch as well as Italian republican writers, and he suggests that whilst the magistrate's 'will' in a mixed state would be bridled, in a mixed state the wills of individual subjects were also held in check.[132] Walsh calls for the Commons to 'persist ... constantly, in the maintenance of the government grounded upon her majesty's laws. Stand firmly upon the certain stays thereof. Restrain that which is to consist upon the uncertain will of any'; and Walsh then makes direct reference to the Roman republican tradition.[133] He openly rejects the reformed protestant position, that only through the dissemination of God's word would man be brought to act well in a political setting. He refers to Cicero and 'his book *de Oratore* in praise of the laws of the twelve tables of Rome, that they did more divert men to live well than did all the words of the philosophers'.[134] In doing so he hints at the distinction drawn in Italian republicanism between political *virtù* and moral or godly virtue.

> So may I say by our laws that they do little less draw men to virtue, and withdraw them from vice, than do the persuasions of preachers for that, alas, man's frailty is such, that the greater number will be sooner moved by the allurements and terrors of this world than by that [which] is to be expected in the world to come. And when some be by this means brought to the love of virtue, and vice is made hateful unto them, then are they easily formed to the frame whereunto preachers desire to bring them.[135]

Thus Walsh moves to attack head on government's fixation on conscience and the internal disposition of Elizabeth's Irish subjects. In effect, he points out that it is quite impossible to examine man's internal condition, meaning the only thing government can base its policies upon is man's outward actions. 'Neither are the outward shows of obedience nor the external badges of benevolence to be omitted', because 'Christians wisheth that people be reputed as they seem until the contrary effect do appear'.[136]

Finally, when we consider that a mixed state model did not gain traction in Ireland, but nevertheless did in the Netherlands, the difference in the make-up of the respective Dutch and Irish political communities helps provide some form of an explanation. In Ireland the catholic population was quite large if not dominant, whilst those in positions of authority in the state remained protestant. For an Irish protestant government maintaining the state meant maintaining its authority over its institutions, which a plurality of confessions might undermine. Tolerating a catholic community that was more numerous meant making the state tacitly catholic. We might add that until the norms and values of political culture became less consciously religious or Christian in character, the state would remain confessional, as it did in the writing of Stubbs and Philip Sidney. In contrast, van Gelderen has argued that in the Netherlands, the external threat posed by Spain required political unity to be pursued despite confessional division. This meant that a very different non-confessional approach to the maintenance of the state could be conceived.[137] Here the fact that reformed protestants were a majority, but not fully dominant in numbers, also encouraged the political community to move further away from the model of the body of Christ than was possible in Ireland or in many other communities in Europe, since it did not automatically entail altering the confessional character of the Dutch state. In short, with a diminution in the idea of a Christian body politic, we have a shift away from a mixed godly polity, linked together by friendship, towards the idea of a more institutional mixed state.[138]

5 IRELAND'S LORDSHIPS AND AN ABSOLUTIST STATE

In light of the failure to construct a godly community in Ireland, and with the conscious exclusion of the traditional gentry from government, this chapter asks what sort of society or political community Irish government actually wished to build. In relation to island-wide reform, a sense of fortune or mutability further solidified in Irish government thinking. As a consequence, there followed a wider deployment of the term 'the state', as political action in general, not simply in relation to the Pale community, was framed in terms of the maintenance of state institutions and authority, as opposed to the common good or a wider godly objective. So whilst the state was separated from a corrupt polity in the form of Dublin and its localities, in relation to the wider island this entailed a more general deconstruction of the lordly community. It is this wider deployment of the terminology of the state that this chapter examines.

As with the inversion of European norms identified in relation to the Pale community, the continued existence of great noble houses in Ireland, who had a significant degree of independence from government, allows us to identify and trace how an emerging notion of an institutional state responded to and was conditioned by a pre-existing lordly model. Why was a lordly model now defunct, and how did the notion of the state seek to supplant such a model? In contrast, in England the strength of the nobility had been more gradually and progressively undermined under Henry VII and Henry VIII, and both protestant and catholic nobles had adapted themselves to courtly and institutional government.[1] Thus there remains a blurred line in England between the noble model of loyalty and fidelity, and the impersonal entity of the state with its oppressive focus on the maintenance of sovereignty.

Our attention should be drawn to two aspects of Irish government correspondence. Whilst common law practice had formed part of government reform proposals through the 1550s, '60s, and '70s, the idea of martial law and arbitrary justice became far more normative (even though the number of commissions issued declined for a period) and in turn the role of the freeholder altered.[2] The freeholder was not necessarily to serve the commonwealth through active participation in political life. Instead, he became more of a structural component of the institutional state. The freeholder's role was to help in the atomization of society and the deconstruction of lordships, where his contribution to political life would be the payment of tax. Within Irish government correspondence, and political writing more generally, Stoic republican and Tacitean values also began to be articulated, where in a world governed by fortune emphasis was placed on man's ability to control his appetites and passions in order to respond appropriately to the vagaries of the world.

Once again, the open deployment of these ideas slightly predates developments in England. Interestingly, Markku Peltonen has identified an early English articulation of civic republican thought and the notion of fortune in Richard Beacon's Irish reform treatise *Solon his Follie* (1594). Reflecting on this, Peltonen suggests that the vagaries of the Irish political environment gave form and clarity to English political thought (something this study has continued to emphasize).[3] Alongside this, the wider context in which such notions were deployed suggests that Stoic republicanism was not simply about coping with the corruption of court life, but about learning how to act in a clearly temporal political sphere where God was absent. In other words, man had to control his corrupt nature (his passions and appetites), because he could no longer rely on grace. Here there is also some indication that the separation of state from polity had allowed room for individuals to begin to rethink the nature of the polity. Instead of the state simply recreating a shadow of the bonds that united a Christian community, the state would regulate, direct and bridle self-interest and man as a natural earthly body.[4]

Bryskett, Italian Republicanism and *Fortuna*

The motif of *fortuna* or mutability, like all aspects of statist thought in Ireland, became more consciously applied and referenced in letters sent by John Perrot as lord deputy and also in Lodowick Bryskett's *A Discourse of Civill Life* (1606), which, although published in the first decade of the seventeenth century, had been written sometime in the 1580s.[5] Significantly, whilst Fenton's translation work might have set out two models for political action and the construction of a polity, Fenton in his published work had not set these two models beside each other. In Bryskett's *Discourse*, however, a godly model for political action was firmly positioned against an alternative statist critique, and Bryskett, unlike Fenton, whose translation work had been carried out before his arrival in Ireland, set his *Discourse* firmly within an Irish context. We encountered Bryskett's *Discourse* at the very opening of this study.

Bryskett's treatise is divided into three books and takes the form of a dialogue between Bryskett himself, who had just retired from crown service to a farm on the outskirts of Dublin, and a set of Bryskett's friends who had journeyed from

Dublin to see him. They included Dr John Long, the archbishop of Armagh, and the poet Edmund Spenser. One of the dedicatees of the *Discourse* was 'the right Honourable Arthur late Lord Grey of Wilton', and as with much of Bryskett's correspondence as clerk to the council under Grey the treatise is rooted in the language of the state.[6] It is explained in the preface that in writing the dialogue it could not be said that on leaving office, he, Bryskett, was 'retiring my selfe from the State'. Bryskett's *Discourse* is also a much embellished translation of Giambattista Giraldi Cinthio's *Tre dialoghi della vita civile* and other Italian republican writing.[7] This draws our attention to a fusion occurring in Ireland between civic republican thought and a growing Irish absolutism. Bryskett discussed how action should be directed towards the maintenance of the state in a context where those state institutions were most certainly not those of a mixed or free state.[8]

In particular, Bryskett attempts to demarcate a basis for political action and virtue which was not reliant on the presence of grace in political life, though he had raised the received view on the centrality of grace in the opening of the work. He explained that the discourse would help bring the reader 'to attaine to that further perfection which the profession of a Christian requireth; and that everlasting felicite, which assisted with God's grace ... thou mayst assuredly purchase'.[9] In book one, however, a variety of types of action are outlined. Following his comments in the prefacing material, the dialogue engages in the perennial problem faced by reformed protestants in Ireland, of how exactly man could be reformed, and significantly in the dialogue it was the archbishop of Armagh, John Long, who set out the reformed protestant position.

This was very much in character, since throughout Perrot's deputyship Long continued to argue that without grace man could not be brought to know what was truly good, and in the treatise the archbishop adopted an extreme reformed protestant position. His character suggests that, because of original sin, man is incapable of properly contributing to political life. Long's character argues that:

> when you seeme to shoot at such a marke as human felicitie, which is without, not your reach onely, but all mens, whiles they are here in this low and muddie world: for I wis[e] that is no where to be found but above the stars: mans felicity is placed only in heave[n], where God of his mercie hath appointed it for him to be found, and not here on earth.[10]

He continues and explains how 'our first father [Adam] by his disobedience ... [had deprived] himselfe and all his posteritie of ... the infinite goodnes and mercie of God'.[11] In identifying, then, the centrality of grace in political life, the treatise arrives at the suggestion that virtuous earthly action may be an impossibility; but it is from this position that two interconnected positions are outlined which might allow for a type of virtuous political action that is neither godly or necessarily dependent on grace. As with many of his contemporaries, Bryskett points to the Italian distinction between virtue and *virtù*.[12]

First, Bryskett's character restates the well-worn renaissance motif of *vita active* and *vita contemplative* explaining that there is 'a contemplative felicite (which some men haply draw neare unto, but cannot perfectly attaine in this life;) the other an active or practicke felicite, consisting in virtuous actions, and reducing of a mans passions under the rule of reason'.[13] Here Bryskett elaborates and describes how this 'civil' felicity 'is an inward reward for morall vertues ... wherein fortune can chalenge no part or interest at all'.[14] He details how man's various appetites and passions can be controlled and trained so man might behave correctly and know how to act in a political setting. The dialogue draws on Stoic republican values and emerging Tacitean sentiment, which suggested that man needed to control his own internal condition so he could withstand the vagaries of fortune and the corruption of the world. This is a theme Bryskett returns to in more detail in book two.

More importantly, considering the type of political language this study has traced, Bryskett explains that the actions of man in such a context should be directed towards the maintenance of the state. In discussing the boundaries of political action, Bryskett explains that he is discussing the public not private actions of individuals. He points out, for example, that 'the name of *Duellum* was given by the Latins, not to a singular fight betweene man and man, but the general war between two nations or states', and in discussing what might lead a man to take up arms in defence of 'the state', he goes on to define treason as 'offences against the Prince's person', which should be seen as an offence against 'the publike State, which resposeth upon the person of the Prince', explaining that the 'injuries of private men' are something very different indeed.[15] Furthermore, a propensity to further private interest, as opposed to the public good, is presented as fuelling civil war. Bryskett clarifies his point by arguing that 'when warre is moved against any Prince, the State and Common-weale is offended', meaning that 'it is the dutie of everyman of vertue and honor, to oppose himselfe against the fury of the enemy'.[16] Political action is to be directed at identifiable institutional structures, not the remoter and more difficult objective of moral or godly reform.

The next two books discuss, therefore, how exactly man could be trained to act in a political setting conditioned by the absence of grace. Bryskett draws on Aristotle's view of the natural body, dividing man's faculties into the vegetative, the sensitive and the rational and on this basis a very different model for the construction of a virtuous individual is detailed. Bryskett argues that virtue arises from man's ability to control his various appetites and passions, which come from his vegetative and sensitive faculties. For Bryskett, man will gain control of his baser passions and appetites through the employment of his rational faculty. For Bryskett 'virtue consisteth in the meane betweene two extremes, which on either side are too much or too little, wherein yong men do most incline to that extreme of too much: for they love too much, they hate too much'.[17] In this respect, Bryskett comments at the end of the first book that 'true fortitude' is a 'convenient mean between rashnesse and fearfulnesse', and man requires 'fortitude' so he can stand firm in the face of 'the inconsistencies and changeablenesse of fortune'. He continues in book two to describe how man might be educated through civil conversation, habit and custom so man could bridle and balance his baser faculties.[18] Interestingly, in the dialogue, in both books two and three, a grace-centred view of political action continues to be raised only to be dismissed. In doing so, Bryskett emphasizes rhetorically the model of grace-based virtue which his dialogue aims to move past.

In particular, what appears most significant about the discussion is that in focusing on the natural or physical body of the subject or citizen, Bryskett starts demarcating an area and a definition of virtue completely distinct from grace and individual conscience. Man, after all, cannot remove his appetites or passions, or stop them arising. But he can learn to respond to them in a way that drives him forward so he can act in a controlled manner for the good of 'the state'. Such a process is distinct from a qualitative change in the internal condition or conscience of man. Bryskett addresses bashfulness and magnanimity, defining bashfulness as 'the one to hold us back from doing of any thing worthy [of] blame and reproach: the other [magnanimity] to put us forward into the way of praise and vertue', these two qualities together helping effect sound political actions.[19] Earlier on Bryskett had also pointed towards the work of Machiavelli, where with regard to education, it was explained that 'knowledge of warre was one of the surest foundations for the upholding of a State or kingdome'.[20]

The wider Irish context of the *Discourse* begins to suggest, then, that the rehabilitation or application of these aspects of Aristotelian thought, and more importantly Stoic and Tacitean values, was not simply a response to the perceived corruption and venality of political life. This is the argument usually extended in discussions addressing the latter half of Elizabeth's reign, where the problem of flattery and the suffocating aspects of an ageing court had become particularly problematic for the younger generation. Here Stoicism and Taciteanism were also about rehabilitating or rediscovering political values in the face of a failure of protestant views on grace and free will, over a number of decades, to deliver usable and successful principles when constructing and governing political communities. This is something the work of Richard Tuck has pointed towards, in contextualizing neo-Stoicism within the fraught climate of confessional division, where the expression of belief or attempts to achieve religious and political consensus became increasingly difficult. However, the extent to which normative Christian values, and a wider conception of unredeemed man, may have driven the use of this new language remains downplayed, because Tuck tends to focus on the problems confronted by an earlier more optimistic humanism and not the more difficult question of the relationship between grace, conscience and right political action.[21] Similarly, more recent work by Ethan Shagan on the aggressive nature of England's ecclesiastical *via media* and the rule of moderation, which entailed forcible restraint of excesses in order to maintain a 'middle way', might also be read as a response (from some quarters) to a failure to build God's kingdom. Again it required the bridling of passions in the absence of definite conscience based reform.[22]

Bryskett's book three addresses this very problem, and the character of Long actually engages directly with a grace-centred model, where after an initial discussion concerning knowledge of the ultimate good or God, Long makes it clear that 'we are here to discourse of Morall Philosophie, we will for this time put Divinitie to silence'. Following this the character of Captain Carleil sets out in detail the wider problem. First, 'whether vertue and vertuous actions be in our power or no'? And secondly, 'whether the good or evill we do, proceed fro[m] the influence of the heavens or from necessitie of destinie, and not from our owne free election'?[23] Bryskett's solution, in line with the aspects of Italian republican writing identified by J. G. A. Pocock, is to turn now more directly to the notion of fortune to demarcate a clearly political and linear sphere of action. Bryskett adopts the position of Virgil:

> who seeing many things to happen by chance or fortune; whereby it appeared that it could not be true, that things came by necessitie [i.e., by the will of God], lest they should denie a thing so manifest as sense, they supposed the beginnings and the endings of things to be of necessitie, but the meanes and circumstance they yeelded to be subject to the changes and alterations of fortune.[24]

Bryskett's position is contradictory in that it raises the simple question as to exactly how events can occur by chance if the sum total of those events actually achieves God's will. Bryskett also engages in quite a challenging, and often strained, interpretation of St Augustine's writing and scripture to draw a distinction between God as universal cause and the vagaries of daily political life. What he would appear to have been trying to do, however, is make it clear that in political life man needs to be trained to address secondary, historical, causes, which from a temporal perspective appear disordered. The critical point for us is that only in a world governed by chance or fortune are the appetites and passions meaningful, since it is the unknown contingent event that causes the natural body to react. The dialogue continues:

> And because fortune ... hath no small part in most of our actions, the wisest men have said, that counsel is the eye of the mind, by helpe whereof, men of prudence see how to defend themselves from the blind strokes of fortune, and eschuing that which may hurt them, they take hold of that which is profitable.[25]

It is in this context that fortitude, temperance, justice and prudence are required in maintaining the state, and again these four principal civil virtues are defined as mean points between various passions. Whilst the original topic of the *Discourse* had been to demonstrate how man could be brought to know and act for the *summum bonum*, which we would rightly equate with God, by the end of the dialogue the meaning of political action has changed. It is now about acting for the good of the state in a world governed by fortune, where virtue arises from the natural body and its appetites and passions, not from the action of God's grace. It is about a physical or natural political virtue, not a spiritual or moral virtue. As Richard McCabe notes, Spenser's presence within the dialogue, and Spenser's reference to his yet unfinished *Faerie Queene*, is indicative of 'a close correspondence' between both projects. Here, then, our reading of Bryskett's dialogue also suggests that notions of civility, reform and godliness, which Spenser himself addressed in the late 1590s, had already started to break down.[26]

Perrot's 1581 Treatise and an Ulster Emergency

It was such an idea of a more clearly political and contingent environment that broadened out and informed an emerging statist model for island-wide reform. The basics of such a wider re-conceptualization of political action can be found as far back as Perrot's 1581 treatise written in an early bid for the deputyship, where the contingent non-godly conditions facing Lord Deputy Grey directly informed how the prospective deputy thought of political reform. The treatise outlined the basics of a godly and commonwealth view, asking 'how ... a people so estranged from God and their duty to him [can] have any grace to know their lawful prince and their duty to her'?[27] Like Bryskett's dialogue, however, Perrot turned to the question of maintaining the state, and he clearly saw this as an alternative.

The treatise departs from earlier thinking, where unlike his predecessors in the 1550s and '60s Perrot does not propose building a rival noble clientage, which would undercut the authority of the Geraldines or Butlers.[28] Instead, it is suggested that a survey be made of all their lands and that 'your majesty by good advice shall take such a third part thereof into your hands as shall be fittest for the furtherance of your service'. Lordships should be reduced significantly in size, which in effect would reduce the lord to the status of a large landowner; and it is in arguing for such a conceptual change in the nature and extent of lordship that 'your majesty's state may be more followed and depended upon than hitherto it hath been and the lords of the counties less'.

Perrot also suggests that the position of the freeholder needs to be reassessed. Instead of simply negotiating directly with the lords, where rents owed to the crown would be fixed in lieu of military service, the lord then altering how he collected rents from his tenants and freeholders, it is suggested that the composition agreements government negotiated should not only involve the crown and a given lord, but that tripartite indentures should be drawn up whereby the agreement would be 'betwixt the queen, the lord and his freeholder'. Whilst the freeholder would continue to pay some form of annual rent to the lord of the manor, as was standard practice in England, the services owed to the prince would be paid directly to the crown without the lord acting as an intermediary.[29] For Ciaran Brady this reflects the continuation of an earlier model of reform involving the imposition of an English model of land tenure and common law.[30] The predominance of the language of the state, not godly reform or commonwealth values, however, suggests that in reality an alternative statist model was being detailed.

In giving clear recognition to this form of tenure, government would significantly diminish the authority of the feudal lord by reinforcing the independent position of the freeholder. As a result, any sense in which a given lord held authority beyond the defined terms of his manorial holdings would be undermined, and in turn any sense in which he held authority independently of the crown. As Perrot himself commented, the freeholders would as a result be at 'the devotion of the state' and their contribution to political life would be to fund directly provincial institutions, not necessarily to participate in a common law jury or more generally in local gentry government.[31]

In this regard, the treatise hints or suggests that a system of martial law should be institutionalized in Ireland, whereby alongside the deputy and provincial presidents it is proposed that two marshals be appointed for life who would join the deputy and presidents in touring the island and administering justice.[32] The treatise concentrates on the way in which the institutional structures of government might be repositioned geographically so that the state can extend its authority throughout Ireland in a context where lord or freeholder would not form a natural resource for government in the localities. For Perrot no part of Ireland should be remote from the chief 'officers of state'. One presidency should be established at Kilmallock in Munster and the other in Ulster, and the lord deputy should reside in Athlone, not in Dublin.

Perrot further commented in another 1581 treatise that 'it is neither honourable nor necessary that a prince should be driven to use *precari imperium* or to suffer any under their government to live in such [a] state of obedience, as at their will and pleasure one of them may enjoy or harm another'.[33] He reinforced the point that sovereign authority or *imperium* needed to be firmly located with the prince, and the state, and not precariously shared out among semi-autonomous feudal and Gaelic Irish lords. As Rapple notes references to *precari imperium* started to appear dotted throughout the correspondence of provincial officeholders in Ireland, as they sought to uphold the authority inherent in their offices in the face of an increasingly hostile lordly class.[34]

Returning to the question of finance, Perrot suggests, quite out of sync with the principles of good government, that coinage in Ireland be debased to reduce the cost of government: base coin should be called in to give the impression that it is being restored to the correct value, but instead a standardized debased coinage should be re-issued. This, it is suggested, would save government money, since it would take time for the general population to realize what had happened. To justify such action a more explicit reference is made to reason of state. The problem of innovation and change is raised, but this is balanced against the fact that the Irish state is so disorderly anyway that duplicitous government activity cannot actually do harm. It is explained that whilst 'imbasing [*sic*] of coin and such like dangerous innovations may breed harm in well governed states, so in Ireland being all out of order it can do no harm at all'.[35]

Beside this, when Perrot's initial actions in Ulster are considered, where he was forced to respond to an emergency situation, both a notion of the state and a sense of the political contingent event can be found very much at the forefront of the deputy's mind. As mentioned, not long after Perrot's appointment as lord deputy the Scot Sorley Boy MacDonald had started to press his claims in the province and to bring large numbers of Scots into the Glens of Antrim. Sorley Boy was also supporting the claims of the sons of the now dead arch-traitor Shane O'Neill. Alongside this it emerged that Turlough Luineach O'Neill, the head of the O'Neill clan, was attempting to exploit political instability in Ulster by fomenting rebellion in Connacht in order to force Irish government to recognize his position. Turlough's authority as the O'Neill was threatened by Hugh O'Neill the baron of Dungannon, who as a rival claimant to the Gaelic title had the support of the Irish administration as the legitimate heir to the earldom of Tyrone.[36] In Perrot's response his broader intention of atomizing Irish society can be identified, as well as the clear application of statist language and neo-Stoicism.

In August 1584 Perrot argued that the invasion of the Scots posed a serious threat to her majesty's 'state' and 'imperial crown', and he explained that 'if we should receive an overthrow it would be hard for her majesty to recover'.[37] He further suggested that 'if an overthrow should happen ... how dangerous the same would be to her majesty and this her state'.[38] He was concerned that any possible alteration in the political *status quo* might undermine the institution of the state; and the deputy's longer-term solution sought to divide the province into three. Turlough Luineach was given control of one third, and jurisdiction over the other two-thirds was given respectively to the baron of Dungannon and Nicholas Bagenal, the leading crown officer in the province. In particular, the composition agreements negotiated meant that in theory the troops Turlough and Dungannon would command would not be their own clients and military retainers, but instead they would command men supported by a composition rent that would be collected throughout the province.[39]

This was important because Gaelic custom gave the heads of Gaelic clans and septs a degree of independent/sovereign authority – so too did the notion of feudal lordship. As Kenneth Nicholls notes, the O'Neill had 'the power to cess troops and other followers at will upon the vassal'.[40] Such titles, therefore, were in direct conflict with a notion of the state, which saw sovereign authority as resting within the offices or apparatus of government. The agreements explained that the troops were to be at the service of 'the state' and 'to be always at the commandment of the lord deputy'.[41] Perrot also described the division of the territory into three as being 'necessary to this state'.[42] He even commented positively on the baron of Dungannon that 'he maketh his whole dependence of the state'.[43] In reality, however, because the military force in the province was maintained by composition, as Hiram Morgan notes, the troops were billeted throughout the province. Irrespective of the notion of the state, then, Turlough and Dungannon remained in effective control of their lordships.[44] At a very basic level Perrot simply institutionalized the pre-existing *status quo*.

Nevertheless, in presenting a medium- to long-term solution to the problem in Ulster, Perrot drew on the Stoic republican values as set out in Bryskett's *Discourse*. The lord deputy argued that those in government needed to find a mean point between their various passions in order to take sound political decisions. Perrot's comment was directed at Elizabeth, who as usual had been reluctant to support military activity in Ulster because of the expense. Perrot had had to raise an army pretty much immediately to repel the Scots, and he proposed that alongside a garrison of 2,000 foot soldiers and 400 horses, seven forts, seven bridges and seven towns should be built in Ulster. Elizabeth, though she supported a composition arrangement that would support 1,100 troops, refused to give the go ahead for the building project.[45] Perrot explained that:

> I cannot but be very sorry to see carelessness in matters of the greatest weight ... together magnanimity and contempt of peril is good, but it is the better and holdeth out longest and surest ... when it is accompanied with wariness and foresight, whereby dangers are known as they are and the easier avoided without confusion or and amazedness the ordinary companions of uncircumspection.[46]

Perrot also presented the agreements he had made with Turlough O'Neill and the baron of Dungannon as responding to a political situation governed by fortune, and his use of the vocabulary of mutability and change was more detailed and expansive than the earlier descriptions of Ireland as a 'broken state'. He explained to Elizabeth that if she did not support the agreements he had made:

> if for want of performance of that plot anything should fall out, contrary to the present stayed appearance, whereof yet I see no cause of doubts, it may please your majesty graciously and gravely to consider how subject the best estates are, much more this torn one, to mutations and change.[47]

He also returned to the motif of fortune later in his deputyship when he once again faced criticism and countermand from Elizabeth regarding his dealings with the Pale community, explaining that 'for my part I cannot assure further in worldly causes than becometh a man'. As lord deputy he could only address secondary 'worldly' causation, and Elizabeth should remember that 'Kent and Middlesex are subject to such mutations as God can call upon the best governed and settled state', so what could be reasonably expected, in reality, in Ireland.[48] He even quoted from the Roman Stoic writer Seneca as he reflected on the level of complaints being levelled against him, 'that I have heard of this good caution given by Seneca', that one should 'strike sail and not try out all seas and weathers', thus man should resign from political life in order to avoid the vagaries of fortune.[49]

It is interesting that when the Irish council began to criticize Perrot, whose often dictatorial behaviour alienated many, the accusation directed at the lord deputy was that he was unable to bridle and control his own passions. The Irish treasurer Wallop explained how Perrot had been advised by the council that there was no need to intervene in Connacht, where rebellion had broken out, because the provincial president Richard Bingham had the situation under control. Wallop referred to the impartial advice given by the council, 'the good faithful advice of such as were no way interested in the matter', which was aimed at 'the service of her majesty', and this he contrasted with the lord deputy's behaviour whose 'passions ... he cannot, nor careth not to bridle before us' – a refrain that was repeated on a number of occasions in a variety of contexts.[50] This suggests that Bryskett's emphasis on Stoic republicanism, whereby man would learn how to act in a world governed by fortune, was an emerging philosophical position known by those on the Irish council – Ireland again giving form and clarity to a position that would later inform how the second earl of Essex and a growing body of younger courtiers in England re-conceived of political virtue in opposition to English courtly life which they thought corrupt and ungodly.[51]

The State in Ulster and the Gaelic World

Returning, then, to government's response to island-wide reform, from 1585 onwards a broader statist model was extended to the rest of the kingdom; although within the thinking of Perrot and his associates, as discussed earlier, there remained the suggestion of a godly model as denoted by the somewhat ambiguous optimism of the first year of his deputyship.[52] In line with Perrot's 1581 treatise, there was a progressive move away from surrender and regrant arrangements, which were based on an earlier notion of lordly government. A growing institutional definition of the state, I would argue, was incompatible with a lordly model, because it could not allow any form of independent political authority to remain within lordships, whilst the continuing doubts about the internal disposition of Elizabeth's Irish subjects made ideas concerning loyalty and fidelity problematic.

Whilst, then, the tendency in Irish government's dealings with the Old English community had been to separate state from polity, the broader notion of acting in order to maintain the state also hardened, where following Bryskett's

Discourse, and Italian republican writing in general, government now sought to maintain the Irish state in a clearly contingent political situation. As Machiavelli commented 'the nobility' because of their 'ambition' and 'boldness' needed a 'bit in their mouths'.[53] This sits in contrast with events in England, where the health of a protestant nobility, as exemplified by Leicester's faction, meant the deconstruction of the English nobility and its replacement by the institutional state was far less pronounced.[54]

The example of the O'Reilly lordship in Ulster allows us to trace the gradual shift in lordly political relationships. Here the language of loyalty and fidelity, usually associated with the lord–prince relationship, was subsumed by the question of state sovereignty. Whilst the surrender and regrant agreement made between Deputy Sidney and O'Reilly in 1567/8 speaks of the bonds of friendship implicit in the feudal relationship, by 1579, alongside initial shifts in the use of the term 'state', O'Reilly's relationship to government was phrased slightly differently. Originally, Elizabeth had described O'Reilly's obligations to her as arising from the fact that he was her 'faithful and loving subject', going on to note O'Reilly's submission 'to us and our crown'.[55] Over a decade later, however, O'Reilly was to be obedient to the 'the precepts and commandments which shall be commanded and ordered' by 'the governor or the council of this realm' and other officers of state.[56] It was to the higher offices of government that O'Reilly was directly answerable, not the prince.

In 1585, in line with Perrot's 1581 treatise, the relationship of the O'Reilly to the state changed further. The new lord deputy negotiated a new agreement with Sir John O'Reilly. The language of surrender and regrant remained in force, because government could not simply dispense with the notion of the prince. But as in 1579, the indenture emphasized that it was the lord deputy and Irish council, by virtue of their authority as officers of 'the state', who had made the agreement; and alongside this a more detailed deconstruction of the pre-existing political order was attempted. John O'Reilly agreed to take four baronies, whilst the other three were to go to other members of the sept who would hold the baronies directly from the crown.[57] The position of the freeholder was not yet directly raised, but the size and extent of O'Reilly's jurisdiction, and any wider jurisdictional authority inherent in the Gaelic title, was significantly reduced as a result of the division of the lordship into independent baronies.

There was also a clear interplay between institutional authority in Ireland and the authority of the prince. Perrot had to ask for further authority to be delegated to him, because the deputy, it would appear, was only allowed to regrant estates 'to lords and their heirs male', in line with a very fixed view of English lordship, whilst each O'Reilly wanted their estates regranted to them and 'their heirs general'.[58] Quite naturally, Elizabeth, in her response, in which she authorized Perrot to make such grants, redeployed the language of fidelity and loyalty, whilst the 'matter of

... importance' for the deputy remained the deconstruction of an alternative point of sovereignty.[59] That 'having the five chief septs [of the O'Reillys] then with me', Perrot 'dissolve[d] their Irish tanistry and ... reduce[d] them to English tenures'.[60]

Another example of this gradualist model for the deconstruction of Gaelic and feudal lordship can be found in government's dealings with Sorley Boy MacDonald in 1586. By this stage troop levels in the province had dropped to 550 and this had allowed Sorley Boy to return. The lord deputy decided to offer the MacDonalds full denization[61] as subjects of the crown. This was not all Perrot's decision, in that pressure was brought to bear by Elizabeth and the privy council in England for some final resolution to be reached. As Fenton noted, something had to be done and the guiding principle was establishing some level of external or 'public peace'.[62] As in the case of O'Reilly, the agreements followed the established language of the personal loyalty owed by the lord to the prince. MacDonald's indenture emphasizes his 'assured loyalty and fidelity to her majesty'.[63] But unlike the case of O'Reilly, the term 'state' was now openly referenced in the actual indenture, even if the deployment of the term was by no means bold.

First, when Roger Wilbraham, the Irish solicitor-general, reported on the denization the next month, the matter was framed both in terms of Sorley's relationship with the prince and his relationship with the Irish state. Wilbraham reported how on the one hand Sorley had given his 'humble submission and unfeigned allegiance to her majesty', but he also emphasized that the 'indenture' had been 'made by the lord [deputy] and the state'.[64] Secondly, in the indenture proper, Sorley, his heirs and successors, as well as their tenants, were to 'always serve her majesty' against any 'enemy to her majesty or state that shall attempt to openly ... invade ... this realm of Ireland'.[65] And as with O'Reilly, the area controlled by the MacDonalds was divided into two, with Sorley being granted the Route and his nephew Angus being allotted the Glens, once again clearly limiting Sorley's jurisdiction as a Gaelic lord – and underlying this there remained the possibility that freeholders would be introduced.[66]

Under Perrot's deputyship, however, it was the continuing problem of the Gaelic title of 'The O'Neill', and the authority that such a title implied, which further drew out the rationale underlying the deconstruction of lordships and the imposition of freeholders. It was argued that a critical problem with the nation of the O'Neills was their claim to an independent sovereign jurisdiction – that the O'Neill's had always sought 'sovereign authority and princely pre-eminence over the rest'. It was for this reason that Turlough and Hugh should have 'allotted to them and their heirs, lands competently bounded with rents and reservations'.[67] This would ensure that whilst they remained significant landowners, they would not be able to claim any significant authority beyond the extent of their manorial holdings. Later it would be noted how the earl of Tyrone, on the death of Turlough Luineach O'Neill, was now exercising 'his own authority incident to his name'; and again the problem was phrased not in terms of the lord's relationship with the prince, but was described as being 'dangerous to the state'.[68]

It was this rationale that informed continued attempts at reform in Ulster, where under Deputy Fitzwilliam, another Ulster lordship, that of the MacMahon, was divided between the seven leading members of the Gaelic sept or clan with 287 freeholders being established within the seven new lordships.[69] As we will discuss below, there was a certain sense of Machiavellianism and reason of state in the way in which Deputy Fitzwilliam achieved such a resolution, where Fitzwilliam framed his actions as being for the maintenance and strengthening of 'the state'. Similarly, Bingham's attack on the Connacht lord Brian O'Rourke in the early 1590s was also conditioned by a notion of state sovereignty and the implications of O'Rourke's attempt to reassert his Gaelic authority.[70]

For Bingham, O'Rourke wanted to recover his 'old seignories, with their unlawful cuttings and Irish custom, according to the Tanist law'. In the aftermath of the Spanish Armada, with many vessels crashing off the coast of Ireland, O'Rourke had refused to deliver the Spaniards notwithstanding the institutional authority of the state, namely 'provincial proclamations'.[71] For Bingham, therefore, O'Rourke could not be 'pardoned and all indignities put up by the state'.[72] The fact that the issue of state sovereignty was in question is further exemplified in the story told concerning O'Rourke's reputed defacing of a makeshift picture of Elizabeth. The suggestion was that he had committed the ultimate crime of *lèse majesté*, though the actual story told is a misrepresentation of a shaming ritual of a local woman.[73] Nevertheless, this facilitated O'Rourke's attainder for treason, and the result was the division of O'Rourke's territory, where, as with O'Reilly, MacMahon and to a degree MacDonald, it was divided into baronies and freeholder properties. The lord deputy drew up agreements and divisions in line with what had been achieved in the MacMahon lordship, 'the country of Monaghan'.[74] O'Rourke's 'powers should be broken', whereby he had now grown 'more dangerous and absolute than before'.[75]

Here it becomes more apparent that the position of freeholder was not necessarily seen as a component of a civil commonwealth, but that the freeholder was viewed as instrumental in building and strengthening the state and its emerging institutions. In effect the position was used to undermine the authority of the lord, such a landholder becoming a component of an emerging absolutist state. Earlier chapters discussed the more normative Irish use of martial law, which alongside the positioning of sovereignty within state institutions (not the polity) left little political or societal role for the Irish freeholder. If we consider the importance within English historiography of the common law mind, Ireland emerges as an important counterpoint. For J. G. A. Pocock, the English notion of common law helped inure English society against a rampant absolutism, because ideas of immemorial custom and trial by one's peers reinforced notions of popular sovereignty.[76] In Ireland, however, alongside a clear deployment of absolutist and statist ideas, a willingness to disregard common law practice arises, where common law was not treated as essential and better just because it was peculiarly English.

Irish practice was noteworthy in England because of its deviation from common political practice. For example, Delvin's report on martial practice, which the previous chapter raised, gained a clear response from Lord Treasurer Burghley who summarized Delvin's proposals in a document returned to the Irish administration.[77] Similarly, in 1590 the new Irish chief justice Robert Gardiner repeated the charge that sheriffs used martial law procedure with little regard for common law practice. Gardiner thought this 'a strange course in a Christian state' – further revealing something of the contrast in language and values involved in the arbitrary and rigid model of the state, where the critical issue for reformed protestants was that, from their perspective, the Irish political community or 'state' was not in fact 'Christian'.[78] For example, in Ulster, between 1587 and 1589 martial law commissions were issued to the sheriff of Down, the governor of upper and lower Clandeboy, Dufferin, the Rout, and the Glynnes, the sheriff of Leitrim, and a province-wide commission was issued to Sir Henry Bagenal.[79] The later repudiation of martial law practice which followed in 1590/1 helps provide some form of an explanation for two incidents involving Lord Deputy Fitzwilliam and the seeming manipulation of existing law in Ireland. Elizabeth, no doubt because such practice jarred with Christian and commonwealth values in England, sent instructions that the use of martial law should be curtailed.[80]

First, one Arthur O'Tool, a Gaelic lord in Leinster, complained in June 1591 that Fitzwilliam had 'proclaimed upon pain of death that no man should draw weapon' in Dublin, on summoning the Gaelic lord to the city, thus Arthur had 'laid away all my weapons'. But O'Tool recounted how he was set upon on his entry into Dublin, and though he showed Fitzwilliam his wounds, he reported that the deputy instead chastized those who had attacked Arthur because they had failed to murder the Gaelic lord. O'Tool suggested that Fitzwilliam had attempted to engineer his death upon summoning him to Dublin – the implication being that Fitzwilliam had attempted to use his authority to issue proclamations in order to pursue a clearly unprincipled and unlawful course of action and end Arthur's life.[81] This followed on from the earlier decision by Perrot to attempt to persuade Arthur and Phelim O'Tool, the two claimants of the O'Tool lordship, to settle their dispute through trial by duel in Dublin castle (a very odd occurrence indeed) – though both refused to co-operate.[82] Quite simply Phelim had taken possession of land which Arthur claimed was his inheritance, and there seems to have been a good degree of ambiguity over the legal right to the land since a long exchange took place over the various genealogies and the supposed content of the title deeds involved.[83] To some extent, then, government was unwilling to alter the *status quo*, when the inheritance was small and the legal right unclear.

More importantly, when dealing with the Gaelic Irish, government was happy to dispense with common law procedure. This suspicion was echoed by Arthur who explained that whilst the deputy 'hath referred me and my suit to be tried by common law', his case had nevertheless sat 'for many years' before the crown and the deputy.[84] Similarly, within the first Munster plantation common law values were wilfully disregarded when Old English and Gaelic Irish lords petitioned to have their estates restored to them. The speed with which the survey of land had been carried out meant a significant number of individuals were dispossessed of land when they had not been involved in the second Desmond rebellion and so had not been attainted. But now the native population understood how to make use of common law practice, the New English simply changed the rules of the game eschewing fair practice for their own advantage. A commission was appointed which simply rejected virtually all of the claims, denying access to common law.[85]

Secondly, returning to Fitzwilliam's deconstruction of the MacMahon lordship, in order to achieve the division of the lordship, the deputy had one of the main competitors for the MacMahon title, Hugh Roe MacMahon, tried, convicted and executed for resisting sheriffs and extorting from his subordinates the exactions associated with Gaelic lordship – such as cattle rustling. Questions remain over Fitzwilliam's actions because he had originally supported Hugh Roe MacMahon's claims after his rival Brian McHugh Og had escaped Dublin and established himself as the MacMahon on the death of Sir Ross MacMahon. Fitzwilliam had sent Hugh Roe with an armed forced to the lordship to dislodge his rival and thus Hugh became the MacMahon. There is a certain ambiguity surrounding proceedings, because it was suggested that Fitzwilliam had actually been bribed by Hugh Roe; and that it was Hugh's subsequent failure to pay the bribe that led to his trial and execution. Somewhat ironically, the Gaelic exactions taken by Hugh, in order to pay the bribe, actually allowed for his trial and conviction by common law jury.[86] In particular, what Hugh Roe did was not unusual and government in similar circumstances did not tend to proceed against Gaelic lords on this basis.

The question arises as to whether Fitzwilliam engaged in the open manipulation of legal procedures in accordance with reason of state in order to deconstruct the lordship, or was he simply mildly incompetent? Did he intend to allow one MacMahon to dislodge the other, then use such a context to attaint the present holder of lordship, thus bringing the lordship into crown hands and therefore allowing the lordship to be divided? What is clear is that Fitzwilliam had originally intended to divide the lordship between the various competitors on the death of Sir Ross MacMahon. He also justified his subsequent behaviour with direct reference to 'the state'. When at an early stage in his various dealings in the lordship, it was alleged he secretly favoured Brian not Hugh, the deputy pointed out that he hoped to bring everything to 'the profit of her majesty and the good of the state, nothing regarding my own private gain'.[87] He suggested that his dealings, however duplicitous they might appear, were directed towards the maintenance of 'the state'. He later explained that he wanted 'the territory divided and the [Gaelic] title extinguished', and in reflecting on his actions after office he argued that the MacMahons had been 'threatening eminent danger to that whole state' and that they would be better 'commanded being so divided, then as it was before united'.[88]

Gaelic Political and Religious Vocabulary

By the 1590s this reassertion of Gaelic vocabulary started to move beyond the suggestion that Gaelic titles simply implied some degree of independent political authority. The customary norms of Gaelic political life were more fully articulated and, more critically, this language combined with the vocabulary of a Gaelic and then pan-catholic commonwealth. Whilst Kenneth Nicholls and Hiram Morgan have sought to recover the political norms of the Gaelic polity, there is still a need in wider British history to re-engage in Gaelic political vocabulary. This formed an additional political language which helped shape statist thought.[89] Here Irish government, in its attempt to construct its own state and institutional structures in Ireland, now faced the somewhat natural emergence of a rival state and polity, which many involved in government then charted in the letters they sent to England. Again the separation of state from polity took place, but we also see the possibilities provided by such separation, whereby the state provided a structural frame below which different bonds of unity could be slowly or quickly formed.

Hugh O'Neill remained a key figure in the articulation of such a position. Hiram Morgan has examined in detail government's progressive attempts to undermine Hugh O'Neill's lordship and authority through the deconstruction of minor Gaelic lordships. This, it was hoped, would undermine the extent of the O'Neill's traditional authority over his Gaelic underlings. Morgan has also pointed to the way in which this elicited a series of well thought out rhetorical responses from O'Neill, which were no doubt partly formulated by his secretary Henry Hovendon who was from an early new English settler family.[90] These various aspects helped contribute to the start of the Nine Years War in Ulster at the end of Fitzwilliam's deputyship.

In the late 1580s Hugh O'Neill justified his decision to execute Hugh Gavelach O'Neill – a son of the arch traitor Shane O'Neill, who continued to act against Tyrone and government in Dublin – by arguing that he not only had the necessary delegated authority as a chief crown officer in the province, but also that he held independent political authority because the political community of Ulster was at a level distinct and separate from the rest of Ireland. O'Neill argued that Ulster was a variant polity with its own customs and laws – 'there is neither magistrate, judge, sheriff, nor course of the laws of this realm, but certain customs by which both O'Neill [Turlough Luineach] and I and others of our sort do govern our followers'.[91]

Similarly, in 1593 the Gaelic lord Hugh Maguire, after his election as head of his country, refused to accept the imposition of a sheriff in his country and all which that implied.[92] No doubt such behaviour was informed by his knowledge of the way in which government had dealt with both O'Reilly and more problematically MacMahon. When Humphrey Willis was given a commission as sheriff with jurisdiction over Maguire's country, the lord of Fermanagh drove him out and raided Connacht, thus making clear that he did not intend to have his lordship atomized and the title of the Maguire abolished. Around this time, the Gaelic world's claims to an independent sovereign jurisdiction then combined with the idea that the wider polity in Ulster should be united in conscience in direct opposition to the godly polity, which Irish government had tried to create. The key attributes of both state and polity now emerged and combined together, and in this respect various individuals took note of the literal building of the bonds of catholic friendship and the creation of an alternative body political.

Bingham in September 1592 suggested that 'the state' would not be 'any better assured of their obediency than before', because the Irish in Ulster and Connacht were 'indeed fed with a vain hope of Hugh Roe O'Donnell and his two popish bishops, James O'Hely and Neale O'Boyle'.[93] In 1592 Hugh O'Donnell, another key Ulster lord, had escaped from Dublin castle, and like Maguire and Hugh O'Neill he had re-asserted his Gaelic title. For Bingham these 'two popish bishops and arch-traitors that be with Hugh Roe O'Donnell [did] ... much harm in seducing the ill Irishry ... and persuading them to fall from their duties'.[94] Alongside this, an account by Patrick McArt Moyle [McMahon], sheriff of the county of Monaghan, noted how one McGauran 'nominated the primate of Ireland by bulls from the pope repaired to Maguire and after O'Donnell and used persuasive speeches unto them to forbear all obedience to the state', with the lords involved swearing 'corporal oaths'.[95] These oaths were the catholic equivalent of those taken in England by recusants re-entering communion with the protestant church or under suspicion of nonconformity.[96]

> In the presence of earl of Tyrone at Dungannon, Maguire took an oath to join with the Spanish forces, and after at another day meeting at Ballymascanlan before the earl of Tyrone these persons combined together and by their corporal oaths taken did conclude to join in arms for aiding of the Spanish navy.[97]

O'Neill and his associates sought direct Spanish intervention. Similarly, in September 1593, the lord deputy and council, in giving an account of their proceedings in the province, described how they had 'charged the earl [of Tyrone] with these points, namely, with entertaining of the traitorous bishop Magawran in his country and with the receiving of the mass', where again 'corporal oaths' had been taken.[98] This was the confederacy of Tyrone, Maguire, O'Donnell, and O'Rourke under the norms of Gaelic lordship and in unity of catholic conscience. What Irish government identified, therefore, were key theoretical attributes of an independent state and political community coalescing in Ulster, where the bonds of conscience and brotherly love sat beside direct claims to absolute sovereignty.

It was described how 'Tyrone is like enough to assume absolute command throughout Ulster as his predecessors', that he preferred to be called 'O'Neill than Caesar' and that he wanted to 'tyrannise with absolute power'.[99] Significantly, it was Fenton writing in December 1594 who identified the consequences of these developments, where there was the potential for Tyrone to be recognised as head of an alternative commonwealth, which would not support the institutions of the protestant state in Ireland – a potential problem not dissimilar to the one identified by Stubbs and Philip Sidney in the context of the Anjou match in England. For Fenton 'if he [Tyrone] publish himself as the protector of the catholic cause he will shake all four provinces'.[100]

Beside this, a wonderful counterpoint to protestant statism in Ireland emerged in Tyrone's later deployment of the language of commonwealth and Catholicism. Once again Morgan has made a very apt comparison between resistance to Spanish rule in the Netherlands and English rule in Ulster, as well as the prince of Orange as *stadtholder* and Hugh O'Neill's position as earl of Tyrone. What Morgan observes are similarities in terms of the calls for liberty of conscience made by Dutch protestants and the catholic Gaelic Irish, as well as the reassertion in both the Netherlands and Ireland of the norms of customary self-government in opposition to a distant monarch in both Philip and Elizabeth.[101] This can be taken further, where the existence of an already developed statist vocabulary in Ireland, as used by Ireland's lord deputies and their associates, suggests that O'Neill was consciously looking for an alternative vocabulary to counter the idea of an Irish absolutist state which had solidified throughout the 1580s. In particular, in the midst of the Nine Years War, O'Neill appealed to notions of faith, fatherland, conscience and the particular bonds of catholic friendship in an attempt to construct a pan-catholic opposition to the crown in Ireland.[102]

In 1597 and 1599, as a resolution to conflict, the idea emerged from O'Neill that catholics in Ireland be given liberty of conscience. This was detailed in a set of articles addressed to government in England, and here an attempt was made to use the general notion of the state and its institutions as a way of overcoming the problem of a political community divided from its ruler on the basis of conscience. On the one hand it was suggested that Catholicism should be restored, and alongside this Tyrone proposed that 'the council of state' and 'all other officers appertaining to the council and law of Ireland, [should] be Irishmen', though those state offices would remain under the control of Elizabeth as prince with 'the governor of Ireland [being] at least an earl, and of the privy council of England'.[103] Like the promulgation of edicts in France, and in particular the 1598 edict of Nantes, quite a blunt idea of institutional obedience was deployed in order to argue that the polity could have a different confession from the prince and still be loyal as long as loyalty was defined in terms of institutions and their function.[104]

Most strikingly, the set of articles drawn up even referred to Ireland as a 'republic', the articles explaining that all Irishmen should be able to 'freely traffic with all merchandises, that shall be thought necessary by the council of state of Ireland for the profit of their republic'. Ireland should be a mixed state not an absolutist state, although what was proposed was clearly fanciful.[105] Morgan also suggests that the language of faith and fatherland may have been designed to garner international catholic support. Some of Tyrone's associates had spent time in France, such as the Jesuit James Archer, and the ideas of nation and faith drew directly on the language of the French Catholic League.[106]

The State in Connacht and Munster

The notion of the state can also be found informing policy, more broadly, in Munster and Connacht, where the question of conscience or the internal condition of the lord or gentlemen, once again, came to the fore in government correspondence. There are obvious exceptions to the shift which took place. As David Edwards points out, the earl of Ormond, through the strength of his own feudal lordship, and a good personal relationship with the prince in England, effectively resisted the encroachment of the Irish state upon his own personal dominion as a great lord.[107] The point which might be made here, however, is that it was the health of Ormond's personal feudal relationship with the prince that meant he could resist the Irish state, where, in contrast, it was the very fact of the wider breakdown in those personal feudal relationships that actually allowed room for a new abstract and impersonal statist model to take root. A more traditional view of the freeholder and gentry community also remained in play in the first plantation of Munster, despite the fact, or probably because of the fact, that the traditional lordly and gentry class had been summarily removed as a result of the act of attainder of Desmond and his associates passed in the 1585–6 parliament.

Here those granted seignories in Munster were not only meant to build market towns, they were also meant to divide out their seignories, which in theory numbered 12,000 acres, between six freeholders with 300 acres, six farmers with 400 acres, and 42 copy holders with 100 acres.[108] The intention was to attract Englishmen to be freeholders on these estates, thus constructing the model of local English county government within Ireland. The instructions also asked that a preacher be maintained; and William Herbert, a key player in the plantation, wanted 'public prayers ... [to] be said in their own [Irish] tongue ... [and] the Lord's prayer and Ten Commandments, and the Articles of Belief, to be translated into Irish'.[109] A godly model, therefore, remained in play as well. This might explain why Perrot never issued martial law commissions for Munster, because common law was instrumental in a more optimistic vision associated with gentry society, which the first plantation was meant to foster. In reality, however, far larger grants were given, undertakers did not arrive, and the model quickly fell far from its original ideal.[110]

In the Munster plantation, nevertheless, the language and vocabulary of the state remained relevant, and here it was openly deployed in connection with the problem of conscience and political virtue in a dispute which developed between William Herbert and another New English settler Sir Edward Denny. The issue at stake was Herbert's determination to receive two full seignories. The problem was that flaws in the initial survey of land in Munster meant that in reality the land granted was less than originally envisaged. As a consequence Herbert attempted to encroach on the land of other undertakers such as Denny, despite Herbert's own self-professed godly credentials, and irrespective of the various actions taken by either individual Herbert clearly felt that Denny did not share his own godly outlook. Herbert suggested that Denny had allowed his soldiers free rein in the area of plantation and that Denny had no intention of making available common law procedures and instead used and abused his tenants.[111] For Herbert, this was because Denny was not a godly individual, and here Herbert identified two motivations for correct political behaviour that might lead Denny to act well. One was God and the other was the state. Herbert argued that besides:

> the pleasing of God and obedience unto his will, which ought more to weigh in a Christian than all other reasons whatsoever, there are many causes to move the most graceless, if there be in them any regard of private credit, commodity, or contentment, or of public utility, fame, or ignominy.[112]

For Herbert a 'Christian' man would seek to act in accordance with God's will, but if 'graceless', the need for 'private credit' amongst your contemporaries should encourage some sort of good behaviour. Herbert even describes this as helping shore up the bonds of 'concord' and 'amity' usually associated with the Christian body politic. Such self-interest should help foster 'good concord, agreement, and amity' if these individuals would consider 'the benefits that will be bereft us, and the mischief that will annoy us' if New English planters refused to co-operate with one another.[113] A divided colonial community, being small in size, would be vulnerable to attack from the native population.

This further encouraged Herbert to identify four different types of relationship in the political community. He pointed to an individual's relationship with God and then the prince, but also as an individual's relationship to institutional authority, 'the estate', and the good of the community, 'the commonwealth'.[114] This distinction is repeated further on in his letter, where Herbert then drew attention to political action as entailing reward from the prince and the state. Denny, it was argued, needed to consider the consequences of not having 'the good opinion of the state', but Denny suffered from 'evil of conscience, evil nature and evil discretion'.

Interestingly, Denny was an associate of Philip Sidney, Sidney having written to Denny advising him on his Irish service. The disjuncture then between Herbert and Denny may be indicative of a wider tension between an earlier godly ideal and an emerging statism. For instance, Philip himself was in the vanguard of English–Irish statist thought, whilst Denny embraced the use of martial law.[115] Earlier Herbert had also contrasted the supposed godly intentions of plantation with what he saw as the actual political agenda. He thought that many planters wanted to pursue a more temporal policy, in line with Machiavellian and other Italian republican thinking, by furthering innovation and change to their own benefit. He had told Burghley how:

> Our pretence in the enterprise of plantation was to establish these parts [in] piety, justice [and] inhabitation ... Our drift now is, being possessed of land, to extort [and] make the state of things turbulent.[116]

In Connacht, moreover, Lord Deputy Perrot had been able to apply his tripartite model in full, as outlined in his 1581 treatise. As Bernadette Cunningham notes, there were clear limitations with the composition scheme in the province. The earls of Thomond and Clanrickard were best placed to collect the composition rent within their former feudal jurisdictions. This is because government still lacked a certain level of institutional capability, and so whilst the earls acted as agents of the crown there emerged a very blurred line between a statist model and former feudal lordship. Alongside this the larger lords, in order to compensate for their loss of feudal rights, were given exemptions from the payment of the composition rent, whilst the book of composition failed to name the individual persons charged. This significantly undermined the purpose of the tripartite indenture, which aimed at separating freeholder from lord, since the specific freeholders were not identified. Cunningham suggests, then, that the regional *status quo* remained unchanged.[117] Here, however, the Irish administration did attempt at least in principle to apply a statist model as best it could. The problems Cunningham identifies simply reveal that we are dealing with an attempt to force a transition towards an institutional state, and as before a clear shift in thinking can be identified.

Within government circles the rebellion of the McWilliam Burkes in Connacht was presented in obvious statist terms. In a 'discourse on the rebellion of the Burkes', which was drawn up by the president of Connacht, Richard Bingham, and others, the leading clan members are recorded explaining the reason for their revolt. This was so Bingham and his associates could protect themselves from the suggestion that they might have fomented rebellion; and it was the deconstruction of the lordship – the removal of the Gaelic title and all which that entailed – and the clear positioning of political authority within state institutions which was at issue. It was argued that the cause of their rebellion did not arise from 'any man belonging to the state', but because they wanted to retain 'the names of McWilliam, and the McWilliamship bestowed upon Edmund Burke and so to run by the course of eldership according to the old custom'. It was the 'taking away of the said McWilliamship and the division of the lands and inheritance', namely the division of the lordship into a series of baronies and freehold properties, that was the 'ground and principal beginning and chief cause of this rebellion and none other'.[118] The solicitor-general Roger Wilbraham added that the Burkes 'utterly refuse [the] government of any other officers but their own'.[119]

Importantly, Connacht formed a key plank in Perrot's grand vision for an island-wide taxation system. The administration sought to regularize composition arrangements throughout the island by equalizing plough lands with 'a respect being had to the differences of both soil and state' – although as discussed the Commons used its opposition to the island-wide tax to resist the implementation of penal legislation.[120] The proposal included Munster, Connacht and Leinster, but not Ulster, which was just in the process of being shired. There was some precedent for such a tax, since Lord Deputy Sidney had attempted to negotiate a similar island-wide composition in late 1570s, and at a practical level it was understood that this would allow government to maintain a larger military force.[121] As Michael Braddick has noted when discussing the emergence of a clearly defined state power in England, this arose, in part, out of a rationalization of the tax system. For Braddick, it was in the 1640s that such a process really took hold due to the Civil War. Again Ireland pre-empts this, where the demands of continuous military activity added urgency to a need to formalize government funding, and by the 1580s the issue of state sovereignty shaped, and was shaped by, such a requirement.[122]

In the 1550s and 60s, political power in Ireland was most certainly a physical entity, where the troops raised by government followed lordly practice and tended to be billeted on the population at large, taking foodstuffs directly from the population. Now, however, a more abstract and theoretical possibility opened up. By shifting away from a hand-to-mouth existence in terms of the support given to the troops, and instead raising a standard cash tax, this had the potential to add an extra step or abstraction in respect to the conception of physical power. For Bodin the sinews of the state, after all, were finance.[123] Perrot himself commented that the proposed tax would 'abate the wonted dependency of the state upon some of them as upon demi-kings', thus emphasizing the question of sovereignty and the state.[124] It might even be suggested that in a very modern sense the freeholder, along with the lord, would serve the state, not through the glory of military action, as found in Italian republican writing, but through the payment of an impersonal and anonymous tax. This impersonal contribution was something that, in a community divided along confessional lines, could be received by government free from confessional suspicion, because any personal animosity or doubts in conscience would not affect the cash payment. In contrast, allowing those suspect in conscience to provide military service might lead to unintended consequences.

We should also note, that as with Ulster, very little role in local government was envisaged for those freeholders in Connacht who had entered into tripartite indentures. Cunningham points out that the indentures did not actually establish a right to freehold. The indentures simply treated those possessing a certain amount of land under certain conditions as if they were freeholders.[125] Martial law, not common law practice, also remained dominant. For Solicitor-General Wilbraham the norms of shire government were consciously ignored. Wilbraham describes how 'upon our new late reviving of our star chamber court, two several bills against two of the sheriffs in Connacht are preferred; the one of them containeth 24 articles of outrageous offences, as unlawful execution by martial law of gentlemen living without cause'.[126] As in Ulster, martial law commissions were issued to Robert Fowl, provost marshal of the province of Connacht and Thomond, Thomas Le Strange, chief commissioner of the province of Connacht and Thomond, and George Bingham in the absence of his brother Richard, as well as Richard Bingham on his return to office in 1588.[127] It was later reported that the Binghams summarily executed a number of the Burkes, O'Tools and O'Flahertys, who conceived of themselves as 'gentlemen' without any recourse to the normal process of law, again reflecting the perception that no equivalent English gentry community existed.[128]

Furthermore, Connacht provides evidence of the continued relevance of the problem of conscience for a wider reconceptualization of Ireland's lordships. Returning to the rebellion of the McWilliam Burkes, for Bingham there was no point in negotiating with them because they were corrupt in conscience. He asked rhetorically in 1589 whether we should 'keep our words with those which have no conscience, but break words daily. I am not of that opinion'.[129] Similarly, in 1591, when the possibility of conciliation was raised, he again stressed the faithlessness of the McWilliam Burkes:

> And for assurance of the said peace, Ulick Burke, of Irris, has delivered in as pledge for himself and the sept of Ulick, his best son, which is indeed a very good tie upon them. Howbeit, we have experience how little they do now and then esteem of their pledges, being so faithless and so inconstant a race.[130]

These doubts about conscience meant that the underlying relationship involved in surrender and regrant agreements could not be sustained. Such agreements relied on fidelity and loyalty and these qualities were based upon an honest conscience. This encouraged the atomization and impersonal abstraction associated with an emerging notion of the state. This was a theme picked up by John Hooker in his extension of the Irish section of Holinshed's *Chronicle* (1587), where Hooker similarly described the unreformed and corrupt consciences of the Clanrickard Burkes, Shane O'Neill, and the earl of Desmond, amongst others (which will be examined more closely in the final chapter). References to conscience are even used in the 1586 discourse concerning the rebellion of the Burkes. Here 'conscience' was deployed to stress the account's veracity. The leading clan members are recorded stressing that 'we can in conscience but clear him [Bingham] thereof' of any suggestion of wrong doing, and in another document the Burkes stress that 'all honest men are bound in conscience to declare the truth'.[131]

Alongside the commonplace reference to 'the state', therefore, the question of conscience was now routinely raised by 1586. Many such references occur in the context of a series of breakdowns in relations between members of the Irish council and the lord deputy. As stated, Perrot's often dictatorial behaviour, his refusal to consult the council, and his violent temper had caused numerous problems. The rhetoric of the letters, nevertheless, can be seen as indicative of a change in atmosphere and perception. In the 1560s and '70s, the general trend in letters sent from Ireland was to sign off with some reference to 'God's glory' or the guidance provided by God's 'holy spirit'.[132] This reflected the belief that as a member of a reformed protestant political community you were part of the visible embodiment of the body of Christ. It was a clear expression that you were confident that all those involved in correspondence with you were united in conscience. The need to explain why you were now rightly disposed in conscience would appear to be an open acknowledgement that these ties of Christian friendship were now highly contested. Not even on the Irish council could they be taken for granted, with Fenton, Wallop and Bagenal all stressing that their criticism of Perrot and the advice they had given had arisen out of a sound 'conscience', not personal animosity or self-interest.[133]

Local Office Holding and the Old English Gentry

Finally, alongside the broader deconstruction of Ireland's lordships, a more specific examination of the limits and conditions of local office holding took place in relation to the established gentry community associated with the city of Dublin, which would eventually extend to include cities such as Cork, Waterford and Galway.[134] At one level this reflects, as many scholars have discussed, the New English desire to monopolize positions in the Dublin government, the presidential councils and other provincial offices.[135] But the growing doubts about conscience detailed throughout this study meant that a new way of thinking about local gentry government was required. If Collinson's work is again recalled, where gentry community was essential in allowing for government in the English localities, in Ireland such a community effectively no longer existed.[136]

Beside the language of the state and conscience another related shift in language can be identified, where references to 'magistrates', 'gentlemen', 'oaths' and the other conditions upon which individuals held office became the subject of considerable attention. This was about somehow recreating externally and institutionally the bonds of Christian friendship which in government thinking had been the basis of an earlier commonwealth or godly model. In particular, an Irish notion of absolute authority was deployed here in order to impose institutional checks upon a community which might not agree or consent to such checks.

As early as 1584 the ecclesiastical commission had begun to investigate recusancy, with a degree of urgency lacking under Sidney and Grey.[137] There had also been an attempt in 1584/5 to administer the oath of supremacy to the entire population of the Pale in order to test consciences to see whether the community would openly acknowledge Elizabeth's supremacy in ecclesiastical affairs as opposed to Rome. Since such action went beyond the limits of statute law, which only allowed the oath to be administered to crown officers or clergy, Perrot had to explain that he knew 'there is no law here in force to touch any man in that sort'.[138] Government also faced the problem that many members of the gentry community had refused to fulfill their commissions as justices of the peace, in order to avoid taking the oath of supremacy and probably in order to avoid enforcing religious conformity. The fact that these men were 'gentlemen', the natural leaders of regional government, was emphasized. As was previously the case, absolutism and pre-existing institutional arrangements were deployed in order to enforce the type of behaviour which government might have expected from the Old English gentry. In this case Irish government turned to the prerogative court of castle chamber, Ireland's star chamber court, to compensate for another lacuna in the statute governing ecclesiastical supremacy. Apart from depriving individuals of office, no other censure was available in order to force them to fulfill their duties. Government 'thought [it] good to bid those justices of the peace that have made refusal to answer the matter in star chamber' – though little seems to have come of this, probably due to continued sensitivity in England over Irish proto-absolutism.[139]

Similarly, Irish government's inclusion of English penal legislation in the 1585–6 parliamentary programme, as was the case in England, was aimed at laying some institutional structure that would compensate for religious disunity in the gentry community, even though such legislation was out of sync with the broader remit of the 1585 parliamentary programme.[140] The bills, if passed, would also have rectified the situation government had confronted in 1584, when during the torture of Dermot O'Hurley it was realized that the necessary penal acts had not actually been placed on the Irish statute book.

Scrutiny of the gentleman of the Pale who held magisterial office only intensified. The act attainting the earl of Desmond and all his associates, which was passed in 1586, quite explicitly removed the gentry community from positions of authority and local government in a large proportion of Munster. Expressing similar sentiments, the attorney general of Munster, Robert Rosyer, described how 'the Irish magistrates' were 'inwardly' suspect.[141] And Andrew Trollope, in his elaborate account of the failure of religious reformation, described how the 'Irish papistical councillors, magistrates and officers', as leaders in the community, easily 'by their authority' mislead the general population. He singled out the various 'teachers and instructors, yes and magistrates'.[142]

Here Loftus criticized Lord Deputy Perrot's laxity in enforcing obedience. As was now usual for the increasingly politicized Loftus, his account of government policy towards recusants was wilfully inaccurate. He suggested that Perrot had favoured religious toleration when he had not. This served to protect Loftus from accusations that he had not done enough. Nevertheless, Loftus noted how the Old English 'gentlemen' and patricians were now internally (at the level of conscience) completely alienated from government. In Dublin 'the mayor, aldermen, and numbers of others of the best and mean sort' no longer attended church services, but now 'most of the Pale do glory to be so accounted' recusants.[143] And others in government explicitly referred to 'the gentlemen and inhabitants of the country generally', stressing how 'the sting of rebellion which in times past [had] remained among the Irishry is transferred ... into the hearts of the civil gentlemen, aldermen and burgesses, and merchants of Ireland'.[144]

In 1592 the problem very much remained unchanged. In his extended document on reform, the ambiguous figure Miler Magrath noted that those who 'exercise public magistracy and office' had not taken the oath of supremacy. As rehearsed earlier, Magrath detailed how 'known recusants' actually made up juries, one of the quintessential aspects of English common law and the local gentry republic.[145] It comes as no surprise, then, that no parliament was held again in Ireland until 1613 and only after widespread plantation had taken place ensuring that sound protestant gentlemen could be found. Lord Deputy Fitzwilliam did have permission to call a parliament in the late 1580s but did not think it expedient.[146]

Alongside this, Old English gentlemen were now consciously excluded from the high offices of state. It emerged at the Irish council board that Perrot had received secret instructions that 'in matters of secrecy and importance, the English council should only be used and the Irish forborn'. This meant the exclusion of the Old English councillors Sir Lucas Dillon and Sir Nicholas White.[147] As Loftus later commented, Lucas Dillon might have been a 'grave and wise councillor, and of great experience in this state, yet his notorious recusancy and wilful absenting himself from church ... [had] draw[n] the greatest number into that corruption wherein they live'.[148] In line with such sentiment, the chief justice of the common pleas, Robert Dillon, was actually accused of conspiring with

O'Rourke.[149] These accusations are unlikely to have been true, but their plausibility arose from the now pervasive concern over the internal condition of the Old English gentleman. A decade into James's reign the Old English gentry would be excluded from the government of their own towns and cities.[150]

Interestingly, Conal Condren argues that scholars frequently make the mistake of only associating a notion of 'office' with the magistrate or those in political power, when in early modern society everyone was thought to hold an office or position in society which entailed obligations or duties (*officiis*) such as husbands, wives and servants. This was because everyone's position or role in society was ordained by God thus by implication it consisted of a set of obligations and duties. For Condren, then, there is a point at which this normative notion of 'office' becomes externalized, whereby it is assumed individuals might not fulfil their obligations as part of the body of Christ if they are no longer thought of as belonging to that body – a process we see vividly occurring in Ireland.[151]

Furthermore, considered against the more dominant motif in Irish historiography, where Nicholas Canny, amongst others, has emphasized the cultural, linguistic and religious aspects of identity formation in Ireland, we can add to such a process a statist or institutional model, where a need to compensate for concerns over a lack of Christian friendship in the polity fed into attempts to use the state to organize and group Old English, Gaelic Irish and New English by locating political authority in institutions.[152] Thus those thought suspect could be excluded from political life – although such exclusion remained contingent, where the underlying hope of redemption remained operative if diminished.

If we continue to read the Irish case alongside developments in England, the English kingdom looks different as well. Neil Younger has examined the expansion of lord lieutenancies throughout England, where the privy council attempted to organize the English counties in readiness for war and possible invasion; he points to the success of such a model, but also its contingent nature. It lacked statutory authority, and it continued to rely on the norms of the local self-governing gentry republic, where various lieutenants remained sensitive to local conditions. But Younger also notes how leading peers were passed over because of a suspect Catholicism, and lesser ranked protestant gentlemen were appointed to office instead. Here the lieutenancies were layered on top of the long established system of justices of the peace - a system that could not be detached, as easily, from suspect gentry communities.[153] Thus by formalizing and institutionalizing local authority, a similar but milder process seems to have taken place in England. Many of the local gentry stayed in place, but many individuals would now exercise authority through formalized state offices which replaced the earlier assumed bonds of friendship and loyalty.

6 AN IRISH STATE THEORY

This book has argued then, in broad terms, that the vocabulary of the state, and attempts to build state structures in Ireland, responded to the perceived absence of grace in Irish political life. Such a view suggested that at the level of conscience man would remain unreformed and that the bonds of Christian friendship, which should have held the community together, would be absent. Beside this, in the absence of such a godly ideal, a sense of moral political action had become increasingly difficult to sustain or articulate. Here the notion of the state responded in two ways. First, in focusing on the need to uphold the authority of the state and the integrity of state institutions, a clear non-godly and discernible point for amoral political action could be articulated. Secondly, the impersonal institutions of the state provided a means by which the increasingly problematic question of interpersonal political relationships, which relied on good conscience, could be sidestepped. The limits placed on office holding, the atomizing of lordships and the closure of customary and constitutional avenues of protest would allow state institutions to recreate externally the impression of Christian unity.

I have argued, moreover, that the nature of Irish policy debate provides us with the opportunity to engage in a more detailed examination of the various dimensions surrounding a shift away from notions of a godly community towards an idea of an institutional state. Irish government's need to build a functional political community from the ground up meant that the various fundamental assumptions behind notions concerning civil obedience and healthy polities had to be openly discussed on a regular basis, and this in turn allows an everyday shift in political vocabulary to be traced. The study has asked how the practical problems of Christian division and a grace-centred theology fed into and drove the articulation and development of a new model which began to emerge as a proto-modern institutional state. It has been argued that a collapse in the notion of a unified Christian community was not incidental but critical in the development and application of statist thought – something not always apparent in the more urbane domain of European political thought or the more settled environment of Elizabethan England. Alongside this there sits the suggestion, at least with regard to an English language of the state, that this new statist vocabulary first emerged in Ireland where the peculiarity of the Irish situation was critical in giving form to important aspects of English political thought.

It seems appropriate to end, therefore, after having discussed how the practical needs of Irish government had given shape to both a godly view of society, and then an Irish notion of the state, by discussing how some of these ideas re-emerged in political theory and extended written texts associated with Elizabethan Ireland. This enables an additional strand to be added concerning the dissemination of Irish government thinking. It allows the study to move beyond the observation that these ideas were simply discussed at the English court and voiced in an exchange of government correspondence – though this remains important. Here the chapter will concentrate on three texts – John Hooker's extension of the Irish section of Holinshed's *Chronicles* (1587), Richard Beacon's *Solon his Follie* (1594) and, quite naturally, Edmund Spenser's *View of the Present State of Ireland* (1596). Both Beacon and Spenser were involved in the first Munster plantation, whilst Spenser had formed part of Arthur Grey's retinue in Ireland serving as Grey's private secretary.

More importantly, what a re-reading of these texts demonstrates is the extent to which knowledge of a specifically Irish political and religious vocabulary is important when considering the normative political languages available in English political thought. An awareness of such an Irish vocabulary alters how we understand the argument and ideas presented in Hooker's Holinshed, Beacon's *Follie* and Spenser's *View*. In turn, how English political thought might be read changes when it is recognized that a heavily accented Irish notion of an institutional state, which was both distinct and somewhat theoretically advanced, was available to government in England. The Irish texts of Hooker, Beacon and Spenser further demonstrate how the long-term reflections of individual writers and thinkers continued to remain important in adding form and clarity to new political vocabulary and ideas, though the original source of these ideas lay in the way various individuals spoke about practical and immediate problems.

Two more observations might be made. First, with regard to Hooker and Beacon we see the continued destabilization of republican ideals of liberty or freedom. In a very blunt manner, this entailed the right to participate actively in political life through service to the state either in civil government, or through military glory. There was also a sense of negative liberty, where constitutional and customary rights acted as checks on the authority of the ruler and could be used to assert the rights of subjects or citizens to a voice in government. These arguments, as Markku Peltonen astutely observed, can be found well before the Jacobean period or the Civil War in texts concerning peripheral areas of English political life, in John Hooker's *Order and Usage* and more crucially his treatise concerning the *Citie of Excester* (1584), as well as in Beacon's *Solon*.[1] As the study has argued, and as this final chapter will re-emphasize, such notions of freedom, even in the texts of Hooker and Beacon, are dependent on a godly ideal and an underlying notion of Christian freedom, where in the absence of grace, ideas of liberty become unstable and contested.

Secondly, with Beacon and Spenser, the importance of the space left by the separation of the state from the polity or body politic becomes apparent. It is possible to identify further attempts to redefine the polity as a natural body, and not the body of Christ, where the state might regulate passions and appetites as opposed to recreating the vague impression of the bonds of Christian love. This second stage in developments, which remained tentative in Ireland, would be important in allowing the state to act as a negative check on man's behaviour, providing room for individual or non-godly behaviour as long as those passions or appetites did not impinge on stability. This is something that was only really to come to the fore with Hobbes's *Leviathan*, where freedom is not determined by a right to participate in government, but is defined simply in terms of an individual's freedom from being coerced to act in a way he or she does not want (a more fully developed notion of negative freedom).[2]

Hooker's Holinshed

To begin with John Hooker has been viewed as one of a number of quintessential early English civic republican and mixed state theorists. His *Order and Usage*, as discussed, presented England and Ireland as mixed polities, whilst his *Citie of Excester* treatise emphasized the patrician rights of the citizens of Exeter, where he discussed the role or duties of the freeman, the 'office of the Maior', and the 'office of the Constables' amongst others.[3] Not only has Peltonen raised the importance of Hooker, McLaren presents Hooker as an important theorizer of a specifically godly mixed polity, where good conscience allowed the gentry to participate in government.[4] Here, however, the position which emerges in his addition to Holinshed presents itself as the other side to English godly theorizing and as an important counterpoint in his thought; and given the popularity of Holinshed, the absolutist position which Hooker took in the *Chronicle of Ireland* would have had a certain currency in England.

Hooker's addition to the second edition of the Irish section of Holinshed picks up the narrative account of government in Ireland from the reign of Edward VI. Hooker extends the narrative from the earlier account written by Richard Stanihurst (and Campion), which had set out an idealized view of the role of the Old English in preserving English civility. In contrast, Hooker recounts the detail of Sidney's 1565 programme for government, the various efforts to evangelize, and in turn acknowledges how inadequate finance and inadequate clerical personnel meant God's word continued not to be preached.[5] The vocabulary used, and the detail given, actually suggests Hooker may have had access to much original government correspondence. His account of government's dealings with the Clanrickard Burkes even parallels the detail and language of Nicholas Malby's letters, whilst Hooker would appear to have had access to a copy of the first earl of Essex's eulogy written by Waterhouse.[6] In this manner, Hooker comes to draw a strong link between attempts to construct a godly political community in Ireland, the failure to achieve such an objective, and the subsequent development of a proto-absolutist position; this mirrors the argument and narrative set out in this book.

The narrative addresses the fact that in the absence of God's word, Christian brotherly love remains absent and stable political relationships highly problematic. This is because, internally, at the level of conscience, many key political and noble players in Ireland remain unreformed. Shane O'Neill's rebellious behaviour is explained with reference to 'his [O'Neill's] conscience', which was 'cauterised' and also 'overladen with an utter despaire to obteine anie grace or favor'.[7] The rebellion of the Butlers and Geraldines in 1569 is framed with direct scriptural paraphrases. The narrative states that the 'waies of peace they know not, and in the paths of righteousnesse they walke not'. Hooker refers to the internal disposition of those involved in rebellion – 'the hardnesse of their hearts' and their lack of 'respect' for 'faith' and 'duty'.[8] And this language is repeated with respect to the 1576 rebellion of the two sons of the earl of Clanrickard. Again the narrative draws on a direct reading of scripture and it is explained how after 'the wicked spirit was gone out of the man ... he goeth and seeketh out other seven wicked spirits ... and the last state of that man is woorse than the first'.[9] Clanrickard's sons, we are told, are 'graceles impes'.[10] Hooker also refers to the action of God in hardening the heart of Pharaoh when describing the second Desmond rebellion of 1579. In reference to the earl of Desmond, 'yet was ... Pharaos heart so hardened and indurated in disobedience, rebellion, and treacherie, that nothing could make him to yeeld and relent' and as a result Desmond had no 'feare of God, obedience to the prince, or regard of himself'.[11] This critique is subsequently applied generally to include the Old English gentry, where 'the nature of the Irishman' is unfaithfulness, lack of duty and ingratitude.[12]

Importantly, it is the continued ungodly nature of the political community that creates or establishes the context for the subsequent deployment of statist language and Hooker's open espousal of a proto-absolutist position. Obviously, this contrasts with Hooker's own earlier mixed polity position, but also the tone of the earlier part of the *Chronicle of Ireland*, which emphasized the participation of the Dublin patricians in government and the constant use of parliament as a consultative body. Very much in line with Hooker's own thinking in the 1560s, the preceding narrative suggests that Ireland is a mixed polity with some aspect of popular sovereignty. As with much of the discussion traced in Ireland, then, but with a more direct sense of a causal relationship, it is the problem of conscience-based reform that invalidates the right of individuals to participate in political life and encourages a more institutional and statist model.

Sovereign authority, throughout Hooker's account, is positioned openly within institutional structures and in particular with the office of the lord deputy. This reflects Irish constitutional peculiarity, in that sovereignty by necessity is disassociated from the person of the prince who is physically absent. But it also reflects the inability to locate sovereignty within a wider community which has been shown to be corrupt and unreformed. Contrasting with Stanihurst's reference to the act of kingly title, which showed sovereignty passing from the people or parliament to the prince, Hooker labours the passing of 'the sword of state', the physical manifestation of sovereignty, from each lord deputy or lord justice to the other, emphasizing institutional continuity and the authority of the office holder.[13] This was something Derricke's *Image of Irelande* had visually portrayed through a set of detailed engravings.[14] Hooker even draws attention to the election of Pelham, on the death of Lord Justice Drury in 1579, by virtue of the authority inherent in the offices of state in Ireland and the act for an election of a lord justice.[15]

Hooker rejects the claims made by the Irish gentry that some level of sovereignty lay with the wider community – though critically this would not appear to be the position Hooker held in relation to England. He recounts how as a representative for Athenry in the Irish Commons in 1569 he had had to explain to the MPs, who refused to pass Poynings' law and so threatened to scupper all parliamentary proceedings, 'what was the office and authoritie of a prince'.[16] If we recall that James Stanihurst (Richard's father), as speaker in the 1569 parliament, as well as Richard, emphasized the constitutional position of parliament, it seems that Hooker was consciously reacting against these views.[17] Partly in line with Annabel Patterson's work on Holinshed, Hooker can be seen using the 'multivocality' of the text (the many authorial voices involved in the *Chronicles*) to make his point.[18] And his emphasis on crown authority expands when he addresses the more general opposition to the levying or commutation of cess. The city of Waterford is praised and its civic liberties extolled, where:

> no officer nor officers of the kings or queenes of England, nor their deputies shall intermeddle, nor exercise anie authoritie nor jurisdiction, within the citie and liberties, but onelie the maior and officers of the same.[19]

Hooker, however, takes a Bodin-esque position and builds on Irish proto-absolutism. The narrative gently warns the citizens of Waterford that in order to preserve civic life they should:

> compare not your privileges not with his [the prince's] authoritie, nor doo you dispute your liberties with his prerogative. For notwithstanding your privileges, liberties, and grants be great and manie: yet they can not abate nor impugne the least part of the princes prerogative: which is so great, as nothing can be greater, if you will take

> the view of Gods owne ordinances, when he first erected and established a king, who gave him so high and so absolute authorite, that (as the apostle saith) it must be with all humblenesse obeied.[20]

This reflects something of the city of Waterford's own litigious practice of maintaining and asserting its corporate rights. In many ways, Waterford encapsulates a lot of the quintessential aspects of the English self-governing gentry republic, having insisted that its charter and liberties be confirmed on the accession of a new king or queen – in particular, the right to import wine free of duty ('prisage wine').[21] But Hooker's comment expands into a general criticism of the Pale community, where the prerogative right to cess, as exercised by Sidney in 1575–6, had been challenged. Here the Pale community is reminded that the prince's 'prerogative dooth not onelie extend to his owne person, and all that which he hath of his owne, but also to all his subjects', with the implication that questioning the prerogative could jeopardize wider civic liberties such as those of Waterford.[22] Finally, it is amongst this repositioning of sovereignty within institutions, and the denial of political rights, that Hooker actively searches for new vocabulary and in doing so draws on the vocabulary charted in Irish government correspondence.

Hooker struggles to draw a distinction between commonwealth and 'the state' and we see a transition in thinking at a half-way point between a godly and a statist objective. In the midst of his various descriptions of Old English and Gaelic Irish lords, Hooker includes a eulogy for the Irish chancellor Robert Weston, as well as the eulogy of the earl of Essex. He also points explicitly to Henry Sidney's godly credentials.[23] At one level these individuals are easily described as serving the 'commonwealth', or the common good, as equated with a clear moral good or God. In the context of the narrative account given, however, whilst Sidney, Weston and others may remain godly, and so act for the commonwealth, this becomes problematic when the goodly polity or commonwealth does not exist. Here Hooker searches for a new term and slides between two. For example, the need to uphold 'the imperiall authority' of the prince begins to be emphasized. But in trying to articulate what this means, he deploys 'commonwealth' and 'state' together, not yet being able to draw a full distinction between sovereignty and state institutions and an earlier sense of good and healthy political relationships.[24]

His narrative account talks of 'the publike state of the commonwealth' and the 'the whole state and government of this realme' in describing the problems government faced and the basis upon which government acted. The sheer variety of what this might mean is expressed in his description of Sidney acting for 'alimightie God, the preservation of hir majestie, and of hir imperiall crowne of this realme, and the safetie of the common-wealth of the whole realme'. Even the Clanrickard Burkes, and government's failure to properly punish them, is set in terms of both 'state' and 'commonwealth', where again Hooker struggles to articulate what state institutions actually are and mean. Because of the Clanrickard Burkes, he tells us, 'the whole state is disturbed, & the commonwealth (as a garden overgrown with weeds) [is] in peril and danger to be overthrowne'.[25]

Read against Hooker's *Citie of Excester* treatise the same instability can be identified in an English context, which actually suggests that the articulation of an absolutist view by English reformed protestants is not that surprising. For Peltonen, Hooker's *Pamphlet* is straightforwardly republican and Ciceronian in quality.[26] In the preface to the work, however, the duties of the patricians are not simply to fulfil their prescribed roles where the mayor guards and protects the 'state of the citie, and liberties of the same', or where the steward makes sure true records of justice are kept.[27] In the preface it is argued that the duties of the magistrates concern in the first place 'God and his service in religion, the other concerning your selves and your office in politike government. The latter dependeth upon the first'. The preface then stresses how the citizens do not attend church to hear sermons, but spend their 'daies most licentiouslie ... in sinne and wickednes', where 'the fault is knowen, a redresse is wished, but nothing is done'.[28] The point for Hooker is that the city's liberties and the mixed polity are endangered and undermined when godly responsibilities are not fulfilled, because at the moment 'the ship of your common wealth being overladen with sinne and iniquitie, is in great danger of shipwracke'; and the consequences of such a situation had been realized in his account of Irish civic life in Holinshed.[29]

Beacon

In contrast, when Beacon's *Solon his Follie* (1594) is considered, the later date of the text, as well as Beacon's direct focus on the specific question of reform, would appear to have allowed a different variant of ideas to emerge. There is a more direct reflection on the notion of an institutional state, and how the distribution of sovereignty within the community might affect stability. The definition of reformation shifts and it becomes about stability, as opposed to good conscience, where external institutions, not internal reform, regulate political behaviour. Again, this reflects practical political developments in Ireland, where those involved in Irish government had applied and drawn on a variety of political theory and vocabulary when discussing and attempting to understand how to build, from their perspective, a stable and functional polity now in the absence of a wider godly community.

More importantly, when Beacon's text is read as appropriating the practical political vocabulary used by Irish government, another important counterpoint can be identified within *Solon* in relation to earlier English civic republicanism and a godly political outlook. Whilst a republican language is clearly present, I would argue that it is combined with a more forthright language of absolutism. This is despite the fact that, as with Hooker's earlier work, Peltonen has held up Beacon's text as a prime example of civic republican thought, arguing that in an Irish context civic republicanism could be developed and applied less controversially because the prince was physically absent.[30] Peltonen points to the way in which Beacon uses Ireland as an arena in which the active English citizen can pursue glory, Beacon arguing that an active political life would help man avoid corruption and so the threat of declination.[31] However, Beacon is neither a die-hard republican, nor an absolutist. In actual fact, sovereignty is not located with any particular estate in society, which was a central tenet of Bodin's position.

Instead, political life in Beacon's text is dominated by a now broader idea of institutional state structures and it is the limits of these institutional forms which guide and direct the behaviour of the citizen or subject. The pursuit of glory, therefore, is not the essential characteristic of the political life which Beacon describes. Instead, political life is more impersonal and slightly more sterile, and it is below this more defined sense of institutional government that the polity begins to be gradually reconceived as a natural body. The state in many senses now works to regulate man in his fallen condition, but that fallen condition needs to be repackaged in a way that allows for a fuller and more beneficial discussion of the type of regulation the state can provide. Hence Beacon begins to address man's appetites and passions.

As before with regard to Hooker's text, Beacon's treatise had a particular resonance in England. His treatise was published when the second earl of Essex was lobbying for his candidate, William Russell, to replace Lord Deputy Fitzwilliam; Russell was appointed to office not long after the publication of *Solon*. The treatise takes the form of a dialogue between *Solon*, the ancient law giver of Athens, and Epimenides, one of his advisors whose attention is directed towards the Athenian colony, Salamina. For Clare Carroll and Vincent Carey, *Solon* can be read as referring to William Russell; Epimenides as referring to Beacon, who is attempting to advise Solon/Russell; Athens as referring to England; and Salamina as referring to Ireland. The treatise is also dedicated to the 'wise Ulysses', whom Carroll and Carey suggest refers to the second earl of Essex.[32] Carroll's and Carey's edition is of immense value because of the level of critical detail provided concerning Beacon's classical and contemporary sources. We should also note that the treatise is divided into three books. Book one sets out an introductory position on what reformation actually means, book two expands on this definition of reformation, and finally book three raises the motif of fortune or declination and attempts to apply the various theoretical models set out in the previous two books in the context of the specific and temporal problem of Irish government.

Book one opens with a broad definition of an 'absolute and a thorough reformation', which encompasses 'the whole bodye of the common-weale, namely of the ancient laws, customes, governementes and manners of the people', and in discussing what this means Beacon refers to Solon's attempts to reform Athens.[33] A thorough reformation was not attempted because Solon did not have the necessary force to back up such radical change. It is explained that he 'did not change the whole state thereof' because if he had 'changed the whole state ..., I might afterwards never have beene able with that smal power and forces then granted unto me, to settle and establish the same againe'.[34] Does 'the state' refer to the institutional structures, the community as a whole or the conditions and customs within the community? This ambiguity, however, quickly dissipates as Beacon engages in a more detailed examination of what reformation entails in book two.

It is explained with regard to the 'reformation universall of the whole state and body of the commonwealth, [that it] is nothing els, but a thorough and absolute mutation ... of the common-wealth ... unto a better forme of government' or 'a new institution'.[35] In moving to discuss what shape reformation should take, Beacon is led to discuss the idea of institutional limits on sovereign authority. The treatise argues concerning the force needed to further reformation, that 'all authority herein graunted is after two sortes: the one absolute, the other limited by time, and other circumstances'.[36] Again drawing on the particular circumstances of Ireland, Beacon raises the problem that sometimes those granted 'absolute power', as governor or in 'provinciall governement', may end up with sufficient authority to threaten state institutions. Those appointed to office should not be so strong and have such natural or lordly authority whereby 'the state may stand in feare of his greatnes'.[37] In line with this, Beacon raises the example of the Venetian republic, where the governor or duke has absolute authority, but points to the fact that such authority is limited in time and its use overseen by 'certaine watchmen'.[38] Interestingly, the importance of the Venetian republic, for Beacon, is not necessarily the fact that it is a quintessential example used in republican or mixed state theory, but that it supports a broadly institutional conception of government.

This institutional sense of the state broadens out later in book two when Beacon attempts to define what he actually means by state institutions. He discusses:

> the institution itselfe, wherein foure matters are found worthie of consideration: first, the soveraintie and commaundment, secondly, the forme of governement; thirdly, the forme and manner of the institution itselfe; lastly, the severall endes and scopes of this institution.[39]

As Sommerville has been at pains to point out here, Beacon expands on a clearly Bodinian definition of the state.[40] 'Common-weales', he tells us, are 'properly distinguished by the soveraintie and commaundement, and not by the diversity which sometimes appeareth in the forme and governement'.[41] But Beacon steps beyond Bodin's insistence on locating such authority with a particular estate in society. Instead, a conception of 'the state' emerges in which an idea of 'institution' and 'form' is more critical, where sovereignty is positioned in the different offices and apparatus of government. Here we approach the critical question as to why Beacon is driven to articulate such a statist and institutional model.

Again reflecting Beacon's Irish experience, it would appear that at one level it is the lack of a Christian community that is critical – though within current interpretations of Beacon's *Solon* the sense of a collapse in a previous model or conception of society is not really considered. What rests below Beacon's focus on the state is an attempt to reconceive of the political community in line with Bryskett's *Discourse*.[42] Enough room seems to have opened up, as a result of a broadening institutional conception, which now allows the political community to be thought of as a natural body, the natural body expressing the conditions and desires of man in a sinful world.

An idea of fortune or mutability is outlined, where in addressing both a monarchy (or an absolutist state) and a free state, Beacon recounts how 'neither the one nor the other may be founde so happy and permanent, but ... with the apple in his ful ripenes, they fall with their owne weight ... to the ground' through discord or effeminacy. Critically, he refers to this as the 'fatall destinie' of all states, where in the absence of grace all things due to their sinful nature move towards declination.[43] This signals Beacon's attempt to detach the state from a Christian world view.

In this context the state and its institutions are seen as responding to man's passions and appetites, where the aim of political action is no longer internal reform, but to stabilize current contingent conditions. When English law is discussed, it is not described as acting to reform through edification or education, but as instilling a 'feare to offende, bred in the hearts of the people'.[44] The examples of both Arthur Grey and Richard Bingham are raised, which points back to an earlier comment on the usefulness of martial law, where 'governours in cases of great extremities, for the avoiding of daungers and difficulties, may proceede against offenders, without observing the usuall ceremonies of lawe'.[45] The maintenance of 'the state' can require amoral political action, which 'in a publike magistrate, the same is rightlie tearmed policie, but in private persons, the same is not unjustly condemned by the name of deceite'.[46] A clear Machiavellian sense of political action emerges.

Furthermore, when Epimenides expands on the reasons why the state may be threatened, man's passions and appetites are addressed more directly. Problems arise 'partly from the contrarietie of humours, and opinions, lodged in the brests even of the wisest; partly from the insolency of the multitude', where in dealing with 'diversitie of humours, opinions, and factions, they must of necessitie remove for a time, or otherwise imploy the leaders and heades of all such factions'.[47] It is this view of man that would appear to inform Beacon's reading and deployment of contemporaneous political theory.

The treatise quotes from Lipsius's *Politickes* and draws out the sense of the political as the profane, Beacon writing that 'God the creator & maker of the world, coupled hatred and a kingdome together'.[48] Interestingly, Lipsius's *Politickes* sets out more explicitly than Beacon the division between a political community as the body of Christ and the political community as an institutional state. Book one of the *Politickes* details how a stable community is built on unity of conscience, the action of grace and the bonds of friendship. The next five books, however, silently assume such a community will not exist and then detail how an impression of such a united community can be built institutionally, whereby it is the integrity of state authority, the impression of a unified religion, and the ability of the state institutionally, fiscally and militarily to control political life that is discussed.[49]

Similarly, when Beacon draws on Fenton's *Guicciardin*, as well as Bodin, more evidence of a direct Irish reading of statist thought can be found. Beacon draws on the example of French oppression in Italy as detailed by Guicciardini, whereby the Italians once favouring French intervention, then sought to expel them. What motivated them on both occasions was the desire to be freed from exploitation and oppression. Beacon also makes reference to Bodin and uses the example of Henry II. The French king had raised a tax in order to fund his army, forgoing the need to billet troops upon his subjects and therefore relieving his subjects from the oppressions of soldiers.[50] This would have had particular resonance in an Irish context where attempts to commute cess into a unified tax had failed quite badly. In each case, therefore, political action is seen as responding to the desires and interests of subjects, who, when they feel oppressed, will push against the ruler. Here again Fenton's *Guicciardin* is referenced where it is described how Lodowick Sforce, the duke of Milan, was removed from office by particular factions of the city and had to flee.[51] This is followed by an account of the actions of the Geraldines and the arch-traitor Shane O'Neill, where again in line with Irish government correspondence they are described as acting against 'the state' and as disturbing 'the politike body'.[52]

There is a need, therefore, for the public magistrate to focus on manipulating 'the affections of the people', and at this juncture the treatise expands further on the subject of passions and appetites. For Beacon:

> The affections which be the first, are in number these; love, hatred, hope, feare, dispaire, and such like; the matter and subject which is the second, is parentage, consanguinity, friendes, goods, possessions, lands, the custome and manner of living, honours, libertie and life; the presence whereof wee love and imbrace, and with their absence wee are soone carried away unto wrath, hatred, revenge, hope, feare, and dispaire.[53]

In contrast with earlier discussion about godly reform, Beacon now redefines preaching. It is not grace that he thinks critical, but the preacher's ability to use oratorical skills in order to pull on the various passions of man.[54] This informs how Beacon understands both the nature of a free state and a monarchy. Turning back to book two, Beacon had argued that state and institutional structures operate best when they 'holde the ... most just temperature ... [and] commeth nearest to the perfection of nature'; that we should think about how nature 'doth temper the foure humours and elements in our natural bodies, by so much we receive a more perfit strength, and a longer being and continuance'. The political community is again thought of as a natural body.[55]

By implication, in book three, a free state or republic now emerges, not as an ideal, but as a set of institutional arrangements that respond to current conditions and man's habits and passions. There is a need to 'make a difference in the manner of reforming of a free and popular estate', as opposed to a monarchy. In a free state those pursuing reform need to leave in 'place onely a shadowe and resemblance of that which is changed, for the better contentment of the people'.[56] Here Beacon is thinking directly of England. In contrast, in a monarchy or a more absolutist state, in this case Ireland, government is able to make a thorough alteration and change.

Thus in book three political corruption and declination are defined in light of such a definition. In a monarchy it is through bad leadership or factional struggles that man comes to act against the state as his passion and humours are not properly controlled and the treatise turns to address how 'every distemperature raigning in this pollitické bodie' might be regulated.[57] Beacon raises the question of office holding in the Irish kingdom and reassesses the limits that should be placed on the offices held. Instead of primarily ensuring those of good conscience are in positions of leadership, offices should provide an outlet and redirect the self-interest of those government does not want to lead the community astray. In effect, subjects should be given offices that provide financial reward, thus satisfying self-interest, but not such offices that will provide political authority. That 'we shall more safely give offices of profite, then of commaundement, whereby the multitude shall rest pleased, and the state acquitted of peril and daunger ... if we shall give any higher places to anie then those of profit and gaine, let us then carefullie with *Antipater* [the lord deputy] make choise of such *Athenians* [Englishmen], as shall not be studious of any innovation'.[58]

An interesting symbiotic relationship also emerges, where the theatre of Ireland, with its scope for glory through colonial projects, is presented as the natural outlet for the ambitions of the English gentleman. The Englishman can pursue glory without damaging the English state, whilst his presence in Ireland will help shore up the institutional checks on the wider Irish population. This has implications for the way in which we read English political ideas. For Peltonen, such an argument is evidence of an active republic virtue in the pursuit of glory. However, the sentiment of Beacon's text is far more contingent. Not only is Ireland a safety valve for the over-ambitious Englishman, political 'liberty', the right to actively participate in civil life, is part of a wider temporal and contingent reading of the English and Irish polities, where the point of acknowledging such rights and liberties is simply about ensuring that current institutional arrangements function in England very much akin to Beacon's perspective on the Irish kingdom.[59] In other words, liberty is important because in a free state man's passions and appetites are framed or set in such a way that man expects such an outlet, with state institutions acting to regulate the polity below.

Spenser

When we turn to consider Spenser's *View*, a similar shift in ideas concerning state and polity can be identified. Spenser tends to be read as a quintessential New English text, where the language of innovation and change is appropriated in order to justify the forced removal of the native population; but Spenser's *View* also emerges as potentially central in our understanding of a broader English statist position. A sense of the distinction between polity and state clarifies, as well as the manner in which the institutional state could give shape to the polity which rests below it. The other important aspect to Spenser's position is the manner in which a proto-secular notion of the state, as articulated, remains caught between a failed godly model and a remaining longer-term hope for godly reform.

As with Hooker and Beacon, a *View* had a significant presence within the English political elite. Whilst a *View* remained in manuscript form, as Andrew Hadfield notes, the text circulated widely amongst the English governing class. The text even indicated that the second earl of Essex should be appointed governor, something which did occur within two years of a *View*'s initial circulation.[60] In the dialogue which Spenser constructs, the text can be divided roughly into three parts. The dialogue involves Ireneus the sceptical New English planter, where Spenser puns or plays on the fact that Ireneus is not in fact offering a peaceful or irenic solution to the Irish problem, and Eudoxus, the naive and inexperienced Englishman, who has no direct experience of Ireland, and displays wanton naivety in continuing to look to various aspects of earlier reform practice in the Irish kingdom.

In the first third, current approaches to reform are addressed, involving both the imposition of an English model of land tenure and law, as well as religious reformation. The second third of the text, on this basis, pushes towards an alternative solution, where an institutional and largely statist model is proposed. But the final part returns to the godly model and Spenser restates the godly view in fulsome detail. This immediately raises the question of what exactly the Irish state and its institutions are meant to do, where underlying these various structures remains a hoped-for godly community. There are also a number of references to 'the state' throughout, Spenser's title again encapsulating the sense of a shift between the condition or 'state' of the island and an emerging institutional definition which concerned the distribution of sovereignty or 'the present state of Ireland' and its need for reform.[61]

To begin with, then, in the first third of a *View* Spenser manages to summarize the full detail of current Irish political and religious vocabulary, which Beacon tended not to engage with. What is important is that akin to Beacon's treatment of civic republicanism, Spenser argues that an English model of land tenure and law cannot have any claims to universal validity. Echoing Beacon, Ireneus opens Spenser's dialogue by referring to Ireland's 'fatall destiny' and how

'Almighty God hath not yet appointed the time of her reformation'.[62] It is this absence of a providential plan or vision for Irish society that sets the tone of the text, where 'change and alteration' are the dominant processes affecting the Irish kingdom and have 'disannulled' the validity of previous attempts to reform the island.[63] This contingent sphere immediately invalidates common law, one of the quintessential structures of English society. That:

> *jus politicum*, though it bee not of it selfe just, yet by application, or rather necessity, it is made just; and this onely respect maketh all lawes just. Now then, if these lawes of Ireland bee not likewise applied and fitted for that realme, they are sure very inconvenient.[64]

This criticism of the universal validity of law and specifically common law is something Ciaran Brady has raised as the particularly controversial aspect of a *View*, considering the presumed dominance of the common law mind.[65] This is certainly true, but combined with the narrative so far traced, Spenser's position actually looks a little more normative, and in this respect it could be suggested that Spenser's position, along with Beacon's discussion of Ireland, can be taken as the start of a far broader shift in English thought. Spenser's text, therefore, should not be read solely within the confines of a colonial discourse.[66]

In particular, if it is recalled that the involvement of the gentry community is an essential characteristic of common law, because freeholders participate in common law juries, what happens if those freeholders are thought to be corrupt? Ireneus explains that the 'Common Law appointeth, that all tryalls, as well of crimes, as title and rights, shall bee made by verdict of a jury, chosen out of the honest and most substantiall free-holders', but 'most of the freeholders of that realme are Irish ... [and] they make no more scruple to passe against an Englishman, and the Queene, though it bee to strayn their oathes, then to drinke milke unstrayned'.[67]

The problem here is one of conscience – something not largely recognized by scholars because of a failure to engage with the vocabulary of godly reform. It is Eudoxus who raises the first objection, asking 'doth many of the people (say you) make no more conscience to perjure themselves in their verdicts, and damne their soules?'[68] Ireneus responds, first, that 'they are most willfully bent', and quickly explains that 'so inconscionable are these common people, and so little feeling have they of God, or their owne soules' that it does not matter what action government takes they will act how they wish.[69] That 'when a people be inclined to any vice, or have no touch of conscience, nor sence of their evill doings; it is bootelesse to thinke to restraine them by any penalities or feare of punishment'.[70] If the position expressed by Goodman, Ponet and Aylmer on the health of a polity is recalled, Spenser can be seen as responding to a key aspect of English political thought. As Aylmer himself raised in *An Harborowe*, trial by jury rested on grace and good conscience.[71]

The problem of the absence of individuals correctly disposed is further developed, when, in line with the broad trend in Irish government thought, any sense of popular sovereignty dissipates. It is suggested by Eudoxus that parliament could be employed to pass statute law which would remedy the various problems detailed: such as the fact that juries will never convict because they are on good terms with the accused or have been threatened by the defendant, or that coyne and livery remains an ever present practice where current statute provision has not effected a remedy. Ireneus responds that 'Parliament must consist of the peeres, gentlemen, freeholders, and burgesses of that realme it selfe'.[72] Nevertheless, it has already been pointed out that those individuals are corrupt in conscience. In this context, Spenser raises the example of Perrot's parliament, where the problem of divisions in conscience had increased, leading to another stepped shift in the deployment of the vocabulary of the state.[73]

Interestingly, Spenser raises three times the idea of liberty or freedom, which is pejorative in tone because it is used to refer to diversity of action and an unbridled will, thus more forcefully articulating the corollary of the position taken by Goodman, Ponet and others, where a notion of Christian freedom, as applied to the political arena, meant conformity of godly action. In turn, there is no sense of negative freedom, as hinted at by the Old English community, whereby White, Delvin, Walsh and others argued that the state or its institutions should bridle the uncontrolled will of those who governed and so allow a level of personal or private freedom with respect to citizens or subjects.

Ireneus describes how 'the lawes themselves they [the Irish] doe specially rage at, and rend in peeces, as most repugnant to their libertie and naturall freedome, which in their madnes they affect'.[74] This position is repeated by Eudoxus, who signals agreement, describing how 'they [the Irish] look after liberty, and shake off all government'.[75] The failure of lords and freeholders to find settled tenants and so foster a stable agricultural society is understood in the same terms. The 'poore husbandman' likes insecurity of tenure, because 'by his continuall liberty of change' he can 'keepe his land-lord the rather in awe from wronging of him'. It is further described how the 'tennant being left at his liberty is fit for every occasion of change that shall be offered by time'.[76]

From here Spenser spills into a discussion of Irish custom, which has been of particular interest to literary scholars such as Andrew Hadfield. A *View* details the origin legend of the Irish, and the dialogue suggests that the Irish are descended from the Scythians which encourages a nomadic or pastoral lifestyle.[77] Spenser raises the issue of degeneracy, which is inflected throughout Irish government thinking, though not to the same extent scholars seem to assume.[78] A *View* details how Old English lords, following Irish custom, have become like the mere Irish in habit and behaviour. In reality, in the 1560s, '70s and '80s, this trope seems to be hardly addressed, though in the 1540s, with a more dominant

Christian humanist position, it seems to have had more weight. Maybe from a Calvinist perspective, the fact that man will degenerate in the absence of God was simply far too obvious to bother discussing. However, the discussion now points towards an attempt to reconceptualize the polity.

As before, the room for a tentative reconceiving of relationships within the polity is provided by a concurrent discussion over the location of sovereignty in the state and its institutional structure. Spenser now tackles the question of sovereignty and state institutions as the one identifiable point for political action in a world governed by fortune. Akin to Beacon, it is now the institutional structures of the state that are seen as giving external form and shape to political relationships, where again the fact that such mechanisms seem to have been removed from the polity allows the body political to be thought of in different ways.

Ireneus describes the fact that 'young children be like apes' and so raises, in line with Bryskett's *Discourse*, the possibly that through habit and education man can be inured into a variety of modes of behaviour. As addressed earlier, and by Richard McCabe, Bryskett provides a clear model for Spenser to follow.[79] Spenser is also concerned with the way in which dysfunctional institutional structures had allowed or facilitated degeneration and undermined the operation of law. Throughout a *View* an account is given of the dislocated nature of sovereign authority, which meant institutions had no strength to enforce government's will, thus allowing a pejorative natural liberty to run rampant. This reflects a Bodinian position, where it is the dislocation of sovereignty, and weak or ambiguous constitutional or institutional structures, which fuelled civil discord, and at worse civil war.[80] Spenser's position also reflects concurrent political discussion in Ireland, with a *View* referring to the way in which Arthur Grey's authority was undermined at the Elizabethan court.[81]

Here Spenser identifies, as had many of his contemporaries, how various major lords had taken upon themselves a degree of sovereign authority thus creating states within the state and further splintering political authority and perpetuating discord and division. In a Bodinian manner, a *View* points to the act of kingly title, where absolute authority passed to the prince, and contrary to the Old English position a *View* refers to the fact that the 'kings of England [are supposed to] have had the absolute dominion thereof'.[82] But it is also recalled throughout the first two-thirds of the dialogue how Henry II at the conquest of Ireland did not remain resident, thus quickly dissipating his sovereign authority and allowing the near immediate independence of the Anglo-Norman lords.[83] A *View* similarly points to the way in which the presence of the duke of Clarence, as governor, brought Ulster under control, but more critically how, on the duke's departure in 1366, O'Neill made open claims to independent political authority.[84]

It is described how the norms of the English political community in Ireland were disregarded as separate political entities emerged, where the Norman lords 'received unto them as their vassalls [the Irish], but scarcely vouchsafed to impart unto them the benefit of those laws ... but every one made his will and commandement a law unto his own vassal'.[85] The major Old English lords, through their palatine jurisdictions, pursued their own agendas, bending 'that regal authority ... one against another', which helped feed into the degeneracy of the colony. The claims of Gaelic lords to an independent political authority are also addressed. Progressive rebellions arose because of the space provided by a dislocated sovereignty, where Gaelic Ireland was able to re-assert itself, the Gaelic Irish lord Feagh McHugh O'Byrne playing a '*Rex*' and 'lift[ing] up hand against that state'.[86]

Spenser approaches then quite a basic point, but one faced by Irish government on a daily basis, of where to locate sovereign authority in order to provide sufficient authority for government to govern and further reform. Like his contemporaries, Spenser cannot locate sovereignty with the wider community, which he has already deemed corrupt. And like his contemporaries, Spenser faces the fact that the prince is absent, so sovereign authority needs to be located with the lord deputy. We encounter another problem, however, because, as Spenser observes, such authority tended to be delegated in an *ad hoc* and ill-defined manner, allowing intrigue at court to undermine a deputy's authority. It has already been addressed how each deputy attempted to claim absolute authority in order to compensate for this and further their various programmes. It is at this point, right at the end of a *View*, that Spenser is led to take quite a bold step. He does not simply assume, like many a lord deputy, that authority should be separated from the prince and located within the institution of the deputyship; he now openly states that this should be the case. For Ireneus, 'this should be one principall in the appointing of the Lord Deputies authority, that it should bee more ample and absolute then it is, and that he should have uncontrouled power to doe any thing'.[87]

Whilst this is a conceptually significant step, in that a clearer notion of a doubly abstract state now emerges, Spenser locates sovereignty here in order to facilitate a wider analysis of how institutional structures might allow the community to be reformed and regulated. Two other significant points arise. First, state structures can now be seen as operating to undermine or break the various cultural bonds that might allow rival communities or factions to arise. Secondly, in line with the earlier sentiment of Stubbs and Philip Sidney, and Fenton's later observations, the state now operates to prevent rival communities or polities subsequently forming again below state structures.

In the first place, Spenser deploys his well-known shift in positions, where after arguing that laws should be made to suit the people, he now suggests that the people should be made to fit the law. There has been some discussion over what exactly Spenser means here; whether or not this is a rhetorical ploy to help mask the duplicitous nature of the dialogue and the detailing of quite a brutal solution?[88] I would suggest, however, that it shows Spenser struggling to find the right language and terminology in order to express, not so much a new system of law, but the institutional restructuring of the island.

In line with established thinking, a *View* tells us that garrisons need to be placed throughout the island and that colonies should be planted to ensure obedience. There is also Spenser's infamous proposal, that after a general pardon, a scorched earth policy should be pursued, leaving most of the population to starve, whereby afterwards the army can easily re-establish order.[89] Despite such brutality, there is a degree of subtlety in what Spenser suggests should happen next. In the initial general pardon that will be proclaimed 'the very principalls and ringleaders ... should [not] finde grace'.[90] This is critical in neutralizing rival polities or states. Ireneus goes on to describe a restructuring that consciously guards against rival political leadership. After everything has been settled and the main leaders removed, it is now proposed that akin to England under 'King Alured, or Aldred', where conditions of outlawry similar to Ireland were the norm, that the kingdom be divided 'into shires, and shires into hundreds, and the hundreds into lathe or wapentackes, and the wapentackes into tythings'. The point of this atomization is to use self-interest – the natural desire for self-preservation – to regulate the community. The idea is that each person within the tything is responsible for the actions of everyone else, with the eldest pledge being held responsible for all, who is called the 'Tythingman or Borsolder'.[91] The tything then is responsible for bringing in an undutiful man, and if the community fails the responsibility slowly extends out to each wider grouping.

These bonds of unity are in stark contrast with bonds of friendship, and Spenser discusses how government can prevent bonds of customary loyalty forming within the smaller groupings and thus creating the rival polities Ireneus fears. Earlier on in a *View* Ireneus argued that various traditional assemblies or gatherings should be prevented, because they end up creating communities which rival the state, that 'dangerous are such assemblies, whether for cesse or ought else, the Constables and Officers being also of the Irish'.[92] As a consequence, it is proposed that the previous bonds of cultural unity be broken before the system is brought into operation; the Irish will be transplanted to different parts of the kingdom, that 'the name of their septs' should be abolished and that in 'time [the Irish man will] learne quite to forget his Irish nation'.[93] A sense of cultural genocide begins to emerge. In particular 'all the O's and the Mac's, which the heads of septs have taken to their names, [are] to bee utterly forbidden and extinguished', and the nobility will be excluded from such a system because they might naturally assume positions of leadership.

What, then, are we to make of Spenser's model? Is 'the state' finally breaking free from the Christian body political? The answer must be emphatically no, because it is at this point that a *View* takes its final about-turn and Spenser now concludes by reprising a call for religious reformation. Ireneus wants preaching in the Irish vernacular, church finances reformed, churches repaired and schools established, as had originally been suggested in the mid-1560s. This connects directly into a strained commentary running throughout a *View*, where Spenser awkwardly sidestepped the question of religious reform at an earlier stage in the dialogue. Ireneus argued that it was too soon to discuss religious reformation, because if a man was dying one would call a physician before the priest suggesting that political reform should take precedence over religious reformation. But Ireneus's comment rests on a clear misappropriation of terminology, because he answers a question of salvation by addressing not the soul but the physical health of the body – a false comparison. After all, the promise of eternal life, or the prospect of eternal damnation, should trump all. Ireneus explained that:

> if you should know a wicked person dangerously sicke, having now both soule and body greatly diseased, yet both recoverable, would you not thinke it evill advertizement to bring the preacher before the phistian? ... it is like that his languishing soule being disquieted by his diseasefull body, would utterly refuse and loath all spirituall comfort.[94]

This says something important about the nature of the political space that the state, in Spenser's perception, makes available. In effect, the ability of the state to make available a space that would provide for diversity of action and behaviour (freedom in a far more modern sense) remains severely limited as long as some form of a Christian world view dominates. This is because the environment the state regulates is a fallen and temporal space and Spenser cannot forget the ideal of the Christian polity. Actually, in attempting to sidestep the issue, Spenser cannot find a way to rationalize away the Christian body political, as his strained metaphor indicates. Interestingly, the same pattern of discussion can be found in William Herbert's own reform treatise *Croftus Sive de Hibernia Liber*, which is usually read beside Beacon and Spenser, where a hoped-for reformation conditions a similar proposal to atomize and restructure Irish civil life.[95] It also says something about Spenser's political outlook, where there has been a debate over his supposed republicanism, where on the one hand he is critical of central government and demands a right to participate in political life, but on the other he upholds the absolute authority of the prince. In this regard, Spenser encapsulates the godly republican, where the mixed polity and the active life are only viable when made good by grace.[96] Thus Spenser, like Hooker, Beacon and both Sidneys, easily looks to an absolutist state when a godly polity is absent.

EPILOGUE: BEYOND THE 1590S

Looking forward to the Jacobean period, the absolutist pretensions of government in both Ireland and England now look far more normative. John Guy's playful identification of Elizabeth's two reigns parallels the more detailed and precocious shift in language and thought found in Irish government correspondence. The gradual death of an earlier group of councillors, who had strong godly credentials, such as Francis Walsingham and the earl of Leicester, meant commitment to a godly mixed polity, and by implication collegiality, was significantly diminished.[1] Patrick Collinson, Stephen Alford and Peter Lake have hinted towards this position, but in Ireland the importance of evangelism, grace and good conscience in establishing a wide set of godly political relationships, and the consequences of a failure to do so, becomes all too apparent.[2]

Guy's other observation, that a more compound idea of the prerogative took hold, where individual prerogative rights merged into one general statement on the absolute nature of royal power, also rings true. For Guy, a more arbitrary and absolutist style of government arose, where it was argued that 'Elizabeth possessed an "imperial" sovereignty, that she alone enacted laws, and that she herself was above the law by the prerogative of her *imperium*'.[3] The vanguard of this movement included Richard Bancroft, who would succeed John Whitgift as archbishop of Canterbury, Thomas Bilson, bishop of Worcester and Winchester, and the ecclesiastical lawyer Richard Cosin.[4] Thus absolutist ideas in England came to the fore within the specific context of discussions concerning church government. Whiftgift pursued non-conformist English clergy through a subscription campaign to root out protestant dissent. Such a move, in and of itself, departed from an idea of the church, established by statute, through the consent of the mixed polity as assembled in parliament.

In the famous case involving the cleric Robert Cawdry, government openly set aside common law, the quintessential customary expression of the mixed polity. Whitgift, in order to curtail protestant dissent, provided judges with the right to proceed *ex officio mero*. This meant that with no grounds for suspicion, clergy could be forced to express beliefs or views which they had not publicly expressed. The judge could also act by virtue of the authority of his office alone. In the case of

Cawdry this went further, because attempts were made to protect the cleric from losing his living by arguing that since he held his benefice as a freehold, common law made it clear he could not be deprived of his livings. Whitgift, and high commission, took the opposite view, that the prerogative as exercised by an officer of state could not and was not bound by such customary precedents.[5]

The fact that such an absolutist position in England was most articulately and openly voiced in the context of religious and confessional discussion should not be a surprise. Alongside Whitgift's actions sit larger treatises, *The True Difference Betweene Christian Subjection and Unchristian Rebellion* (1585) by Bilson, *Dangerous Positions and Proceedings* (1593) by Bancroft, and *Conspiracie for Pretended Reformation* (1592) by Richard Cosin. These were written against an emerging English Presbyterianism and a more radical Catholicism. Like earlier protestant resistance theory, radical English catholics drew on popular sovereignty arguments to mandate the people to act against the ruler.[6] Such a discussion reflected the need to curtail or stymie a level of freedom of conscience, when the hoped-for godly polity had not emerged. If Cartwright's Presbyterian model is taken as an ecclesiastical manifestation of a wider hoped-for godly equality, which should have come from word and grace, the absence of widespread evangelism and the absence of a dominant godly community can be seen as invalidating this model.

Akin to Ireland, therefore, an absolutism emerged in order to shut down the avenues those not fully reformed in conscience might use in order to voice their views and act, thus destabilizing an increasingly shaky *status quo*. The difference was that in Ireland the distinction between the political and the religious had become especially blurred because of the basic remit of reform and the question of civil obedience, although in the Irish kingdom clergy and theologians also started to dominate the debate. It was the bishop of Meath, Thomas Jones, who penned a long rebuttal of O'Neill's 1599 proclamation. Jones drew on various examples, including the investiture contest, to prove that the papacy did not have the right to free subjects from their obedience to the prince or to depose rulers. This was not published as it was thought too controversial, since it would draw too much attention to O'Neill's position.[7] Similarly, under James I and VI Archbishop James Ussher became a dominant voice in theological controversy.[8] In many ways, the increasingly technical nature of the debate explains the reliance on clergymen, because a more specialist knowledge was required, thus leading to a division between the religious and the political simply on the grounds of a rarefied expertise (which the earlier years of reformation had purposefully eschewed).

The increasing dominance or use of the language of 'the state' in England, I think, should also be read within the context of Irish discussions. Alexandra Gajda has drawn attention to the second earl of Essex's use of statist vocabulary in the 1590s to articulate or express a distinction between a corrupt council, termed 'commonwealth' men, and his service to the wider notion of England and its institutions. Lord Burghley and his son Robert, Essex perceived, monopolized all positions at court and on the council, thus he needed a language through which to express his opposition and exclusion from political life. Essex argued for a more interventionist foreign policy and war with Spain.[9]

Essex's service in Ireland against Hugh O'Neill at the start of the Nine Years War, and his disastrous return to court to salvage his reputation, suggests that Essex's awareness or use of a statist vocabulary had Irish roots. In particular, Thomas Wilson's 'The State of England' directly referenced Essex's service in Ireland and the condition of the Irish kingdom more generally.[10] There are indications that Wilson, reputedly the nephew of Elizabeth's secretary of the same name, was connected to Essex's circle. In 'The State of England' Wilson tells us he had written a 'Treatyse of the State of Ireland' – although his Irish treatise is not extant. And like Spenser's *View of the Present State of Ireland*, within Wilson's English treatise a transition in meaning takes place.[11] In the first instance, 'the state' refers to the present political condition of both kingdoms, but by the end of the treatise discussion involves the nature of the prince's authority, the delegation of that authority through commissions, the problem of a community divided in religion and other 'matters of state'.[12] As Elizabeth's Irish lord lieutenant, Essex's own letters patent delegated to him near full absolute authority – something Spenser's *View* had suggested should take place.[13]

Interestingly, Gadja does observe that Essex was accused of using the language of commonwealth, not state, because he courted popular opinion.[14] This is suggestive of an increasingly disparaging or angst-ridden view of the wider polity and a contested notion of the common and public good. Gadja also explores how members of Essex's circle, including a prominent catholic exile, Thomas Wright, used the notion of service to the state to express an idea of national and institutional loyalty to England which might facilitate a level of religious toleration.[15] In England statist language could be less absolutist in character, where already-stable English conditions meant more open political participation was less threatening to the *status quo*. Nevertheless, the point remains, that a notion of state was used to sidestep and rethink a breakdown in the idea of a godly polity or commonwealth.

Here Francis Bacon, in his apology concerning Essex's attempt to raise rebellion in London, can be seen shifting between strained notes of loyalty and friendship to Essex and Bacon's service and concern for the wider interests of the state. Essex was ostensibly motivated by the desire to free the queen from corrupt councillors. Bacon expresses the dichotomy the language of the state attempted to solve, where in an increasingly contested and factional environment loyalty and friendship with your peers no longer equates with service to the wider community if a diversity of interests and outlooks exist.[16] This makes any conception of service to the commonwealth fraught with tension.

This dichotomy should inform our understanding of a subsequent Jacobean discussion concerning the nature of the political community and state. For Glenn Burgess, there was no disjuncture between an absolutist and a constitutionalist position in England under James. Instead, there was a general consensus that royal authority was defined by common law, which was regarded as a set of 'customary and conventional' practices that governed kingship. The broader position taken is that the Civil War arose out of a breakdown in such a model. It was a later generation's attempt to reinterpret earlier aspects of monarchy as tyrannical that has erased our awareness of an earlier Jacobean consensus. If it is acknowledged, however, that a set of previously normative notions of commonwealth and godly unity had come under strain under Elizabeth, such a 'to and fro' over the position of sovereignty and the limits on royal authority appears more genuine and more akin to the wider absolutist and constitutionalist dichotomy, which, amongst others, J. P. Sommerville identified.[17] As it did in Ireland, it involves the wider question of how government and political life should be organized when religious division and diversity had removed previous bonds of trust. This is the critical context surrounding Bodin's own decision to discuss the nature and position of sovereign or absolute authority in the French kingdom.

Returning again to Ireland, Linda Levy Peck's identification of a definite absolutism in the writing of one John Cusacke, an Old English catholic under James, points as before to the centrality of Irish political discourse. This is made all the more compelling by an already acute and precocious Irish political vocabulary identified under Elizabeth.[18] Cusacke's absolutism may reflect an adherence to an abstracted state authority by catholics, since strong institutional structures could be used to enforce and uphold the rights of persecuted religious communities. This can be seen in France where Huguenots came to support a catholic monarchy since it supported the edict of Nantes which protected the rights of French protestants.[19] Spenser also looms large here, with the eventual publication of a *View* in 1633 and Milton's own interest in the poet.[20]

Nevertheless, the transition towards an institutional notion of 'the state' was far from complete. A new lord deputy, Lord Mountjoy, felt curtailed in his dealings with O'Neill from 1600–1603; and Mountjoy's deputyship expresses fully the ambiguity and contradictions in the emergent statist position. After Essex's botched return to England and Elizabeth's displeasure with the peace he had negotiated with O'Neill, the new deputy, unlike many of his predecessors, was unwilling to act in negotiations without express command from his sovereign. However, a certain 'reason of state' did predominate, where Mountjoy saw little hope of fully rooting out O'Neill and so asked that he be allowed to negotiate some reasonable settlement – though Elizabeth, asserting notions of honour, duty and fidelity refused to countenance such a policy.[21] Mountjoy, like his predecessors, also understood well enough the significance of the O'Neill's claims to an independent sovereign jurisdiction, smashing the inauguration stone of the O'Neill at the end of the Nine Years War.[22]

The issue of the nature of sovereignty further resurfaced in Mountjoy's negotiations with O'Neill. Whilst he knew Elizabeth had died a week before, Mountjoy, for good reason, did not inform O'Neill, who would have held out for better terms with the accession of James I and VI.[23] At a level, therefore, Mountjoy negotiated on the basis of a more institutional notion of sovereignty, negotiating on behalf of 'the state' not the prince *per se*. But again the restructuring of the political community did not immediately follow. O'Neill's earldom was restored, and whilst defeat had clearly curtailed his authority, with garrisons being stationed within his earldom, the extent of his earldom and his claims over many lesser lords remained intact.[24] It would take a more long-term assault on his wider jurisdictional claims and the 'flight of the earls' to ultimately change the character of Ulster by necessitating plantation.[25]

Within the Old English gentry community the Irish statist position is both more complex and straightforward. There was a further reassertion of values of the English local self-governing republic within the corporate towns of Waterford, Cork, Limerick, Kilkenny, Drogheda, Wexford, Clonmel and Cashel – though this was spurred on by Old English Catholicism.[26] Waterford led the way and, with news of Elizabeth's death, shut the gates of the city to Lord Deputy Mountjoy and openly celebrated Catholicism, claiming they had the right to refuse the deputy admittance on the basis of a charter granted by King John. In response Mountjoy threatened to cut the charter and thus negate the liberties of the city.[27] When commissioners arrived at Cork, Mayor Sarsfield took a more traditionalist interpretation of delegated authority, arguing that the commissioners' authority had lapsed with the death of Elizabeth and so the city expelled them.[28]

This spilled into a more open and concerted negation of the rights of the traditional gentry community in Ireland, making true the tone and intent of Hooker's addition to Holinshed. As Hans Pawslich notes, attempts were made to revive the court of high commission as a means of tendering the oath of supremacy to all administrative officials in Dublin (very much in line with Perrot's deputyship). And with the inability to gain parliamentary consent to various proposals, 'the state' acted arbitrarily. The rest of the penal laws (not passed in Perrot's parliament) came into force through 'royal fiat' and mandates were issued demanding the chief gentlemen attend church services.[29] In a more extreme case in Munster, the lord president deposed the mayors of all of the towns of the province because they had refused to attend church or take the oath of supremacy with the suggestion that the towns forfeit their charters (though the litigious Waterford was excluded from such a proposal).[30] Civic life became closed to the Old English gentry, whose customary liberties and rights stood for nothing if they were not of right conscience, though the distasteful proposition existed that with conversion participation in civic life would become an option.

An emerging notion of 'the state', therefore, solved nothing, because despite having the institutional components to construct a more pluralistic political life, conceptually this remained impossible. With the confederacy of Kilkenny in 1642 and the trumpeting of an Irish catholic republic, where notions of lordship, self-government and religion were reasserted, an even more aggressive and uncompromising assertion of state authority emerged in response. Not only does Oliver Cromwell's appointment as lord general of Irish forces encapsulate the clear relocation of the authority of a now dead king within the institution of the council of state; Cromwell exemplifies the inability of that state to free itself from an increasingly dogmatic religious outlook, where at the siege of Drogheda more than the town's charter was lost.[31] In effect, whilst early on the problem of conscience and Christian friendship had been pushed to the side or obfuscated by the deployment of the different languages of the state, such language remained caught in a failed attempt to move past a godly model.

It took Hobbes in *Leviathan*, in the aftermath of the English Civil War, to find a solution, where Hobbes simply abolished conscience as an invented category of little relevance.[32] In many ways, however, this left the general notion of 'the state' and its institutions as anti-ideological, where they simply provided for stability and the regulation of self-interest. As a consequence, no area or space remained where a reformative vision of society was necessarily welcome. This is something with which pluralistic Western state structures still have to cope, where strong ideological commitments easily fracture a *status quo* of rights and liberties, which in its first manifestation was designed to cope with the absence of a godly ideal and so the prevalence of sin.

WORKS CITED

Primary Works

Manuscripts

Alnwick Castle: Northumberland Papers, VI.

Bodleian Library, Oxford: Carte MS 242; Perrot MS 1; Willis MS 58.

British Library, London. Additional MSS 5845, 33271, 48023; Cotton MSS Titus BX & Titus BXII; Harleian MS 3292; Sloane MS 2172; Lansdowne MS 23.

Denbighshire Record Office, Ruthin: Plas Power MSS DD/PP/839.

Lambeth Palace Library, London: Carew MSS 609, 611, 614; LPL, MS 2003.

The National Archives, Kew: State Papers Ireland, SP63: English Privy Council Register, PC2.

Printed Manuscript Sources

Fitzwilliam, W., 'The Deputy's Defence: Sir William Fitzwilliam's Apology on the Outbreak of the Nine Years War', ed. H. Morgan, *Proceedings of the Royal Irish Academy*, section c 114 (2014), pp. 1–34.

Gerrard, W., 'Gerrard Papers: Sir William Gerrard's Notes of his Report on Ireland, 1577–8', ed. C. McNeill, *Analecta Hibernica*, 2 (1931), pp. 93–182.

Knox, J., 'Some Unpublished Letters from John Knox to Christopher Goodman', ed. J. E. A. Dawson and L. K. J. Glassey (eds), *Scottish Historical Review*, 84:2 (2005), pp. 166–201.

Ó Cearnaigh, S. [Kearney, J.], 'A Brefe Declaration of Certeine Pryncipall Articles of Religion: Set out by Order and Aucthoritie Aswel of the Right Honorable Sir Henry Sidneye' (1567), in *Aibidil Gaoidheilge & Caiticiosma: Seaán Ó Cearnaigh's Irish Primer of Religion*, ed. B. Ó Cuív, (1571; Dublin: School of Celtic Studies, 1994), appendix 2, reproduced in full from the only surviving copy in the library of Trinity College Dublin.

O'Neill, H., 'Faith and Fatherland or Queen and Country', ed. H. Morgan, *Duiche Neill: Journal of the O'Neill Country Historical Society*, 9 (1994), pp. 9–65.

Perrot, J., *A Critical Edition of Sir James Perrot's the Life, Deedes and Death of Sir John Perrot*, ed. R. Turvey (Lampeter: Edwin Mellen, 2002).

Perrot, J., 'The Perrot Papers: The Letter-Book of Lord-Deputy Sidney Sir John Perrot between 9 July 1584 and 26 May 1586', ed. C. McNeill, *Analecta Hibernica*, 12 (1943), pp. 3–65.

Sidney, H., *Sidney State Papers 1565–70*, ed. T. Ó Laidhin (Dublin: Irish Manuscript Commission, 1926).

—, *A Viceroy's Vindication: Sir Henry Sidney's Memoir of Service in Ireland, 1556–78*, ed. C. Brady (Cork: Cork University Press, 2002).

Sidney, P., *The Miscellaneous Works of Philip Sidney, Knight*, ed. W. Gray (Boston, MA: T. O. H. P., 1880).

Walsh, N., 'Nicholas Walsh's Oration to the Irish House of Commons, May 1586', ed. M. A. Hutchinson, *Analecta Hibernica*, 45 (2014), pp. 35–47.

Calendars and Indexes

Calendar of the Patent and Close Rolls of Chancery in Ireland, ed. J. Morrin, 3 vols (Dublin: A. Thom and sons, for H. M. Stationery Office, 1861), vols 1–2.

Calendar of State Papers Ireland, 1509–1603, ed. H. C. Hamilton, 11 vols (London: H. M. Stationary Office, 1860–1912).

Calendar of the Carew Manuscripts Preserved at Lambeth Palace, ed. J. S. Brewer and W. Bullen, 6 vols (London: Longman & Co., 1867–73).

'Fiants of the Reign of Queen Elizabeth', in *The Sixteenth Report of the Deputy Keeper of the Public Records in Ireland* (Dublin: Alex. Thom & Co., 1884), appendix 2.

The Great Charter of the Liberties of the City of Waterford (Kilkenny: J. Reynolds, 1806).

The Statutes at Large Passed in the Parliaments Held in Ireland, 1310–1800 (Dublin: George Grierson, 1786–1801).

The Statutes of the Realm (London: Records Commission, 1810–1828).

Contemporaneous Printed Treatises and Other Works

Aylmer, J., *An Harborowe of Faithfull and Trewe Subjectes* (Strasborowe [i.e. London: John Day], 1559).

Bacon, F., *Sir Francis Bacon his Apologie, in Certain Imputations Concerning the Late Earle of Essex* (London: [Richard Field for] Felix Norton, 1604).

Beacon, R., *Solon his Follie; or, A Politique Discourse Touching the Reformation of Common-Weales Conquered, Declined or Corrupted*, ed. C. Caroll and V. Carey (Binghampton, NY: Medieval and Renaissance Texts and Studies, 1996).

Bodin, J., *On Sovereignty*, ed. J. H. Franklin (Cambridge: Cambridge University Press, 1992).

Brutus, the Celt, S. J. [attributed to Du Plessis Morney and Languet], *Vindiciae, Contra Tyrannos*, ed. G. Garnett (Cambridge: Cambridge University Press, 1994).

Bryskett, L., *A Discourse of Civill Life* (London: [R. Field for] William Aspley, 1606).

Calvin, J., *Institutes of the Christian Religion*, trans. Henry Beveridge (Peabody, MA: Hendrickson Publishers, 2008).

—, 'On Civil Government', in *Luther and Calvin on Secular Authority*, ed. H. Höpfl (Cambridge: Cambridge University Press, 1991), pp. 47-86.

Campion, E., *A Historie of Ireland* (Dublin: Societie of Stationers, 1633).

Campion, E., and R. Holinshed, *The Historie of Irelande* [first two books], in R. Holinshed, *Chronicles* (London: [Henry Bynneman], 1577), pp. 1-75.

Cartwright, T., *A Replye to an Answere Made of M. Doctor Whitgifte Agaynste the Admonition to Parliament* ([Hemel Hempsted?: John Stroud?], 1575).

Churchyard, T., *A Generall Rehearsal of Warres* (London: [John Kingston for] Edward White, 1579).

Derricke, J., *The Image of Irelande, with a Discoverie of Woodkarne* (London: [J. Kingston for] Jhon Daie, 1581)

Erasmus, D., *The Education of a Christian Prince*, trans N. M. Cheshire and M. J. Heath, ed. L. Jardine (Cambridge: Cambridge University Press, 1997).

Fenton, G., *An Epistle of Godlie Admonition* (London: Henry Bynneman, 1569).

—, *A Discourse of the Civile Warres and Late Troubles in Fraunce* (London: Henry Bynneman for Lucas Harrison and George Bishop, 1570).

—, *Actes of Conference in Religion* (London: H. Bynneman for William Norton and Humfire Toye, 1571).

—, *A Forme of Christian Pollicie* (London: H. Middleton for Rafe Newbery, 1574).

—, *Golden Epistles* (London: Henry Middleton for Rafe Newbery, 1575).

—, *The Historie of Guicciardin* (London: Thomas Vautrollier, 1579).

Goodman, C., *How Superior Powers Oght to be Obeyd of their Subjects* (Geneva: John Crispin, 1558).

Herbert, W., *Croftus Sive de Hibernia Liber*, ed. A. Keaveney and J. Madden (Dublin: Irish Manuscripts Commission, 1992).

Hooker, J., *A Pamphlet of the Offices, and Duties of Everie Particular Sworne Officer, of the Citie of Excester* (London: Henry Denham, 1584).

—, 'The Supplie of this Irish Chonicle ... until this present yeare 1586', in R. Holinshed, *Chronicles*, 2nd edn (London: [Henry Denham], 1587), pp. 109–83.

—,'Order and Usage', in *Parliament in Elizabethan England: John Hooker's Order and Usage*, ed. V. F. Snow (New Haven, CT: Yale University Press, 1977), pp. 111-214.

Lipsius, J., *Sixe Bookes of Politickes; or, Civil Doctrine* (London: Richard Field for William Ponsonby, 1596).

Luther, M., 'On Secular Authority', in *Luther and Calvin on Secular Authority*, ed. H. Höpfl (Cambridge: Cambridge University Press, 1991), pp. 3–43.

—, *The Bondage of the Will*, trans. Henry Cole (Peabody, MA: Henrickson, 2008).

Machiavelli, N., *The Prince*, ed. Q. Skinner and R. Price (Cambridge: Cambridge University Press, 1998).

More, T., *Utopia*, trans. Paul Turner (London: Penguin, 1965).

Norton, T., *To the Quenes Majesties Poore Deceived Subjects of the North Countrey, Drawen into Rebellion by the Earles of Northumberland and Westmerland* ([London]: Henry Bynneman for Lucas Harrison, 1569).

— [published under Lord Burghley's name], *Execution of Justice in England for the Maintenaunce of Publique and Christian Peace* (London: Christopher Barker, 1583).

Ponet, J., *A Short Treatise of Politike Power* (Strausbourg: by the heirs of W. Köpfel, 1556).

Rich, B., *Allarme to England* (London: Christopher Barker, 1578).

—, *A Short Survey of Ireland* (London: N[icholas] O[kes], 1609).

Smith, T., *A Letter Sent by I. B. Gentleman* (London: Henry Binneman for Anthonhson [i.e. Anthony Kitson]1572).

—, *De Republica Anglorum* (London: Henrie Middleton for Gregorie Seton, 1583).

Spenser, E., *A View of the State of Ireland*, ed. A. Hadfield and W. Maley (Oxford: Blackwell, 1997).

Stanihurst, R., 'Description of Ireland', in R. Holinshed, *Chronicles* (London: [Henry Bynneman] for George Bishop, 1577), pp. 1-29.

—, 'The Thirde Booke of the Historie of Ireland', in R. Holinshed, *Chronicles* (London: [Henry Bynneman] for George Bishop, 1577), pp. 76–115.

Stubbs, J., *The Discoverie of a Gaping Gulf* (London: H. Singleton for W. Page, 1579).

Wilson, T., 'The State of England anno dom. 1600', ed. F. J. Fisher, *Camden Miscellany*, 16 (1936).

Winter, E. F. (ed. and trans.), *Discourse on Free Will: Erasmus and Luther* (London: Bloomsbury Academic, 2005).

Secondary Works

Adams, S., *Leicester and the Court: Essays on Elizabethan Politics* (Manchester: Manchester University Press, 2002).

Alford, S., *The Early Elizabethan Polity: William Cecil and the British Succession Crisis, 1558–1569* (Cambridge: Cambridge University Press, 1998).

—, *Burghley: William Cecil at the Court of Elizabeth I* (New Haven, CT: Yale University Press, 2008).

Bagwell, R., *Ireland under the Tudors*, 3 vols (London: Longmans & Co., 1885–90), with a succinct account of the earlier history.

Ballériaux, C., 'The Idea of Freedom in the Missionary Writings about the New World', in Q. Skinner and M. van Gelderen (eds.), *Freedom and the Construction of Europe*, 2 vols (Cambridge: Cambridge University Press, 2013), vol. 2, pp. 247–65.

Berlin, I., *Essays on Liberty*, ed. Hardy, H. (Oxford: Oxford University Press, 1990).

Boran, E., and C. Gribben (eds), *Enforcing Reformation in Ireland and Scotland, 1550–1700* (Aldershot: Ashgate, 2006).

Bottingheimer, K. S., 'Kingdom and Colony: Ireland in the Westward Enterprise', in K. R. Andrews, N. P. Canny and P. E. H. Hair (eds), *The Westward Enterprise: English Activities in Ireland, the Atlantic and America, 1480–1650* (Manchester: Manchester University Press, 1978), pp. 45–65.

—, 'The Failure of the Reformation in Ireland: *Une Question Bien Posée*', *Journal of Ecclesiastical History*, 36:2 (1985), pp. 196–207.

Bouwsma, W. J., *John Calvin: A Sixteenth Century Portrait* (Oxford: Oxford University Press, 1989).

Braddick, M., *The Nerves of State: Taxation and the Financing of the English State, 1558–1714* (Manchester: Manchester University Press, 1996).

—, *State Formation in Early Modern England* (Cambridge: Cambridge University Press, 2000).

Bradshaw, B., 'Sword, Word and Strategy in the Reformation in Ireland', *Historical Journal*, 21:3 (1978), pp. 475–502.

—, *The Irish Constitutional Revolution of the Sixteenth Century* (Cambridge: Cambridge University Press, 1979).

—, 'More on Utopia', *Historical Journal*, 24:1 (1981), pp. 1–27.

—, 'The Christian Humanism of Erasmus', *Journal of Theological Studies*, 32:2 (1982), pp. 411–47.

—, 'Robe and Sword and the Conquest of Ireland', in C. Cross, D. Loades and J. J. Scarisbrick (eds), *Law and Government under the Tudors: Essays Presented to Sir Geoffrey Elton on his Retirement* (Cambridge: Cambridge University Press, 1988), pp. 139–62.

—, 'Transalpine Humanism', in J. H. Burns and M. Goldie (eds), *Cambridge History of Political Thought* (Cambridge: Cambridge University Press, 1991), pp. 95–134.

Brady, C., 'Faction and the Origins of the Desmond Rebellion of 1579', *Irish Historical Studies*, 22:88 (1981), pp. 289–312.

—, 'Conservative Subversives: The Community of the Pale and the Dublin Administration, 1556–86', in P. J. Corish (ed.), *Radicals, Rebels and Establishments: Historical Studies* XV (Belfast: Appletree Press, 1985), pp. 11–32.

—, 'The O'Reillys of East Breifne and the Problem of Surrender and Regrant', *Breifne*, 6 (1985), pp. 233–62.

—, 'Spenser's Irish Crisis: Humanism and Experience in the 1590s', *Past and Present*, 111 (1986), pp. 17–49.

—, *The Chief Governors: The Rise and Fall of Reform Government in Tudor Ireland, 1536–1588* (Cambridge: Cambridge University Press, 1994).

—, 'The Attainder of Shane O'Neill, Sir Henry Sidney and the Problems of Tudor State-Building in Early Modern Ireland', in C. Brady and J. Ohlmeyer (eds), *British Interventions in Early Modern Ireland* (Cambridge: Cambridge University Press, 2008), pp. 28–48.

Brady, C., and R. Gillespie (eds.), *Natives and Newcomers: Essays on the Making of Irish Colonial Society* (Dublin: Irish Academic Press, 1986).

Brady, C., and J. Murray, 'Sir Henry Sidney and the Reformation in Ireland', in A. Boran and C. Gribben (eds), *Enforcing Reformation in Ireland and Scotland, 1550–1700* (Aldershot: Ashgate, 2006), pp. 14–39.

Brady, T. A., Jr., 'Confessionalization: The Career of a Concept', in J. M. Headley, H. J. Hillerband and A. J. Papalas (eds), *Confessionalization in Europe, 1555–1700: Essays in Honor and Memory of Bodo Nischan* (Ashgate: Aldershot, 2004), pp. 5–17.

Brady, W. M., *The Alleged Conversion of the Irish Bishops to the Reformed Religion at the Accession of Queen Elizabeth* (London: Longmans & Co., 1866).

Burke, P., 'Tacitism, Scepticism, and Reason of State', in J. H. Burns and M. Goldie (eds), *Cambridge History of Political Thought* (Cambridge: Cambridge University Press, 1991), pp. 479–98.

Canning, J. P., 'Law, Sovereignty and Corporation Theory, 1300–1450', in J. H. Burns (ed.), *The Cambridge History of Medieval Political Thought, c.350–c.1450* (Cambridge: Cambridge University Press, 1998), pp. 339–66.

Canny, N. P., 'The Formation of the Old English Elite in Ireland', O'Donnell Lecture, Dublin, 1975.

—, *The Elizabethan Conquest of Ireland: A Pattern Established, 1565–76* (Hassocks: Harvester Press, 1976).

—, 'Dominant Minorities: English Settles in Ireland and Virginia, 1550–1650', *Historical Studies*, 12 (1977), pp. 51–69.

—, 'The Permissive Frontier: Social Control in English Settlements in Ireland and Virginia', in K. R. Andrews et al. (eds), *The Westward Enterprise* (Manchester: Manchester University Press, 1978), pp. 17–44.

—, 'Why the Reformation Failed in Ireland*: Une Question Mal Posée*', *Journal of Ecclesiastical History*, 30:4 (1979), pp. 423–50.

—, 'Edmund Spenser and the Development of an Anglo-Irish Identity', *Yearbook of English Studies*, 13 (1983), special issue: *Colonial and Imperial Themes Special*, pp. 1–19.

–, 'Identity Formation in Ireland: The Emergence of the Anglo-Irish', in N. P. Canny and A. Pagden (eds), *Colonial Identity in the Atlantic World 1500–1800* (Princeton, NJ: Princeton University Press, 1987), pp. 159–212.

—, *Making Ireland British* (Oxford: Oxford University Press, 2001).

—, 'Writing Early Modern History: Ireland, Britain, and the Wider World', *Historical Journal*, 46:3 (2006), pp. 723–47.

Carey, V. P., 'The Irish Face of Machiavelli: Richard Beacon's *Solon his Follie* and Republican Ideology in the Conquest of Ireland', in H. Morgan (ed.), *Political Ideology in Ireland, 1541–1641* (Dublin: Four Courts, 1999), pp. 83–109.

—, *Surviving the Tudors: The 'Wizard' Earl of Kildare and English Rule in Ireland, 1537–1586* (Dublin: Four Courts Press, 2002).

—, 'Atrocity and History: Grey, Spenser and the Slaughter at Smerwick (1580), in D. Edwards, P. Lenihan and C. Tait (eds), *Age of Atrocity: Violence and Political Conflict in Early Modern Ireland* (Dublin: Four Courts Press, 2007), pp. 79–94.

Charlton, K., *Education in Renaissance England* (London: Routledge and K. Paul, 1965).

Christianson, P., *Reformers and Babylon: English Apocalyptic Visions from the Reformation to the Eve of the Civil War* (Toronto: University of Toronto Press, 1978).

Coffey, J., 'Quentin Skinner and the Religious Dimension of Early Modern Political Thought', in A. Chapman, J. Coffey, and B. S. Gregory (eds), *Seeing Things their Way: Intellectual History and the Return of Religion* (Notre Dame, IN: Notre Dame University Press, 2009), pp. 116–74.

—, 'The Language of Liberty in Calvinist Political Thought', in Q. Skinner and M. van Gelderen (eds), *Freedom and the Construction of Europe*, 2 vols (Cambridge: Cambridge University Press, 2013), vol. 1, pp. 296–316.

Collinson, P., *The Elizabethan Puritan Movement* (London: Jonathan Cape, 1967).

—, *Archbishop Grindal 1519–1583: The Struggle for the Reformed Church* (Berkeley, CA: University of California Press, 1979).

—, 'England and International Calvinism 1558–1640', in M. Prestwich (ed.), *International Calvinism, 1541–1715* (Oxford: Oxford University Press, 1985), pp. 197–223.

—, 'The Monarchical Republic of Queen Elizabeth I', in P. Collinson, *Elizabethan Essays* (London: Hambledon, 1994), pp. 31–58.

—, 'Windows in a Woman's Soul: Questions about the Religion of Queen Elizabeth', in P. Collinson, *Elizabethan Essays* (London: Hambledon, 1994), pp. 870–118.

—, 'Puritans, Men of Business and Elizabethan Parliaments', in P. Collinson, *Elizabethan Essays* (London: Hambledon, 1994), pp. 59–86.

—, *The Birthpangs of Protestant England: Religious and Cultural Change in the Sixteenth and Seventeenth Centuries* (Basingstoke: St Martin's Press, 1998).

Condren, C., *Argument and Authority in Early Modern England: The Presupposition of Oaths and Offices* (Cambridge: Cambridge University Press, 2006).

Connolly, S. J., *Contested Island: Ireland 1460–1630* (Oxford: Oxford University Press, 2007).

Crawford, J. G., *Anglicizing the Government of Ireland: The Irish Privy Council and the Expansion of Tudor Rule, 1556 to 1578* (Dublin: Irish Academic Press, 1993).

Cromartie, A., *The Constitutionalist Revolution: An Essay on the History of England, 1450–1642* (Cambridge: Cambridge University Press, 2006).

Cunningham, B., 'The Composition of Connacht in the Lordships of Clanrickard and Thomond, 1577–1641', *Irish Historical Studies*, 24:93 (1984), pp. 1–14.

Dawson, J. E. A., 'Resistance and Revolution in Sixteenth-Century Thought: The Case of Christopher Goodman', in J. van den Berg and P. Hoftijzer (eds), *The Church, Change and Revolution* (Leiden: Brill, 1991), pp. 69–79.

—, 'Calvinism and the Gaidhealtach in Scotland', in A. Pettegree, A. Duke and G. Lewis (eds), *Calvinism in Europe 1540–1620* (Cambridge: Cambridge University Press, 1996), pp. 231–53.

—, 'John Knox, Goodman and the Example of Geneva', in P. Ha and P. Collinson (eds), *The Reception of the Continental Reformation in Britain* (Oxford: Oxford University Press, 2010), pp. 107–35.

Dewar, M., *Sir Thomas Smith: A Tudor Intellectual in Office* (London: Athlone Press, 1964).

Doran, S., 'Elizabeth I's Religion: The Evidence from her Letters', *Journal of Ecclesiastical History*, 51:4 (2000), pp. 699–720.

Edwards, D., 'The Butler Revolt of 1569', *Irish Historical Studies*, 28:111 (1993), pp. 228–55.

—, 'Beyond Reform: Martial Law and the Tudor Re-conquest of Ireland', *History Ireland*, 5:2 (1997), pp. 16–21.

—, 'Ideology and Experience: Spenser's *View* and Martial Law in Ireland', in H. Morgan (ed.), *Political Ideology in Ireland, 1541–1641* (Dublin: Four Courts, 1999), pp. 127–57.

—, *The Ormond Lordship in County Kilkenny, 1515–1642: The Rise and Fall of Butler Feudal Power* (Dublin: Four Courts, 2003).

Edwards, R. Dudley and T. W. Moody, 'The History of Poynings' Law: Part I, 1494–1615', *Irish Historical Studies*, 2:8 (1941), pp. 415–24.

Ellis, S., 'Economic Problems of the Church: Why the Reformation Failed in Ireland', *Journal of Ecclesiastical History*, 41:2 (1990), pp. 239–65.

—, 'Tudor State Formation and the Shaping of the British Isles', in S. G. Ellis and S. Barber (eds.), *Conquest and Union: Fashioning a British State 1485–1725* (London: Longman, 1995), pp. 40–63.

—, *Ireland in the Age of the Tudors 1447–1603: English Expansion and the End of Gaelic Rule* (New York: Longman, 1998).

Elton, G. R., *The Tudor Constitution* (Cambridge: Cambridge University Press, 1960).

—, 'Henry VIII's Act of Proclamations', *English Historical Review*, 75:294 (1960), pp. 208–22.

—, *Reform and Renewal: Thomas Cromwell and the Common Weal* (Cambridge: Cambridge University Press, 1973).

—, *Parliament in England 1559–1581* (Cambridge: Cambridge University Press, 1986).

Flanagan, E., 'The Anatomy of Jacobean Ireland: Captain Barnaby Rich, Sir John Davies and the Failure of Reform, 1609–22', in H. Morgan (ed.), *Political Ideology in Ireland, 1541–1641* (Dublin: Four Courts, 1999), pp. 158–80.

Fletcher, A. and D. Macculloch, *Tudor Rebellions* (1967; London: Routledge, 2014).

Ford, A., 'The Irish Historical Renaissance and the Shaping of Protestant History', in A. Ford and J. McCafferty (eds), *The Origins of Sectarianism in Early Modern Ireland* (Cambridge: Cambridge University Press, 2005), pp. 133–40.

—, *James Ussher: Theology, History and Politics in Early-Modern Ireland and England* (Oxford: Oxford University Press, 2007).

—, Apocalyptic Ireland: 1580–1641', *Irish Theological Quarterly*, 78:123 (2013), pp. 123–48.

Franklin, J. H., *Jean Bodin and the Rise of Absolutist Theory* (Cambridge: Cambridge University Press, 1973).

—, 'Sovereignty and the Mixed Constitution: Bodin and his Critics', in J. H. Burns and M. Goldie (eds), *The Cambridge History of Political Thought* (Cambridge: Cambridge University Press, 1991), pp. 298–328.

Gajda, A., *The Earl of Essex and Late Elizabethan Political Culture* (Oxford: Oxford University Press, 2012).

Goldie, M., 'The Unacknowledged Republic: Office-Holding in Early Modern England', in T. Harris (ed.), *The Politics of the Excluded* (New York: Palgrave, 2001), pp. 153–94.

Gorski, P., *The Disciplinary Revolution: Calvinism and the Rise of the State in Early Modern Europe* (Chicago, IL: Chicago University Press, 2003).

Graves, M. A. R., *Elizabethan Parliaments, 1559–1601* (Routledge: Abingdon, 2003).

Greenblatt, S., *Renaissance Self-Fashioning: From More to Shakespeare* (Chicago, IL: Chicago University Press, 2005).

Guy, J., *Tudor England* (Oxford: Oxford University Press, 1988).

—, 'The 1590s: The Second Reign of Elizabeth I?', in J. Guy (ed.), *The Reign of Elizabeth I* (Cambridge, Cambridge University Press, 1995), pp. 1–19.

—, 'The Elizabethan Establishment and the Ecclesiastical Polity', in J. Guy, *The Reign of Elizabeth I* (Cambridge: Cambridge University Press, 1995), pp. 126–49.

—, 'The Rhetoric of Counsel in Early Modern England', in Dale Hoak (ed.), *Tudor Political Culture* (Cambridge: Cambridge University Press, 1995), pp. 292–310.

Hadfield A., 'Briton and Scythian: Tudor Representations of Irish Origins', *Irish Historical Studies*, 28:112 (1993), pp. 390–408.

—, 'Spenser, Ireland and Sixteenth Century Political Theory', *Modern Language Review*, 84:4 (1994), pp. 1–18.

—, *Spenser's Irish Experience: Wilde Fruit and Salvage Soyl* (Oxford: Oxford University Press, 1997).

—, 'Was Spenser a Republican?', *English*, 47 (1998), pp. 169–82.

—, *Edmund Spenser: A Life* (Oxford: Oxford University Press, 2012).

Haigh, C., 'Puritan Evangelism in the Reign of Elizabeth I', *English Historical Review*, 92:342 (1977), pp. 30–58.

—, *Elizabeth I* (London: Longman, 1988).

Hammer, P. E. J., 'Patronage at Court, Faction and the Earl of Essex', in J. Guy (ed.), *The Reign of Elizabeth I* (Cambridge: Cambridge University Press, 1995), pp. 65–86.

Harrington, J. F., and H. W. Smith, 'Confessionalization, Community and State Building in Germany, 1555–1870', *Journal of Modern History*, 69:1 (1997), pp. 77–101.

Haugaard, W. P., 'Elizabeth Tudor's Book of Devotions: A Neglected Clue to the Queen's Life and Character', *Sixteenth Century Journal*, 12:2 (1981), pp. 79–106.

Hayes-McCoy, G. A., 'The Royal Supremacy and Ecclesiastical Revolution, 1534–47', in T. W. Moody, F. X. Martin and F. J. Byrne (eds), *A New History of Ireland*, 9 vols (Oxford: Oxford University Press, 1976), vol. 3, pp. 39–68.

Heal, F., and H. Summerson, 'The Genesis of the Two Editions', in P. Kewes, I. W. Archer and F. Heal (eds), *The Oxford Handbook of Holinshed's Chronicles* (Oxford: Oxford University Press, 2013), pp. 3–19.

Heinze, R. W., *The Proclamations of the Tudor Kings* (Cambridge: Cambridge University Press, 1976).

Helgerson, R., *Forms of Nationhood: The Elizabethan Writing of England* (Chicago, IL: Chicago University Press, 1992).

Hindle, S., *The State and Social Change in Early Modern England, c. 1550–1640* (Basingstoke: Palgrave, 2000).

Holt, M. P., *The French Wars of Religion, 1562–1629* (Cambridge: Cambridge University Press, 1995).

Höpfl, H., *The Christian Polity of John Calvin* (Cambridge: Cambridge University Press, 1982).

Hoyle, R. W., *The Pilgrimage of Grace and the Politics of the 1530s* (Oxford: Oxford University Press, 2001).

Hunt, A., 'Tuning the Pulpits: The Religious Context of the Essex Revolt', in P. McCullough (ed.), *The English Sermon Revised: Religion, Literature and History, 1600–1750* (Manchester: Manchester University Press, 2001), pp. 86–114.

Hutchinson, M. A., 'Reformed Protestantism and the Government of Ireland, c. 1565–1582: The Lord Deputyships of Henry Sidney and Arthur Grey', *Sidney Journal*, 29:1–2 (2011), pp. 71–104.

—, 'The Emergence of the State in Elizabethan Ireland and England, *c.* 1575–99', *Sixteenth Century Journal*, 45:3 (2014), pp. 659–82.

—, '"The State": Ireland's Contribution to the History of Political Thought', *Irish Review*, 48 (2014), pp. 28–35.

—, 'An Irish Perspective on Elizabeth's Religion: Reformation Thought and Henry Sidney's Irish Deputyship, *c.* 1560 to 1580', in B. Kane and V. McGowan-Doyle (eds), *Elizabeth I and Ireland* (Cambridge: Cambridge University Press, 2014), pp. 142–62.

Ingram, M., 'Reformation of Manners in Early Modern England', in P. Griffiths (ed.), *The Experience of Authority in Early Modern England* (Basingstoke: Palgrave, 1996), pp. 47–88.

Jardine, L., and A. Grafton, '"Studied for Action": How Gabriel Harvey Read his Livy', *Past and Present*, 129 (1990), pp. 30–78.

Jefferies, H. A., *The Irish Church and the Tudor Reformations* (Dublin: Four Courts, 2010).

Jones, F. M., *Mountjoy 1563–1606: The Last Elizabethan Deputy, 1563–1606* (Dublin: Clonmore and Reynolds Ltd., 1958).

Kane, B., 'Elizabeth on Rebellion in Ireland and England: *Semper Eadem?*', in B. Kane and V. McGowan-Doyle (eds.), *Elizabeth I and Ireland* (Cambridge: Cambridge University Press, 2014), pp. 261–86.

Kewes, P., 'Henry Saville's Tacitus and the Politics of Roman History in Late Elizabethan England', *Huttington Library Quarterly*, 74:4 (2011), pp. 515–51.

Lake, P., *Anglicans and Puritans? Presbyterianism and English Conformist Thought from Whitgift to Hooker* (London: Unwin Hyman, 1988).

—, 'The Politics of "Popularity" and the Public Sphere: The "Monarchical Republic" of Elizabeth I Defends Itself', in P. Lake and S. Pinus (eds), *The Politics of the Public Sphere in Early Modern England* (Manchester: Manchester University Press, 2007), pp. 59–94.

—, '"The Monarchical Republic of Queen Elizabeth I" (and the Fall of Archbishop Grindal) Revisited', in J. F. McDiarmid (ed.), *The Monarchical Republic of Elizabethan England: Essays in Response to Patrick Collinson* (Aldershot: Ashgate, 2007), pp. 129–48.

Lennon, C., *Richard Stanihurst the Dubliner 1547–1618: A Biography with a Stanihurst Text on Ireland's Past* (Dublin: Four Courts, 1981).

—, *Sixteenth Century Ireland: The Incomplete Conquest* (Dublin: Gill and MacMillan, 1994).

—, 'Ireland', in P. Kewes, I. W. Archer and F. Heal (eds), *The Oxford Handbook of Holinshed's Chronicles* (Oxford: Oxford University Press, 2013), pp. 663–78.

Lotz-Heumann, U., *Die doppelte Konfessionalisierung in Irland: Konflikt und Koexistenz im 16. und in der ersten Hälfte des 17. Jahrhunderts* (Tübingen: Mohr Siebeck, 2000).

MacCaffrey, W., *Queen Elizabeth and the Making of Policy, 1572–1588* (Princeton, NJ: Princeton University Press, 1992).

—, *Elizabeth I: War and Politics, 1588–1603* (Princeton, NJ: Princeton University Press, 1994).

MacCarthy-Murrough, M. *The Munster Plantation: English Migration to Southern Ireland, 1583–1611* (Oxford: Oxford University Press, 1986).

MacCulloch, D., *Tudor Church Militant: Edward VI and the Protestant Reformation* (London: Penguin, 2000).

Maginn, C., 'The Baltinglass Rebellion, 1580: English Dissent or a Gaelic Uprising', *Historical Journal*, 47:2 (2004), pp. 205–32.

—, '"Surrender and Regrant" in the Historiography of Sixteenth-Century Ireland', *Sixteenth Century Journal*, 38:4 (2007), pp. 962–6.

—, *William Cecil, Ireland and the Tudor State* (Oxford: Oxford University Press, 2012).

Malette, R., *Spenser and the Discourses of Reformation England* (Lincoln, NE: University of Nebraska Press, 1997).

Matthew, H. C. G., and B. Harrison (eds), *Oxford Dictionary of National Biography* (Oxford: Oxford University Press, 2000).

McCabe, R. A., *Spenser's Monstrous Regiment: Elizabethan Ireland and the Poetics of Difference* (Oxford: Oxford University Press, 2002).

McConica, J., *English Humanists and Renaissance Politics under Henry VIII and Edward VI* (Oxford: Oxford University, 1965).

McCormack, A. M., *The Earldom of Desmond 1463–1583: The Decline and Crisis of a Feudal Lordship* (Dublin: Four Courts, 2005).

McGowan-Doyle, V., *Book of Howth: Elizabethan Conquest and the Old English* (Cork: Cork University Press, 2011).

McGuire, J., and Quinn, J. (eds.), *Dictionary of Irish Biography: From the Earliest Times to the Year 2002* (Cambridge: Cambridge University Press, 2009).

McLaren, A., *Political Culture in the Reign of Elizabeth I: Queen and Commonwealth 1558–1585* (Cambridge: Cambridge University Press, 1999).

—, 'Rethinking Republicanism: *Vindiciae, Contra Tyrannos* in Context', *Historical Journal*, 49:1 (2006), pp. 23–52.

Mears, N., 'Counsel, Public Debate, and Queenship: John Stubbs's "The Discoverie of a Gaping Gulf", 1579', *Historical Journal* 44:3 (2001), pp. 629–50.

Mentzer, R. A., 'The Edict of Nantes and its Institutions', in R. A. Mentzer and A. Spicer (eds), *Society and Culture in the Huguenot World 1559–1685* (Cambridge: Cambridge University Press, 2002), pp. 98–116.

Montano, J. P., *The Roots of English Colonialism in Ireland* (Cambridge: Cambridge University Press, 2011).

Morgan, H., 'The Colonial Adventure of Sir Thomas Smith in Ulster, 1571 to 1575', *Historical Journal*, 2:28 (1985), pp. 261–78.

—, *Tyrone's Rebellion: The Outbreak of the Nine Years' War in Tudor Ireland* (Woodbridge: Royal Historical Society, 1993).

—, 'Hugh O'Neill and the Nine Years War in Tudor Ireland', *Historical Journal*, 36:1 (1993), pp. 21–37.

—, 'The Fall of Sir John Perrot', in J. Guy (ed.), *The Reign of Elizabeth I* (Cambridge, Cambridge University Press, 1995), pp. 109–25.

—, 'Beyond Spenser? A Historiographical Introduction to the Study of Political Ideas in Early Modern Ireland', in H. Morgan (ed.), *Political Ideology in Ireland, 1541–1641* (Dublin: Four Courts, 1999), pp. 9–21.

—, '"Overmighty Officers": The Irish Lord Deputyship in the Early Modern British State', *History Ireland*, 7:4 (1999), pp. 17–21.

—, 'Policy and Propaganda in Hugh O'Neill's Connection with Europe', in M. A. Lyons and T. O'Connor (eds), *The Ulster Earls and Baroque Europe: Refashioning Irish Identities, 1600–1800* (Dublin: Four Courts, 2010), pp. 28–30.

Moroney, M. '"The Sweetness of Due Subjection"; Derricke's Image of Ireland (1581) and the Sidneys', *Sidney Journal*, 29:1–2 (2011), pp. 147–72.

Murray, J., 'St Patrick's Cathedral and the University Question in Ireland, *c.* 1547–1585', in H. Robinson-Hammerstein (ed.), *European Universities in the Age of Reformation and Counter Reformation* (Dublin: Four Courts, 1998), pp. 1–33.

—, *Enforcing the English Reformation in Ireland: Clerical Resistance and Political Conflict in the Diocese of Dublin* (Cambridge: Cambridge University Press, 2009).

Neale, J. E., *Elizabeth I and her Parliaments, 1559–1581* (Jonathan Cape: London, 1953).

Nicholls, K., *Gaelic and Gaelicized Ireland in the Middle Ages* (Dublin: Lilliput, 1972).

Nischan, B., 'Confessionalism and Absolutism: The Case of Brandenburg', in A. Pettegree, A. Duke and G. Lewis (eds), *Calvinism in Europe 1540–1620* (Cambridge: Cambridge University Press, 1996), pp. 181–201.

Orr, D. A., 'Inventing the British Republic: Richard Beacon's *Solon his Follie* (1594) and the Rhetoric of Civilization', *Sixteenth Century Journal*, 38:4 (2007), pp. 975–94.

Ó Siochrú, M., *God's Executioner: Oliver Cromwell and the Conquest of Ireland* (London: Faber and Faber, 2008).

Patterson, A., *Reading Holinshed's Chronicles* (Chicago, IL: Chicago University Press, 1994).

Pawlisch, H. S., *Sir John Davies and the Conquest of Ireland: A Study in Legal Imperialism* (Cambridge: Cambridge University Press, 1985).

Peck, L. L., 'Beyond the Pale: John Cusacke and the Language of Absolutism in Early Stuart Britain', *Historical Journal*, 41:1 (1998), pp. 121–49.

Peltonen, M., *Classical Humanism and Republicanism in English Political Thought 1570–1640* (Cambridge: Cambridge University Press, 1995).

Pocock, J. G. A., *The Machiavellian Moment: Florentine Political Thought and the Atlantic Republican Tradition* (Princeton, NJ: Princeton University Press, 1975).

—, *The Ancient Constitution and the Feudal Law: A Study of English Historical Thought in the Seventeenth Century: A Reissue with a Retrospect* (Cambridge: Cambridge University Press, 1987).

Questier, M. C., *Conversion, Politics and Religion in England, 1580–1625* (Cambridge: Cambridge University Press: 1996).

Quillet, J., 'Community, Counsel and Representation', in J. H. Burns (ed.), *The Cambridge History of Medieval Political Thought, c.350–c.1450* (Cambridge: Cambridge University Press, 1998), pp. 522–72.

Racaut, L., 'Nicolas Chesneau, Catholic Printer in Paris during the French Wars of Religion', *Historical Journal*, 52:1 (2009), pp. 23–41.

Rapple, R., 'Taking up Office in Elizabethan Connacht: The Case of Sir Richard Bingham', *English Historical Review*, 123:501 (2008), pp. 277–99.

—, *Martial Power and Elizabethan Political Culture: Military Men in England and Ireland, 1558–1594* (Cambridge: Cambridge University Press, 2009).

Robinson-Hammerstein, H., 'Aspects of the Continental Education of Irish Students in the Reign of Queen Elizabeth I', in T. D. Williams (ed.), *Historical Studies VIII* (Dublin: Gill and MacMillan, 1971), pp. 137–54.

—, 'The Confessionalisation of Ireland? Assessment of a Paradigm', *Irish Historical Studies*, 32:128 (2001), pp. 567–78.

Salmon, J. H. N., *The French Religious Wars in English Political Thought* (Oxford: Oxford University Press, 1959).

—, 'Stoicism and Roman Example: Seneca and Tacitus in Jacobean England', *Journal of the History of Ideas*, 50:2 (1989), pp. 199–225.

Schilling, H., *Konfessionskonflikt und Staatsbildung* (Guetersloh: Guetersloher Verlgasanstalt, 1981).

—, 'Comparative and Interdisciplinary Paradigm', in J. M. Headley, H. J. Hillerband and A. J. Papalas (eds), *Confessionalization in Europe, 1555–1700: Essays in Honor and Memory of Bodo Nischan* (Ashgate: Aldershot, 2004), pp. 21–36.

Scott, J., *Commonwealth Principles: Republican Writing of the English Revolution* (Cambridge: Cambridge University Press, 2004).

Shagan, E. H., *The Rule of Moderation: Violence, Religion and the Politics of Restraint in Early Modern England* (Cambridge: Cambridge University Press, 2011).

Sheehan, A., 'Official Reaction to Native Land Claims in the Munster Plantation', *Irish Historical Studies*, 23:92 (1983), pp. 297–317.

Simms, K., *From Kings to Warlords* (Woodbridge: The Boydell Press, 1987).

Skinner, Q., *The Foundations of Modern Political Thought*, 2 vols (Cambridge: Cambridge University Press, 1978).

—, 'Meaning and the Understanding of Speech Acts', in J. H. Tully (ed.), *Meaning and Context: Quentin Skinner and his Critics* (Oxford: Oxford University Press, 1988), pp. 29–67.

—, *Liberty Before Liberalism* (Cambridge: Cambridge University Press, 1997).

—, 'From the State of the Prince to the Person of the State', in Q. Skinner, *Visions of Politics*, 3 vols, vol. 2: *Renaissance Virtues* (Cambridge: Cambridge University Press, 2002), pp. 368–413.

—, 'Machiavelli on *Virtù* and the Maintenance of Liberty', in Q. Skinner, *Visions of Politics*, 3 vols, vol. 2: *Renaissance Virtues* (Cambridge: Cambridge University Press, 2002), pp. 160–85.

—, *Hobbes and Republican Liberty* (Cambridge: Cambridge University Press, 2008).

Sommerville, J, *Royalists and Patriots: Politics and Ideology in England 1603–1640* (Abingdon: Routledge, 1986).

—, '*Leviathan* and its Anglican Context', in P. Springborg (ed.), *The Cambridge Companion to Hobbes's Leviathan* (Cambridge: Cambridge University Press, 2007), pp. 358–74.

—, 'Early Modern Absolutism in Theory and Practice', in C. Cuttica and G. Burgess (eds), *Monarchism and Absolutism in Early Modern Europe* (London: Pickering & Chatto, 2011), pp. 117–30, 240–3.

Starkey, D. (ed.), *The English Court from the Wars of the Roses to the Civil War* (London: Longman, 1987).

Stone, L., *The Crisis of the Aristocracy* (Oxford: Clarendon Press, 1965).

Stillman, R., *Philip Sidney and the Poetics of Renaissance Cosmopolitanism* (Ashgate: Aldershot, 2008).

Tawney, R. H., *The Agrarian Problem in the Sixteenth Century* (London: Longmans Green and Co., 1912).

Todd, M., *Christian Humanism and the Puritan Social Order* (Cambridge: Cambridge University Press, 1987).

Treadwell, V., 'The Irish Parliament of 1569–71', *Proceedings of the Royal Irish Academy*, section c 65 (1966), pp. 55–89.

—, 'Perrot and the Irish Parliament of 1585–6', *Proceedings of the Royal Irish Academy*, section c 85 (1985), pp. 259–308.

Tuck, R., *Philosophy and Government 1572–1651* (Cambridge: Cambridge University Press, 1993).

van Gelderen, M., *The Political Thought of the Dutch Revolt 1555–1590* (Cambridge: Cambridge University Press, 1992).

—, 'So Merely Humane': Theories of Resistance in Early-Modern Europe', in A. Brett and J. Tully (eds), *Rethinking the Foundations of Modern Political Thought* (Cambridge: Cambridge University Press, 2006), pp. 149–170.

Viroli, M., *From Politics to Reason of State: The Acquisition and Transformation of the Language of Politics 1250–1600* (Cambridge: Cambridge University Press, 1992).

Voogt, G., 'Primacy of Individual Conscience or Primacy of the State? The Clash between Dirck Volckertsz Coornhert and Justus Lipsius', *Sixteenth Century Journal*, 28:4 (1997), pp. 1231–49.

Williams, P., *The Council and the Marches of Wales under Elizabeth I* (Cardiff: University of Wales Press, 1958).

Woodworth, A., 'Purveyance for the Royal Household in the Reign of Queen Elizabeth', *Transactions of the American Philosophical Society*, new series, 35:1 (1945), pp. 1–89.

Worden, B., *The Sound of Virtue: Philip Sidney's 'Arcadia' and Elizabethan Politics* (New Haven, CT: Yale University Press, 1996).

Younger, N., *War and Politics in the English Counties* (Manchester: Manchester University Press, 2012).

Zeeveld, W. G., *The Foundations of Tudor Policy* (Cambridge, MA: Harvard University Press, 1948).

NOTES

Introduction

1. L. Bryskett, *A Discourse of Civill Life* (London: [R.Field] for William Aspley, 1606). Also N. P. Canny, *Making Ireland British* (Oxford: Oxford University Press, 2001), pp. 1–4.
2. L. Jardine and A. Grafton, '"Studied for Action": How Gabriel Harvey Read his Livy', *Past and Present*, 129 (1990), pp. 40–2.
3. S. Adams, *Leicester and the Court: Essays on Elizabethan Politics* (Manchester: Manchester University Press, 2002), 'The Dudley Clientele, 1553–63', pp. 151–75, and 'A Godly Peer? Leicester and the Puritans', pp. 225–34; S. Alford, *The Early Elizabethan Polity: William Cecil and the British Succession Crisis, 1558–1569* (Cambridge: Cambridge University Press, 1998); and P. Collinson, 'England and International Calvinism 1558–1640', in M. Prestwich (ed.), *International Calvinism, 1541–1715* (Oxford: Oxford University Press, 1985), pp. 197–223.
4. C. Brady, *Chief Governors: The Rise and Fall of Reform Government in Tudor Ireland 1536–1588* (Cambridge: Cambridge University Press, 1994), pp. 112, 114.
5. P. Collinson, *The Elizabethan Puritan Movement* (London: Jonathan Cape, 1967), pp. 29–83.
6. Q. Skinner, *The Foundations of Modern Political Thought*, 2 vols (Cambridge: Cambridge University Press, 1978), vol. 1, pp. ix–x; Q. Skinner, 'Meaning and Understanding of Speech Acts', in J. H. Tully (ed.), *Meaning and Context: Quentin Skinner and his Critics* (Oxford: Polity, 1988), pp. 29–67; and Q. Skinner, 'From the State of the Prince to the Person of the State', in Skinner, *Visions of Politics*, 3 vols (Cambridge: Cambridge University Press, 2002), vol. 2, pp. 368–9 and pp. 394–406.
7. See the introduction - 'Normative Political and Religious Vocabulary'.
8. M. Todd, *Christian Humanism and the Puritan Social Order* (Cambridge: Cambridge University Press, 1987), p. 19.
9. M. Peltonen, *Classical Humanism and Republicanism in English Political Thought 1570–1640* (Cambridge: Cambridge University Press, 1995), pp. 1–17 and pp. 54–118.
10. B. Bradshaw, 'The Christian Humanism of Erasmus', *Journal of Theological Studies*, 32:2 (1982), pp. 411–47; and K. Charlton, *Education in Renaissance England* (London: Routledge and K. Paul, 1965), p. 34 on a wider renaissance vision of man.
11. M. Luther, *The Bondage of the Will*, trans. H. Cole (Peabody, MA: Henrickson, 2008), p. 58; and J. Calvin, *Institutes of the Christian Religion*, trans. Henry Beveridge (Peabody, MA: Henrickson, 2008), book 2, ch. 2: 'Man Now Deprived of Freedom of Will, and Miserably Enslaved', pp. 155–76.

12. See the introduction – 'Re-interpreting State Theory'.
13. Q. Skinner, *The Foundations of Modern Political Thought* (Cambridge: Cambridge University Press, 1978), vol. 2, pp. 189–348. Here an important counterpoint to Skinner and his method is J. Coffey, 'Quentin Skinner and the Religious Dimension of Early Modern Political Thought', in A. Chapman, J. Coffey, and B. S. Gregory (eds), *Seeing Things their Way: Intellectual History and the Return of Religion* (Notre Dame, IN: Notre Dame University Press, 2009), pp. 116–74.
14. See H. Höpfl, *The Christian Polity of John Calvin* (Cambridge: Cambridge University Press, 1982), pp. 154–160 and pp. 190–3. H. Höpfl (ed.), *Luther and Calvin on Secular Authority* (Cambridge: Cambridge University Press, 1991), pp. xvi–xxiii. Also W. J. Bouwsma, *John Calvin: A Sixteenth Century Portrait* (Oxford: Oxford University Press, 1989), p. 214 and p. 217 – Calvin argued that 'the minister of the word should help the magistrate in order that fewer may sin. Their responsibilities [that of magistrate and minister] should be so joined that each helps rather than impedes the other'.
15. Skinner, *Foundations*, vol. 2, pp. 329–31.
16. P. Collinson, 'The Monarchical Republic of Queen Elizabeth I', in Collinson, *Elizabethan Essays* (London: Hambledon, 1994), pp. 31–58.
17. Skinner, *Foundations*, vol. 2, pp. 286–90 and pp. 292–3; and J. H. Franklin, *Jean Bodin and the Rise of Absolutist Theory* (Cambridge: Cambridge University Press, 1973), chs 3–4.
18. J. G. A. Pocock, *The Machiavellian Moment: Florentine Political Thought and the Atlantic Republican Tradition* (Princeton, NJ: Princeton University Press, 1975), in particular pp. 83–113.
19. Q. Skinner, 'Meaning and the Understanding of Speech Acts', in J. H. Tully (ed.), *Meaning and Context: Quentin Skinner and his Critics* (Oxford: Oxford University Press, 1988), pp. 29–67.
20. N. P. Canny, 'Identity Formation in Ireland: The Emergence of the Anglo-Irish', in N. P. Canny and A. Pagden (eds), *Colonial Identity in the Atlantic World 1500–1800* (Princeton, NJ: Princeton University Press, 1987), pp. 159–212. Also see K. S. Bottingheimer, 'Kingdom and Colony: Ireland in the Westward Enterprise', in K. R. Andrews, N. P. Canny and P. E. H. Hair (eds), *The Westward Enterprise: English Activities in Ireland, the Atlantic and America, 1480–1650* (Manchester: Manchester University Press, 1978), pp. 45–65 and C. Brady and R. Gillespie (eds.), *Natives and Newcomers: Essays on the Making of Irish Colonial Society* (Dublin: Irish Academic Press, 1986). Nevertheless, there has been an attempt to see the Old English community in particular drawing on medieval English political and cultural values. C. Brady, 'Reform Government and the Community of the Pale', in Brady, *The Chief Governors: The Rise and Fall of Reform Government in Tudor Ireland, 1536–1588* (Cambridge: Cambridge University Press, 1994), pp. 209–44 and J. Murray, *Enforcing the English Reformation in Ireland: Clerical Resistance and Political Conflict in the Diocese of Dublin* (Cambridge: Cambridge University Press, 2009).
21. R. Rapple, *Martial Power and Elizabethan Political Culture: Military Men in England and Ireland, 1558–1594* (Cambridge: Cambridge University Press, 2009); and D. Edwards, 'Ideology and Experience: Spenser's *View* and Martial Law in Ireland', in H. Morgan (ed.), *Political Ideology in Ireland, 1541–1641* (Dublin: Four Courts, 1999), pp. 127–57.
22. Brady, *Chief Governors*, p. xi.
23. B. Bradshaw, 'Sword, Word and Strategy in the Reformation in Ireland', *Historical Journal*, 21:3 (1978), pp. 475–502.

24. N. P. Canny, *The Elizabethan Conquest of Ireland: A Pattern Established, 1565–76* (Hassocks: Harvester Press, 1976), pp. 123–8 and N. P. Canny, *Making Ireland British* (Oxford: Oxford University Press, 2001), ch. 4.
25. For a more direct discussion of what I see as the misinterpretation of reformed theology within Irish historiography, see M. A. Hutchinson, 'Reformed Protestantism and the Government of Ireland, c. 1565–1582: The Lord Deputyships of Henry Sidney and Arthur Grey', *Sidney Journal*, 29:1–2 (2011), pp. 71–104. See C. Brady and J. Murray, 'Sir Henry Sidney and the Reformation in Irėland', in A. Boran and C. Gribben (eds), *Enforcing Reformation in Ireland and Scotland, 1550–1700* (Aldershot: Ashgate, 2006), pp. 14–39. Also see N. P. Canny, 'Why the Reformation Failed in Ireland: Une Question Mal Posée', *Journal of Ecclesiastical History*, 30:4 (1979), pp. 423–50 and K. Bottingheimer, 'The Failure of the Reformation in Ireland: Une Question Bien Posée', *Journal of Ecclesiastical History*, 36:2 (1985), pp. 196–207. The wider idea of confessionalization, which Murray and Brady would appear to be drawing upon is discussed in chapter two 'Confessionalization and Statism'.
26. H. Morgan, 'Beyond Spenser? A Historiographical Introduction to the Study of Political Ideas in Early Modern Ireland', in H. Morgan (ed.), *Political Ideology in Ireland*, pp. 9–21; and N. P. Canny, 'Writing Early Modern History: Ireland, Britain, and the Wider World', *Historical Journal*, 46:3 (2006), pp. 723–47, in particular p. 744.
27. M. van Gelderen, *The Political Thought of the Dutch Revolt 1555–1590* (Cambridge: Cambridge University Press, 1992), pp. 115–19, 229–56.
28. A. N. McLaren, *Political Culture in the Reign of Elizabeth I: Queen and Commonwealth 1558–1585* (Cambridge: Cambridge University Press, 1999), pp. 134–97.
29. van Gelderen, *Dutch Revolt*, pp. 213–59.
30. A similar point is made by Isaiah Berlin concerning modern political thought and notions of freedom in his *Essays on Liberty*, ed. H. Hardy (Oxford: Oxford University Press, 1990). See 'Two Concepts of Liberty', in particular section 8, 'The One and the Many', pp. 212–17.
31. M. P. Holt, *The French Wars of Religion, 1562–1629* (Cambridge: Cambridge University Press, 1995), in particular pp. 3, 99–122
32. J. Bodin, *On Sovereignty*, ed. J. H. Franklin (Cambridge: Cambridge University Press, 1992), p. 1.
33. J. H. Franklin, 'Sovereignty and the Mixed Constitution: Bodin and his Critics', in J. H. Burns and M. Goldie (eds), *The Cambridge History of Political Thought* (Cambridge: Cambridge University Press, 1991), pp. 298–328, on pp. 298–9, 307.
34. J. Guy, 'The 1590s: The Second Reign of Elizabeth I?', in J. Guy (ed.), *Reign of Elizabeth I* (Cambridge, Cambridge University Press, 1995), pp. 1–19.
35. McLaren, *Political Culture*, pp. 10–11.
36. S. Alford, *The Early Elizabethan Polity: William Cecil and the British Succession Crisis, 1558–1569* (Cambridge: Cambridge University Press, 1998), pp. 4–5, 209–10.
37. This is discussed throughout the study, and in particular in chapter 6 in relation to John Hooker, Richard Beacon and Edmund Spenser.

1 Building a Godly Polity in Ireland

1. For an interesting recent restatement of the notion that English civility was thought self-evidently true see J. P. Montano, *The Roots of English Colonialism in Ireland* (Cambridge: Cambridge University Press, 2011). Montano examines the interplay between

notions of cultivation, which relate to the civility of man and the cultivation of the earth through the introduction of English settled arable farming.

2. B. Bradshaw, *The Irish Constitutional Revolution of the Sixteenth Century* (Cambridge: Cambridge University Press, 1979), pp. 49–57.
3. See J. P. Canning, 'Law, Sovereignty and Corporation Theory, 1300–1450', in J. H. Burns (ed.), *The Cambridge History of Medieval Political Thought, c.350–c.1450* (Cambridge: Cambridge University Press, 1998), pp. 473–6; and J. Quillet, 'Community, Counsel and Representation', in Burns (ed.), *Medieval Political Thought*, pp. 522–6.
4. See G. A. Hayes-McCoy, 'The Royal Supremacy and Ecclesiastical Revolution, 1534–47', in T. W. Moody, F. X. Martin and F. J. Byrne (eds), *A New History of Ireland*, 9 vols (Oxford: Oxford University Press, 1976), vol. 3, pp. 39–68. Since Ireland was held as a lordship from the pope, a basic consequence of Henry's break with Rome was to raise questions about his right to the lordship of Ireland.
5. B. Bradshaw, *The Irish Constitutional Revolution of the Sixteenth Century* (Cambridge: Cambridge University Press, 1979), pp. 193–222.
6. Bradshaw, *Constitutional Revolution*, pp. 46–57.
7. For Bradshaw's more general intellectual position see B. Bradshaw, 'Transalpine Humanism', in J. H. Burns and M. Goldie (eds), *Cambridge History of Political Thought* (Cambridge: Cambridge University Press, 1991), pp. 95–134. Brady in the *The Chief Governors* puts forward an alternative view and suggests that St Leger was involved in bribery and corruption which was really the *leitmotif* of his policy. See C. Brady, *The Chief Governors: The Rise and Fall of Reform Government in Tudor Ireland, 1536–1588* (Cambridge: Cambridge University Press, 1994), ch. 1. I think a middle ground is probably apt here, where a distinction should be made between the philosophical assumptions or principles informing St Leger's overall position and the need for political expediency.
8. G. R. Elton, *Reform and Renewal: Thomas Cromwell and the Common Weal* (Cambridge: Cambridge University Press, 1973), p. 4. Here Elton drew on an already established view concerning the importance of Christian humanism in English thought of the period. See W. G. Zeeveld, *The Foundations of Tudor Policy* (Cambridge, MA: Harvard University Press, 1948) and J. McConica, *English Humanists and Renaissance Politics under Henry VIII and Edward VI* (Oxford: Oxford University, 1965).
9. Fitzwilliam and Irish council to Elizabeth, 27 June 1572, The National Archives SP63/36/46.
10. Fitzwilliam and Irish council to Elizabeth, 24 July 1572, TNA SP63/37/13.
11. Fitzwilliam to Burghley, December 1573, TNA SP63/43/21.
12. Part of this challenge is paralleled in Greenblatt's account of Elizabethan literature where the need to outwardly self-fashion in a courtly setting arises out of a difficulty in speaking about the imitation of Christ due to confessional division and doubt. Edmund Spenser is a critical figure for Greenblatt. See S. Greenblatt, *Renaissance Self-Fashioning: From More to Shakespeare* (Chicago, IL: Chicago University Press, 2005), p. 3.
13. D. Edwards, 'Beyond Reform: Martial Law and the Tudor Re-conquest of Ireland', *History Ireland*, 5:2 (1997), pp. 16–21.
14. Ciaran Brady's account of Elizabethan reform in *The Chief Govenors* points towards a similar shift in positions, though Brady emphasizes that this was not what Irish government ever intended. Brady argues that despite a hope amongst Elizabethan officials in the 1560s that provincial presidencies and a seneschal system would allow the norms of English shire government to come into force, the pressure for results and the fact that the political situation failed to stabilize quickly enough meant these structures came

to support a more militarized solution. For a good summary of Brady's argument, see 'Interlude', in *Chief Governors*, pp. 159–66.

15. C. Maginn, '"Surrender and Regrant" in the Historiography of Sixteenth-Century Ireland', *Sixteenth Century Journal*, 38:4 (2007), pp. 962–6.
16. C. Brady (ed.), *A Viceroy's Vindication: Sir Henry Sidney's Memoir of Service in Ireland, 1556–78* (Cork: Cork University Press, 2002), pp. 57–8. TNA SP63/22/60, 65 and TNA SP63/23/12, 17, 19, 51, 56–8.
17. For a good account of the position of coyne and livery in Elizabethan thinking, see Brady, *Chief Governors*, pp. 73–5, 131, 141–55.
18. Brady, *Chief Governors*, pp. 74–5, 131–9.
19. T. More, *Utopia*, trans. P. Turner (London: Penguin, 1965), p. 79.
20. N. P. Canny, 'Dominant Minorities: English Settlers in Ireland and Virginia, 1550–1650', in A. C. Hepburn (ed.), *Historical Studies*, 12 (1977), pp. 51–69. Also see N. P. Canny, *The Elizabethan Conquest of Ireland: A Pattern Established, 1565–76* (Hassocks: Harvester Press, 1976).
21. 'Sussex his Opinion', 1560, Carew MSS 614, London, Lambeth Palace Library, fol. 272v.
22. *De Republica* was published in 1583 but had circulated in manuscript since the early 1560s.
23. H. Morgan, 'The Colonial Adventure of Sir Thomas Smith in Ulster, 1571 to 1575', *Historical Journal*, 2:28 (1985), pp. 269–70. Also see M. Dewar, *Sir Thomas Smith: A Tudor Intellectual in Office* (London: Athlone Press, 1964), pp. 156–70.
24. T. Smith, *A Letter Sent by I. B. Gentleman* (London: Henry Binneman for Athonhson [i.e. Anthony Kitson], 1572), fol. 5r.
25. Fitzwilliam to Elizabeth, 25 September 1572, TNA SP63/37/59.
26. Sidney to Cecil, 17 April 1566, TNA SP63/17/14.
27. 'Articles of Interrogatory as to the Peaceable State of Ireland, at the Time Sussex Left', 19 April 1566, TNA SP63/17/23.
28. Sidney to Cecil, 17 April 1566, TNA SP63/17/14. Also see Brady, *Chief Governors*, pp. 133–4.
29. R. W. Hoyle, *The Pilgrimage of Grace and the Politics of the 1530s* (Oxford: Oxford University Press, 2001); M. A. Jones, 'Lee, Rowland (*c.* 1487–1543)', *ODNB*; and P. Williams, *The Council and the Marches of Wales under Elizabeth I* (Cardiff: University of Wales Press, 1958), pp. 33–5.
30. See D. MacCulloch, *Tudor Church Militant: Edward VI and the Protestant Reformation* (London: Penguin, 2000).
31. For the long-term influence of the constitutionalist position up to the glorious revolution, see M. van Gelderen, '"So Merely Humane": Theories of Resistance in Early-Modern Europe', in A. Brett and J. Tully (eds), *Rethinking the Foundations of Modern Political Thought* (Cambridge: Cambridge University Press, 2006), pp. 149–170.
32. H. Höpfl (ed.), *Luther and Calvin on Secular Authority* (Cambridge: Cambridge University Press, 1991), pp. vii–xxiii, passim.
33. J. Ponet, *A Short Treatise of Politike Power* (Strasbourg: by the heirs of W. Köpfel, 1556), fols 2r–4r.
34. See Höpfl, *Christian Polity*, pp. 154–60, 190–3; and Höpfl, *Secular Authority*, pp. vii–xxiii.
35. Ponet, *Politike Power*, fol. 6r.
36. C. Goodman, *How Superior Powers Oght to be Obeyd of their Subjects* (Geneva: John Crispin, 1558), pp. 153–4. For a discussion of the specific context surrounding Good-

man's text, see J. E A. Dawson, 'Resistance and Revolution in Sixteenth-Century Thought: The Case of Christopher Goodman', in J. van den Berg and P. Hoftijzer (eds), *The Church, Change and Revolution* (Leiden: Brill, 1991), pp. 69–79.

37. Goodman, *Superior Powers*, p. 154.
38. J. Aylmer, An Harborowe of Faithfull and Trewe Subjectes (Strasborowe [i.e. London: John Day],1559), fol. 41r.
39. Aylmer, *An Harbowre*, fol. 41 r.
40. For McLaren, Aylmer's *Harbowre* is a response to the writings of Knox, Goodman and Ponet, where the concept of grace, as equated with political virtue, is used to rehabilitate the notion of female rule, because a mixed polity allows the godly elite a voice in decisions, which meant Elizabeth's incapacity to rule as a female was negated. Because resistance writing had been aimed at Mary Tudor, a female prince, resistance theory was understood as being directed against female rule in general. A. McLaren, *Political Culture in the Reign of Elizabeth I: Queen and Commonwealth 1558–1585* (Cambridge: Cambridge University Press, 1999), pp. 49–74.
41. Ponet, *Politike Power*, fol. 6r.
42. Ponet, *Politike Power*, fols 73–91.
43. Goodman, *Superior Powers*, pp. 57–9, 148–9.
44. M. van Gelderen, *The Political Thought of the Dutch Revolt 1555–1590* (Cambridge: Cambridge University Press, 1992), pp. 229–42; and J. Coffey, 'The Language of Liberty in Calvinist Political Thought', in Q. Skinner and M. van Gelderen (eds), *Freedom and the Construction of Europe* (Cambridge: Cambridge University Press, 2013), pp. 296–316.
45. See Chapter 2, 'An Irish View of "Civil Obedience" Restated', in this study.
46. P. Collinson, 'The Monarchical Republic of Queen Elizabeth I', in P. Collinson, *Elizabethan Essays* (London: Hambledon, 1994), pp. 31–58; P. Collinson, 'Puritans, Men of Business and Elizabethan Parliaments', in Collinson, *Elizabethan Essays*; and P. Lake, '"The Monarchical Republic of Queen Elizabeth I" (and the Fall of Archbishop Grindal) Revisited', in J. F. McDiarmid (ed.), *The Monarchical Republic of Elizabethan England: Essays in Response to Patrick Collinson* (Aldershot: Ashgate, 2007), pp. 129–48.
47. See 'Instructions to Sir Henry Sidney' (Draft), 4 July 1565, The National Archives SP63/14/2; 'Sir Henry Sidney's Opinion upon the Minute of the Instructions First Devised for Him', 9 July 1565, TNA SP63/14/3; and 'Instructions for Sir Henry Sidney, Lord Deputy, and the Council', 5 October 1565, TNA SP63/15/4.
48. Sidney to English privy council, 13 April 1566, TNA SP63/17/8.
49. Appropriated benefices were held by laymen who provided a stipend for the employment of clergy. Many had been held by monasteries, but with the dissolution the benefices came into crown hands. S. Ellis, 'Economic Problems of the Church: Why the Reformation Failed in Ireland', *Journal of Ecclesiastical History*, 41:2 (1990), pp. 239–65 is revealing of the long-term financial problems faced by the church in Ireland.
50. Michael Fitzwilliam to English privy council, July 1571, TNA SP63/33/17.
51. Elizabeth to Sidney, 28 March 1566, *Sidney State Papers 1565–70*, ed. T. Ó Laidhin (Dublin: Irish Manuscript Commission, 1926), pp. 16–20; Sidney to Cecil, 18 May 1566, TNA SP63/17/53; Sidney to Cecil, 19 August 1566, TNA SP63/18/93; Sidney to Cecil, 18 November 1566, TNA SP63/19/51; and Sidney to English privy council, 12 December 1566, TNA SP63/19/71.
52. Sidney to English privy council, 8 June 1566, TNA SP63/18/6 and Loftus to Cecil, 17 June 1566, TNA SP63/18/20.

53. Loftus to Cecil, 3 November 1566, TNA SP63/19/31 and Loftus to Cecil, 7 November 1566, TNA SP63/19/35. Gaffney was to be appointed to Ossory but it would appear that McCaghwell was not appointed to Cashel.
54. See the various letters from Sidney and the Irish council in January and February 1566 addressing Terence Daniel's role in negotiations and dealings with Shane O'Neill, TNA SP63/16/17, 27, 30; there was also the suggestion Daniel be made archbishop of Armagh, SP63/21/49. R. Bagwell, *Ireland under the Tudor*, 3 vols (London: Longmans & Co., 1885–90), vol. 2, p. 114. W. M. Brady, *The Alleged Conversion of the Irish Bishops to the Reformed Religion at the Accession of Queen Elizabeth* (London: Longmans & co., 1866). The table of contents provides an excellent and concise summary of the episcopacy in Ireland.
55. Sidney to English privy council, 28 April 1576, Cotton MSS Titus BX, London, British Library (hereafter Titus BX), fol. 43v.
56. See 'Robert Weston and an Irish Definition of Civil Obedience' in this chapter.
57. Sidney to Elizabeth, 28 April 1576, Titus BX, fol. 47v–50r.
58. Some aspects of this are discussed in M. A. Hutchinson, 'An Irish Perspective on Elizabeth's Religion: Reformation Thought and Henry Sidney's Irish Deputyship, *c.* 1560 to 1580', in B. Kane and V. McGowan-Doyle (eds), *Elizabeth I and Ireland* (Cambridge: Cambridge University Press, 2014), pp. 142–62. For the views of historians of England see C. Haigh, *Elizabeth I* (London: Longman, 1998), pp. 38–41, W. P. Haugaard, 'Elizabeth Tudor's Book of Devotions: A Neglected Clue to the Queen's Life and Character', *Sixteenth Century Journal*, 12:2 (1981), pp. 79–106; P. Collinson, 'Windows in a Woman's Soul: Questions about the Religion of Queen Elizabeth', in Collinson, *Elizabethan Essays*, pp. 87–118; and S. Doran, 'Elizabeth I's Religion: The Evidence from her Letters', *Journal of Ecclesiastical History*, 51:4 (2000), pp. 699–720.
59. Sidney to Elizabeth, 28 April 1576, Titus BX, fol. 47v–50r.
60. J. E. A. Dawson, 'Calvinism and the Gaidhealtach in Scotland', in A. Pettegree, A. Duke and G. Lewis (eds), *Calvinism in Europe 1540–1620* (Cambridge: Cambridge University Press, 1996), pp. 231–53.
61. With this in mind the judgement of many scholars concerning the positioning of church reform in various programmes of Irish government seems misplaced, where it is suggested that it was simply a rhetorical nod towards God lacking any real critical intent. In particular, Christopher Maginn commented, concerning William Cecil's Irish policy, that Cecil 'accorded the establishment of Protestantism a secondary role in his thinking on Ireland'. Although in the various memoranda on Ireland, which Maginn sees as forming the basis of Cecil's assessment of the Irish situation, church reform is in many cases listed as one of the first points for consideration. See C. Maginn, *William Cecil, Ireland and the Tudor State* (Oxford: Oxford University Press, 2012), p. 165. See Cecil/Burghley TNA SP63/13/51; SP63/13/75 and SP63/14/11, 12, 25. In an extreme case, H. Jefferies simply dismisses protestant evangelical motivation, whilst incongruously arguing that Old English and Gaelic Ireland possessed a residual piety that aided in the triumph of Catholicism. H. A. Jefferies, *The Irish Church and the Tudor Reformations* (Dublin: Four Courts, 2010).
62. 'Instructions' for Lord Justice Drury, 29 May 1578, Carew MSS 611, London, Lambeth Palace Library, fols 351–60.
63. R. Turvey (ed.), *A Critical Edition of Sir James Perrot's the Life, Deedes and Death of Sir John Perrot* (Lampeter: Edwin Mellen, 2002), p. 46. The editor notes in a footnote to p. 45 that 'as far as is known' the copy of Perrot's Munster articles contained in the biography 'is the only extant copy of Perrot's plan which he presented to the queen and

the privy council early in 1574'.

64. Perrot to the bishop, sheriff and justices of several places, 4 March 1585, TNA SP63/115/11; and Perrot to Burghley, 24 September 1585, TNA SP63/119/32. Also see 'A Book of Instructions Touching the Province of Connaught and the Country of Thomond', 11 July 1588, TNA SP63/135/80, where again evangelism is emphasized – although with altered circumstances this is now article 15 – 'And forasmuch as the principal ... way to reform, is to bring the people to the fear and knowledge of God .. care [should] be had to the re-edifying of all decayed churches ... [and that] all such persons ... repair to the said churches at the time of divine service'.
65. Jones to Walsingham, 15 August 1585, TNA SP63/118/66. The bishops complained and so nothing really came of the commission.
66. See J. Murray, 'St Patrick's Cathedral and the University Question in Ireland, *c.* 1547–1585', in H. Robinson-Hammerstein (ed.), *European Universities in the Age of Reformation and Counter Reformation* (Dublin: Four Courts, 1998), pp. 1–33. Murray provides a detailed account of the various unsuccessful attempts to found a university – Trinity College Dublin would be founded in 1592 after much of the original evangelical intent had been exhausted.
67. See V. Treadwell, 'Sir John Perrot and the Irish Parliament of 1585–6', *Proceedings of the Royal Irish Academy*, section c 85 (1985), pp. 270, 303. There seems in this regard to have been tension over whether the leading clergymen or the lord deputy should head a religious reform agenda, as well as tension over how such an agenda should be financed.
68. The English Privy Council Register records that the topic of an Irish translation of the New Testament was raised and in particular the delay in the production of a translation despite the outlay of money by the crown, 26 August 1584, TNA PC2/14, fol. 428. A translation was eventually produced in 1602/3. A first attempt at translation and publication was made around 1573. Also see N. J. A. Williams, 'Walsh, Nicholas (d. 1585), Church of Ireland Bishop of Ossory', *ODNB*.
69. P. Collinson, 'The Monarchical Republic of Queen Elizabeth I', in Collinson, *Elizabethan Essays* (London: Hambledon, 1994), pp. 31–58.
70. J. Calvin, *Institutes of the Christian Religion*, trans. Henry Beveridge (Peabody, MA: Hendrickson Publishers, 2008), book 4, ch. 1: 'Of the True Church: Duty of Cultivating Unity with her, as the Mother of All the Godly', p. 672.
71. Calvin, *Institutes*, book 4, ch. 3: 'Of the Teachers and Ministers of the Church: Their Election and Office', pp. 699–708.
72. P. Lake, *Anglicans and Puritans? Presbyterianism and English Conformist Thought from Whitgift to Hooker* (London: Unwin Hyman, 1988), pp. 37–53; P. Lake, 'The Politics of "Popularity" and the Public Sphere: The "Monarchical Republic" of Elizabeth I Defends Itself', in P. Lake and S. Pinus (eds), *The Politics of the Public Sphere in Early Modern England* (Manchester: Manchester University Press, 2007), pp. 59–94; and J. Guy, 'The Elizabethan Establishment and the Ecclesiastical Polity', in Guy (ed), *The Reign of Elizabeth I* (Cambridge: Cambridge University Press, 1995), pp. 127–9.
73. Knox to Goodman, 27 October 1566, in J. E. A. Dawson and L. K. J. Glassey (eds), 'Some Unpublished Letters from John Knox to Christopher Goodman', *The Scottish Historical Review*, 84:2 (2005), pp. 183–5. The reference was kindly provided by Professor Dawson.
74. Goodman to Loftus, 11 April 1575, Denbighshire Record Office, Plas Power MSS DD/PP/839 p. 130. Once again, the transcript of this letter was kindly provided by Professor Dawson. Also see J. E. A. Dawson, 'John Knox, Goodman and the Example of Geneva', in P. Ha and P. Collinson (eds), *The Reception of the Continental Reformation in Britain* (Oxford: Oxford University Press, 2010), pp. 107–35, which explores

some of the aspects of Goodman's and Knox's links to Ireland.

75. S. Ó Cearnaigh [J. Kearney], 'A Brefe Declaration of Certeine Pryncipall Articles of Religion: Set out by Order and Aucthoritie Aswel of the Right Honorable Sir Henry Sidneye' (1567), in B. Ó Cuív (ed.), *Aibidil Gaoidheilge & Caiticiosma: Seaán Ó Cearnaigh's Irish Primer of Religion* (1571; Dublin: School of Celtic Studies, 1994), appendix 2, reproduced in full from the only surviving copy in the library of Trinity College Dublin.
76. See N. J. A. Williams, 'Kearney , John [Seán Ó Cearnaigh] (b. *c.*1545, d. after 1572)', *ODNB*; and C. Brady and J. Murray, 'Sir Henry Sidney and the Reformation in Ireland', in A. Boran and C. Gribben (eds), *Enforcing Reformation in Ireland and Scotland, 1550–1700* (Aldershot: Ashgate, 2006), pp. 14–39, on p. 19.
77. Elizabeth to Sidney, 10 June 1567, in *Sidney State Papers 1565–70*, ed. T. Ó Laidhin (Dublin: Irish Manuscript Commission, 1926), no. 40, p. 60.
78. 'Instructions to Sir Henry Sidney', 1 May 1568, The National Archives SP63/24/29.
79. Loftus to Cecil, 25 January 1568, TNA SP63/23/18. Here Loftus is referring to the post of lay clerk or vicar choral which still forms the backbone of sung services in Anglican cathedral worship.
80. Loftus to Cecil, 26 October 1570, TNA SP63/30/89.
81. Loftus to Walsingham, 16 March 1577, TNA SP63/57/36.
82. T. Cartwright, *A Replye to an Answere Made of M. Doctor Whitgifte Agaynste the Admonition to Parliament* ([Hemel Hempstead?: John Stroud?], 1575), p. 2 of the opening preface.
83. Lake, *Anglicans and Puritans*, pp. 53–64.
84. Loftus to Cecil, 10 June 1566, The National Archive, SP63/18/13.
85. Loftus to English privy council, 10 June 1566, TNA SP63/18/12.
86. A. Lyall, 'Weston, Robert (b. in or before 1522, d. 1573)', *ODNB*. See the discussion of Hooker in chapter 2.
87. See C. Brady, *The Chief Governors: The Rise and Fall of Reform Government in Tudor Ireland, 1536–1588* (Cambridge: Cambridge University Press, 1994), pp. 127–9.
88. Weston to Cecil, 3 April 1568, TNA SP63/24/2.
89. Weston to Cecil, 3 April 1568, TNA SP63/24/2.
90. Weston to Elizabeth, 18 April 1568, TNA SP63/24/9.
91. See 'A Brief Abstract of Such Bills as the Lord Deputy and Council Have Certified the Queen as Matters Thought Meet to Be Enacted by Parliament', January 1569, TNA SP53/27/12–15.
92. See 'A Brief Abstract of Such Bills'.
93. See V. Treadwell, 'The Irish Parliament of 1569–71', *Proceedings of the Royal Irish Academy*, section c 65 (1966), pp. 55–89, on p. 76 and p. 84.
94. Poynings' act was eventually suspended, but only after agreement for an amendment to the act - that any suspension had to have the prior consent of an Irish parliament before the bill was pass to England for consent. See R. Dudley Edwards and T. W. Moody, 'The History of Poynings' Law: Part I, 1594–1615', *Irish Historical Studies*, 2:8 (1941), p. 420.
95. Brady, *Chief Governors*, pp. 134–7. For a different interpretation from Brady see D. Edward, 'The Butler Revolt of 1569', *Irish Historical Studies*, 28:111 (1993), pp. 228–55.
96. Treadwell, 'The Irish Parliament of 1569–71'; and Brady, *Chief Governors*, pp. 134–6.
97. Weston to Cecil, 18 March 1569, TNA SP63/27/48.
98. Weston to Cecil, 12 March 1570, TNA SP63/30/29.
99. Weston to Cecil, 12 March 1570, TNA SP63/30/29.
100. Weston to Cecil, 12 March 1570, TNA SP63/30/29.
101. Loftus to Cecil, 16 February 1571, TNA SP63/31/11.
102. Sidney to Walsingham, 13 June 1576, TNA SP63/55/57.

103. Piers to Burghley, 6 July 1571, TNA SP63/33/2.
104. Fitzwilliam to Burghley, 8 May 1571, TNA SP63/32/29.
105. [?] to Hugh Brady, Essex eulogy, 22 September 1576, TNA SP63/56/35; or Add. MS 5845, London, British Library, fols 337–49. Also see J. J. N. McGurk, 'Devereux, Walter, first earl of Essex (1539–1576)', *ODNB*.
106. 'The Efficient and Accidental Causes of the Civility of Ireland', 1579, TNA SP63/70/82.
107. Middleton to Walsingham, 21 July 1580, TNA SP63/74/53.
108. Middleton to Walsingham, 21 July 1580, TNA SP63/74/53.
109. Long to Walsingham, 20 January 1585, TNA SP63/114/39. Also see Long to Walsingham, 4 June 1585, TNA SP63/117/7; Long to Walsingham, 8 July 1585, TNA SP63/118/12; Long to Walsingham, December 1585, TNA SP63/121/50; and Long to Walsingham, 22 January 1586, TNA SP63/122/37. More broadly speaking, this may point to a need to reappraise whether Elizabethan evangelism should be understood as educative in intent or as involving a wider grace-based redefinition of political relationships.
110. See E. F. Winter (trans. and ed.), *Discourse on Free Will: Erasmus and Luther* (London: Bloomsbury Academic, 2005), p. 17. Also see D. Erasmus, *The Education of a Christian Prince*, trans. N. M. Cheshire and M. J. Heath, ed. L. Jardine (Cambridge: Cambridge University Press, 1997), p. 79.
111. E. Campion, *A Historie of Ireland* (Dublin: Societie of Stationers, 1633), p. 131.
112. Campion, *A Historie of Ireland*, p. 133.
113. *The Statutes at Large Passed in the Parliaments Held in Ireland* (Dublin: George Grierson, 1786–1801) I, Elizabeth12 c. 1.
114. C. Brady,*The Chief Governors: The Rise and Fall of Reform Government in Tudor Ireland, 1536–1588* (Cambridge: Cambridge University Press, 1994), pp. 116–25. Also see C. Brady, 'The Attainder of Shane O'Neill, Sir Henry Sidney, and the Problems of Tudor State-Building in Ireland', in C. Brady and J. Ohlmeyer (eds), *British Interventions in Early Modern Ireland* (Cambridge: Cambridge University Press, 2008), pp. 28–48.
115. R. Stanihurst, 'Description of Ireland', in R. Holinshed, *Chronicles* (London: [Henry Bynneman] for George Bishop, 1577), p. 23. Also see, C. Lennon, *Richard Stanihurst the Dubliner 1547–1618: A Biography with a Stanihurst Text on Ireland's Past* (Dublin: Four Courts, 1981); and C. Lennon, 'Ireland', in P. Kewes, I. W. Archer and F. Heal (eds), *The Oxford Handbook of Holinshed's Chronicles* (Oxford: Oxford University Press, 2013), pp. 663–78.
116. Stanihurst, 'Description of Ireland', p. 23.
117. Stanihurst, 'Description of Ireland', p. 29.
118. Stanihurst, 'Description of Ireland', p. 29.
119. E. Campion and R. Holinshed, 'The Historie of Ireland' [first two books], in R. Holinshed, *Chronicles*, p. 11. Also see F. Heal and H. Summerson, 'The Genesis of the Two Editions', in P. Kewes, I. W. Archer and F. Heal (eds), *Oxford Handbook of Holinshed's Chronicles*, pp. 8–11.
120. Campion and Holinshed, 'The Historie of Ireland', pp. 71–3.
121. R. Stanihurst, 'The Thirde Booke of the Historie of Ireland', in R. Holinshed, *Chronicles*, pp. 104–11.
122. Gerrard to Walsingham, 8 February 1577, TNA SP63/57/16.
123. Gerrard to Walsingham, 8 February 1577, TNA SP63/57/16.
124. W. Gerrard, 'Gerrard Papers: Sir William Gerrard's Notes of his Report on Ireland, 1577–8', in C. McNeill (ed.), *Analecta Hibernica* 2 (1931), pp. 95, 122.

125. R. Malette, *Spenser and the Discourses of Reformation England* (Lincoln, NE: University of Nebraska Press, 1997), p. 46; and P. Christianson, *Reformers and Babylon: English Apocalyptic Visions from the Reformation to the Eve of the Civil War* (Toronto: University of Toronto Press, 1978).

2 The Failure of Reformed Protestant Plans

1. For a good account of the second Desmond rebellion, see A. M. McCormack, *The Earldom of Desmond 1463–1583: The Decline and Crisis of a Feudal Lordship* (Dublin: Four Courts, 2005), pp. 164–89. Also see C. Brady, 'Faction and the Origins of the Desmond Rebellion of 1579', *Irish Historical Studies*, 22:88 (1981), pp. 289–312.
2. See 'Normative Political and Religious Vocabulary' in the introduction to this study.
3. Nicholas White to Burghley, 15 May 1571, The National Archives SP63/32/31.
4. N. White to Burghley, 15 May 1571, TNA SP63/32/31.
5. See 'The Stanihursts and Some Ambiguities Concerning God's Grace', in chapter 1 of this study.
6. R. White to Cecil, 23 March 1571, TNA SP63/31/32.
7. R. White to Cecil, 23 March 1571, TNA SP63/31/32.
8. R. White to Cecil, 23 March 1571, TNA SP63/31/32.
9. K. R. Bartlett, 'Tremayne, Edmund (c. 1525-1582)', *ODNB*.
10. 'The Causes Why Ireland Is Not Reformed', June 1571, TNA SP63/32/65.
11. See TNA SP63/56/34; SP63/57/40 and SP63/69/43.
12. For an account of the wider factional interests and their eventual intermingling with religious dynamics, see S. Ellis, *Ireland in the Age of the Tudors 1447–1603: English Expansion and the End of Gaelic Rule* (New York: Longman, 1998), p. 298 and C. Lennon, *Sixteenth Century Ireland: The Incomplete Conquest* (Dublin: Gill and MacMillian, 1994), p. 246.
13. Malby to Walsingham, 17 March 1577, TNA SP63/57/40
14. Malby to Walsingham, 17 March 1577, TNA SP63/57/40.
15. Malby to Walsingham, 17 March 1577, TNA SP63/57/40.
16. Malby to Walsingham, 17 March 1577, TNA SP63/57/40.
17. Malby to Walsingham, 12 October 1579, TNA SP63/69/52.
18. Malby to Walsingham, 17 March 1577, TNA SP63/57/40.
19. Malby to Walsingham, 10 November 1577, TNA SP63/59/43.
20. Malby to Elizabeth, 20 September 1576, TNA SP63/56/34
21. Rapple, *Martial Power and Elizabethan Political Culture: Military Men in England and Ireland, 1558–1594* (Cambridge: Cambridge University Press, 2009), p. 270.
22. Googe, 11 March 1584, TNA SP63/108/13.
23. R. Lyne, 'Googe, Barnabe (1540–1594)', *ODNB*.
24. Fitton to Burghley, 9 August 1573, TNA SP63/42/2.
25. Fitton to Cecil, 15 April 1570, TNA SP63/30/43.
26. Fitton and Dillon to Burghley, 20 March 1574, TNA SP63/45/15.
27. Fitton and Dillon to Burghley, 20 March 1574, TNA SP63/45/15.
28. Fitton to Burghley, 5 January 1575, TNA SP63/49/11.
29. Fitton to Burghley, 5 January 1575, TNA SP63/49/11.
30. D. Edwards, *The Ormond Lordship in County Kilkenny, 1515–1642: The Rise and Fall of Butler Feudal Power* (Dublin: Four Courts, 2003), p. 225.
31. Malby to Walsingham, 10 December 1579, TNA SP63/70/51.
32. Drury to privy council, 24 March 1578, TNA SP63/60/25.

33. See B. Bradshaw, *The Irish Constitutional Revolution of the Sixteenth Century* (Cambridge: Cambridge University Press, 1979), ch. 9; and N. P. Canny, *The Formation of the Old English Elite in Ireland*, O'Donnell Lecture, Dublin, 1975, and N. P. Canny, 'Dominant Minorities: English Settlers in Ireland and Virginia 1550–1650', *Historical Studies*, 12 (1977), pp. 51–69.
34. See 'Inverting Resistance Theory' in chapter 1.
35. S. Mendyk, 'Hooker, John (c. 1527–1601), *ODNB*.
36. J. Hooker, 'Order and Usage' in V. F. Snow ed., *Parliament in Elizabethan England: John Hooker's Order and Usage* (New Haven, CT: Yale University Press, 1977), p. 122. As is discussed, this quote is to be found in the dedicatory epistle to the English but not the Irish edition.
37. See Hooker, *Order and Usage*, pp. 123–4. This is different from the dedicatory epistle to Fitzwilliam on pp. 205–12.
38. V. P. Carey, *Surviving the Tudors: The 'Wizard' Earl of Kildare and English Rule in Ireland, 1537–1586* (Dublin: Four Courts Press, 2002), pp. 180–1; and V. P. Carey, 'Atrocity and History: Grey, Spenser and the Slaughter at Smerwick (1580)', in D. Edwards, P. Lenihan and C. Tait (eds), *Age of Atrocity: Violence and Political Conflict in Early Modern Ireland* (Dublin: Four Courts Press), pp. 79–94.
39. See 'An Irish Preaching Ministry' in chapter 1 of this book.
40. Grey to Elizabeth, 28 January 1581, The National Archives SP63/80/38; and Grey to Walsingham, 24 April 1581, TNA SP63/82/48.
41. Grey to Elizabeth, 24 April 1581, TNA SP63/82/54.
42. See 'Robert Weston and an Irish Definition of "Civil Obedience"' in chapter 1 of this book. Also Middleton to Walsingham, 21 July 1580, TNA SP63/74/53.
43. Burghley to Sidney, 10 July 1576, TNA SP63/56/7.
44. Malby to Walsingham, 10 December 1579, TNA SP63/70/51.
45. P. Collinson, *Archbishop Grindal 1519–1583: The Struggle for the Reformed Church* (Berkeley, CA: University of California Press, 1979), pp. 225–8.
46. P. Lake, '"The Monarchical Republic of Queen Elizabeth I" (and the Fall of Archbishop Grindal) Revisited', in J. F. McDiarmid (ed.), *The Monarchical Republic of Elizabethan England: Essays in Response to Patrick Collinson* (Aldershot: Ashgate, 2007), pp. 129–48.
47. Elizabeth to Grindal, May 1577, MS 2003, London, Lambeth Palace Library, fols 40–1.
48. Grindal to Elizabeth, endorsed December 1577, Lansdowne MS 23 no. 4, London, British Library. See P. Collinson, *The Birthpangs of Protestant England: Religious and Cultural Change in the Sixteenth and Seventeenth Centuries* (Basingstoke: St Martin's Press, 1998), pp. 28–59, for a wider discussion of the lay response to preaching and prophesying in England.
49. Grindal to Elizabeth, endorsed December 1577, Lansdowne MS 23, no. 4.
50. BL Additional MSS 33271, fol. 13v.
51. See C. Haigh, 'Puritan Evangelism in the Reign of Elizabeth I', *English Historical Review*, 92:342 (1977), pp. 30–58. Also see M. Braddick, *State Formation in Early Modern England* (Cambridge: Cambridge University Press, 2000), part 4: 'The Confessional State'.
52. S. Adams, *Leicester and the Court: Essays on Elizabethan Politics* (Manchester: Manchester University Press, 2002), pp. 102–3.
53. T. Norton, *To the Quenes Majesties Poore Deceived Subjects of the North Countrey, Drawen into Rebellion by the Earles of Northumberland and Westmerland* ([London: Henry Bynneman for Lucas Harrison, 1569), fol. 16v. A. J. Fletcher and D. Macculloch,

Tudor Rebellions (1967; Abingdon: Routledge, 2014), pp. 9–16, does point, overall, to the religious dimension to obedience, which demanded obedience to God and thus the prince – a language that could be used in different ways and which broke down in a post-reformation world of confessional division. Also B. Kane 'Elizabeth on Rebellion in Ireland and England: *Semper Eadem*?', in B. Kane and V. McGowan-Doyle (eds.), *Elizabeth I and Ireland* (Cambridge: Cambridge University Press, 2014), pp. 261–86 suggests that the categorization of rebellion in Ireland by historians as particularly 'Irish' by nature is strained, where in effect all rebellion was thought to be of similar provenance and nature – something which supports the broader comparative point this study attempts to make.

54. Norton to Walsingham, December 1581, Additional MS 48023, London, British Library, fol. 43r. The sense in which many of these individuals, such as Norton, acted on behalf of a godly ideal confirms very much Patrick Collinson's reading of the dynamics of Elizabethan parliaments. P. Collinson, 'Puritans, Men of Business and Elizabethan Parliaments', in P. Collinson, *Elizabethan Essays* (London: Hambledon, 1994), pp. 59–86. In this respect, Collinson was attempting to rehabilitate the arguments set forward by Neale, that there was a form of proto-factional dynamic involving parties of the political left and right. J. E. Neale, *Elizabeth I and her Parliaments, 1559–1581* (London: Jonathan Cape, 1953). For the revisionist position see, G. R. Elton, *Parliament in England 1559–1581* (Cambridge: Cambridge University Press, 1986) and M. A. R. Graves, *Elizabethan Parliaments, 1559–1601* (Abingdon: Routledge, 2003). In opposition to Neale's view, Elton suggested there was more of a procedural dynamic, which required consensus and discussion.
55. 'The Efficient and Accidental Causes of the Civility of Ireland', 1579, The National Archives SP63/70/82.
56. 'The Efficient and Accidental Causes of the Civility of Ireland', 1579, TNA SP63/70/82. Also see H. Robinson-Hammerstein, 'Aspects of the Continental Education of Irish Students in the Reign of Queen Elizabeth I', in T. D. Williams (ed.), *Historical Studies VIII* (Dublin: Gill and MacMillan, 1971), pp. 137–54.
57. Malby to Walsingham, 31 August 1580, TNA SP63/75/82.
58. R. Turvey, 'Perrot, Sir John (1528–1592)', *ODNB*.
59. Perrot to Walsingham, 20 February 1586, TNA SP63/122/77.
60. Rosyer, 25 September 1586, TNA SP63/126/22.
61. See 'Local Office Holding and the Old English Gentry' in chapter 5 of this book.
62. C. Maginn, 'Magrath, Meiler (*c.*1523–1622)', *ODNB*.
63. Trollope to Burghley, 27 October 1587, TNA SP63/131/64.
64. 'Book Set Down in Writing by the Archbishop of Cashel', 30 May 1592, TNA SP63/164/47, article 15.
65. 'Book Set Down in Writing by the Archbishop of Cashel', 30 May 1592, TNA SP63/164/47, article 25.
66. See lord deputy and council to privy council, 20 January 1589, TNA SP63/140/51; St Leger to Elizabeth, May 1589, TNA SP63/144/82; Dowdall to Burghley, 9 March 1596, TNA SP63/187/19; and Jones to Lord Deputy, September 1592, TNA SP63/165/69i.
67. Lyons to Burghley, 23 September 1595, TNA SP63/183/47.
68. See V. Treadwell, 'Sir John Perrot and the Irish Parliament of 1585–6', *Proceedings of the Royal Irish Academy* 85C (1985), pp. 259–308.
69. For Ireland see J. Murray, *Enforcing the English Reformation in Ireland: Clerical*

Resistance and Political Conflict in the Diocese of Dublin (Cambridge: Cambridge University Press, 2009), pp. 308–20; and H. Robinson-Hammerstein, 'Loftus, Adam (1533/4–1605), Church of Ireland Archbishop of Dublin', ODNB. For England, see M. C. Questier, *Conversion, Politics and Religion in England, 1580–1625* (Cambridge: Cambridge University Press: 1996), pp. 129–67. Questier's main evidence for the activity of various high commission agents would appear to date from around the 1580s onwards.

70. J. E. Neale, *Elizabeth I and her Parliaments, 1559–1581* (Jonathan Cape: London, 1953), p. 391; and C. Haigh, *Elizabeth I* (London: Longman, 1988), ch. 2: 'The Queen and the Church'. Also see Questier, *Conversion, Politics and Religion in England*, in particular, p. 167. Questier writes, 'The state's political rhetoric of unity was not the reformed evangelical rhetoric of grace and renewal'. This view also seems to be implicit in the suggestion that the regime by the late 1580s was frightened of Elizabethan puritans and their demands for further reform which threatened ideas of political conformity. See, for example, J. Guy, 'The 1590s: The Second Reign of Elizabeth I?', in J. Guy (ed.), *Reign of Elizabeth I* (Cambridge, Cambridge University Press, 1995), pp. 1–19.
71. T. Norton, *Execution of Justice in England for the Maintenaunce of Publique and Christian Peace* (London: Christopher Baker, 1583), pp. 4, p. 6.
72. S. Alford, *Burghley: William Cecil at the Court of Elizabeth I* (New Haven, CT: Yale University Press, 2008), pp. 241–3. Alford attributes the *Execution of Justice* to Norton, though it was published under Burghley's name. Alford would also appear to accept at face value the suggestion that Burghley and government more generally did not actually intend to examine consciences.
73. Norton, *Execution of Justice*, p. 6.
74. Norton, *Execution of Justice*, p. 8.
75. Norton, *Execution of Justice*, pp. 36, 29–30.
76. Questier, *Conversion, Politics and Religion in England*, ch. 6 details a concurrent English process where attempts were made to exclude the catholic gentry from office.
77. See Murray, *Enforcing the English Reformation in Ireland*, pp. 308–11. Also see, for example, lords justices to privy council, 25 Match 1584, TNA SP653/108/50.
78. Treadwell, 'Sir John Perrot and the Irish Parliament of 1585–6'; and 'Note of English Statutes to be Enacted in Ireland', TNA SP63/112/36.
79. 'Articles and Ordinances to Be Straightly Observed', April 1585, Carte MS 242, Oxford, Bodleian Library, fols 285r–286v. Perrot set 'down certain orders' and appointed 'certain ordinary officers' such as 'justices of the peace, escheaters [and] coroners', and gave instruction that 'all men and women above the age of 16 years shall be sworn for allegiance to her majesty renouncing all foreign authority, powers and jurisdictions'.
80. Treadwell, 'Sir John Perrot and the Irish Parliament of 1585–6', pp. 259–308.
81. The various ways in which Ireland might fit into a confessionalization paradigm is discussed in E. Boran and C. Gribben 'Introduction', in Boran and Gribben (eds.), *Enforcing Reformation in Ireland and Scotland, 1550–1700* (Aldershot: Ashgate, 2006), pp. 1–13. It is within this model that Brady and Murray, to an extent, position Ireland under Henry Sidney, thus viewing religious reform as an extension of law reform and not as an evangelical effort. See 'Normative Political and Religious Vocabulary' in the introduction to this book for more detail on Murray's and Brady's position, as well as M. A. Hutchinson, 'Reformed Protestantism and the Government of Ireland, *c.* 1565–1582: The Lord Deputyships of Henry Sidney and Arthur Grey', *Sidney Journal*, 29:1–2 (2011), pp. 71–104.

82. H. Schilling, *Konfessionskonflikt und Staatsbildung* (Guetersloh: Guetersloher Verlgasanstalt, 1981). For the wider debate and development of the paradigm see, T. A. Brady, Jr., 'Confessionalization: The Career of a Concept', in J. M. Headley, H. J. Hillerband and A. J. Papalas (eds), *Confessionalization in Europe, 1555–1700: Essays in Honor and Memory of Bodo Nischan* (Ashgate: Aldershot, 2004), pp. 1–20; H. Schilling, 'Comparative and Interdisciplinary Paradigm', in Headley, Hillerband and Papalas, *Confessionalization in Europe*, pp. 21–36; and J. F. Harrington and H. W. Smith, 'Confessionalization, Community and State Building in Germany, 1555–1870', *Journal of Modern History*, 69:1 (1997), pp. 77–101.
83. B. Nischan, 'Confessionalism and Absolutism: The Case of Brandenburg', in A. Pettegree, A. Duke and G. Lewis (eds), *Calvinism in Europe* (Cambridge: Cambridge University Press, 1996), pp. 181–201.
84. U. Lotz-Heumann, *Die doppelte Konfessionalisierung in Irland: Konflikt und Koexistenz im 16. und in der ersten Hälfte des 17. Jahrhunderts* (Tübingen: Mohr Siebeck, 2000), vol. 13. Also see H. Robinson-Hammerstein, 'The Confessionalisation of Ireland? Assessment of a Paradigm', *Irish Historical Studies*, 32:128 (2001), pp. 567–78.
85. See 'Gaelic Political and Religious Vocabulary' in chapter 5.
86. P. S. Gorski, *The Disciplinary Revolution: Calvinism and the Rise of the State in Early Modern Europe* (Chicago, IL: Chicago University Press, 2003). H. Höpfl, *Christian Polity of John Calvin* chs 7–9, discusses in more detail the relationship or elision between Calvin's ideas on grace and man's internal reform, the need to bridle the sinner, and the resulting notion of discipline where notions of internal reform and external bridle were combined. The English equivalent to such shifts in thinking was the reformation of manners, which we might argue had arisen out of a recognized failure to successfully evangelize and effect godly reform. See M. Ingram, 'Reformation of Manners in Early Modern England', in P. Griffiths (ed.), *The Experience of Authority in Early Modern England* (Basingstoke: Palgrave, 1996), pp. 47–88.
87. J. Derricke, *The Image of Irelande, with a Discoverie of Woodkarne* (London: [J. Kingston for] Jhon Daie, 1581). For a more extended discussion of Derricke see M. Moroney, '"The Sweetness of Due Subjection"; Derricke's Image of Ireland (1581) and the Sidneys', *Sidney Journal*, 29:1–2 (2011), pp. 147–72.
88. Derricke, *Image*, fol. 23v [marginalia].
89. Derricke, *Image*, fol. 23v [marginalia].
90. A. Ford, 'Apocalyptic Ireland: 1580–1641', *Irish Theological Quarterly*, 78:123 (2003), pp. 123–48: also A. Ford, 'Force and Fear of Punishment: Protestants and Religious Coercion in Ireland, 1603–33', in A. Boran and C. Gribben (eds), *Enforcing Reformation in Ireland and Scotland, 1550–1700* (Aldershot: Ashgate, 2006), pp. 91–130.
91. Derricke, *Image*, fol. 24r.
92. See 'Henry Sidney and the Levying of Cess' in chapter 3 of this study, and 'Philip Sidney, John Stubbs and Anjou' in chapter 4 of this study.
93. Hiram Morgan has made some similar observations in H. Morgan, '"Overmighty Officers": The Irish Lord Deputyship in the Early Modern British State', *History Ireland*, 7:4 (1999), p. 17.
94. Q. Skinner, *Hobbes and Republican Liberty* (Cambridge: Cambridge University Press, 2008), pp. 124–77.
95. T. Churchyard, *A Generall Rehearsal of Warres* (London: [John Kingston for] Edward White, 1579), fol. 2v.
96. Fitton to Burghley, 9 Aug. 1573, TNA SP63/42/2.

97. Churchyard, *Warres*, fol. 72r.
98. R. Rapple, 'Gilbert, Sir Humphrey (1537–1583)', *ODNB*.
99. Churchyard, *Warres*, fol. 73r.
100. Churchyard, *Warres*, fol. 4r.
101. Churchyard, *Warres*, fols 77r–78v.
102. E. Flanagan, 'The Anatomy of Jacobean Ireland: Captain Barnaby Rich, Sir John Davies and the Failure of Reform, 1609–22', in H. Morgan (ed.), *Political Ideology in Ireland, 1541–1641* (Dublin: Four Courts, 1999), pp. 158–80.
103. B. Rich, *Allarme to England* (London: Christopher Baker, 1578), fol. 9v.
104. Rich, *Allarme*, fol. 12v.
105. Rich, *Allarme*, fols 25r–27v, on fol. 27v.
106. B. Rich, 'Epistle', in B. Rich, *A Short Survey of Ireland*, (London: N[icolas] O[kes], 1609), fol. 2v.
107. Rich, *Survey*, pp. 15–16.

3 Irish Constitutional Peculiarity

1. Sidney and Irish council to Elizabeth, 12 September 1577, Titus BX, fols 124v–127r.
2. Sidney to English privy council, 20 February 1578, Titus BX, fol. 146r.
3. 'Walter Gall's Submission in Kilkenny', 6 November 1578, The National Archives SP63/63/15.
4. Drury to English privy council, 16 December 1578, TNA SP63/65/6. The use of the term 'state' in Ireland was noted by W. T. MacCaffrey, *Elizabeth I: War and Politics 1588–1603* (Princeton, NJ: Princeton University Press, 1992), pp. 355–6, though he made little comment upon its possible significance.
5. J. Guy, *Tudor England* (Oxford: Oxford University Press, 1988), pp. 352–3.
6. W. T. MacCaffrey, *Queen Elizabeth and the Making of Policy, 1572–1588* (Princeton, NJ: Princeton University Press, 1992), p. 214.
7. A similar observation has been made in M. Peltonen, *Classical Humanism and Republicanism in English Political Thought 1570–1640* (Cambridge: Cambridge University Press, 1995), pp. 54–118. Part of the argument as laid out here is also found in M. A. Hutchinson, 'The Emergence of the State in Elizabethan Ireland and England, *c.* 1575–99', *Sixteenth Century Journal*, 45:3 (2014), pp. 659–82. Also see M. A. Hutchinson, '"The State": Ireland's Contribution to the History of Political Thought', *Irish Review*, 48 (2014), pp. 28–35.
8. The influence of Geoffrey Fenton and Lodowick Bryskett will be addressed in chapters 4 and 5.
9. J. H. Franklin, 'Sovereignty and the Mixed Constitution: Bodin and his Critics', in J. H. Burns and M. Goldie (eds), *The Cambridge History of Political Thought* (Cambridge: Cambridge University Press, 1991), pp. 298–328, on pp. 298–9, 307.
10. See Q. Skinner, 'From the State of the Prince to the Person of the State', in Skinner, *Visions of Politics*, 3 vols, vol. 2: *Renaissance Virtues* (Cambridge: Cambridge University Press, 2002), pp. 368–413, on pp. 368–9, 394–406; Q. Skinner, *The Foundations of Modern Political Thought*, 2 vols (Cambridge: Cambridge University Press, 1978), vol. 2, pp. 284–301; and Skinner, 'From the State of the Prince', pp. 387–99, where he revises the conclusions drawn about Bodin's significance in *Foundations*, vol. 2, p. 355 and clearly sets Bodin at least one step behind Hobbes.
11. See H. Morgan, '"Overmighty Officers": The Irish Lord Deputyship in the Early Mod-

ern British State', *History Ireland*, 7:4 (1999), pp. 17–21, on p. 17, as well as the various extant instructions issued to lord deputies such as The National Archives SP63/14/2, SP63/15/4, SP63/25/50, SP63/91/4 and SP63/132/55.

12. See A. McLaren, *Political Culture in the Reign of Elizabeth I: Queen and Commonwealth 1558–1585* (Cambridge: Cambridge University Press, 1999), pp. 59–68 in particular. Also see S. Alford, *The Early Elizabethan Polity: William Cecil and the British Succession Crisis, 1558–1569* (Cambridge: Cambridge University Press, 1998), pp. 2–8 and passim; and J. Guy, 'The Rhetoric of Counsel in Early Modern England', in Dale Hoak (ed.), *Tudor Political Culture* (Cambridge: Cambridge University Press: 1995), pp. 292–310.
13. C. Brady, *The Chief Governors: The Rise and Fall of Reform Government in Tudor Ireland, 1536–1588* (Cambridge: Cambridge University Press, 1994), pp. 209–44. Also N. P. Canny, 'Identity Formation in Ireland: The Emergence of the Anglo-Irish', in N. P. Canny and A. Pagden (eds), *Colonial Identity in the Atlantic World 1500–1800* (Princeton, NJ: Princeton University Press, 1987), pp. 159–212.
14. C. Brady, *Chief Governors*, pp. 141–7, 216–17.
15. See W. Gerrard, 'Gerrard Papers: Sir William Gerrard's Notes of his Report on Ireland 1577–8', ed. C. McNeill, *Analecta Hibernica*, 2 (1931), p. 132.
16. Sidney to Walsingham, 20 June 1577, TNA SP63/58/50.
17. 'Collection of the Matters of Cess', [January] 1579, TNA SP63/65/27; and Brady, *Chief Governors*, p. 154.
18. See R. Rapple, *Martial Power and Elizabethan Political Culture: Military Men in England and Ireland, 1558–1594* (Cambridge: Cambridge University Press, 2009), pp. 194–6.
19. Quote taken from A. Woodworth, 'Purveyance for the Royal Household in the Reign of Queen Elizabeth', *Transactions of the American Philosophical Society*, new series, 35:1 (1945), pp. 21–2.
20. This informed an embryonic notion of negative liberty which was set out by Nicholas White, Baron Delvin and Nicholas Walsh. This is discussed at the end of 'Arthur Grey's Proto-Absolutism and the Irish Mixed Polity' in chapter 4.
21. B. Bradshaw, *The Irish Constitutional Revolution of the Sixteenth Century* (Cambridge: Cambridge University Press, 1979), p. 232 views the act of kingly title as part and parcel of the model of surrender and regrant (which we discussed at the start of chapter 1). Bradshaw also saw this as the Irish equivalent of Thomas Cromwell's 'national sovereignty' and the establishment of Henry VIII's *imperium*. In Murray, *Enforcing the English Reformation in Ireland*, pp. 128–30, it is suggested that questions had begun to be asked in Ireland about Henry VIII's authority to the reform the Irish church, and that 'the act' was meant to bolster Henry's claim to supremacy in ecclesiastical affairs.
22. *The Statutes at Large Passed in the Parliaments held in Ireland* (Dublin: George Grierson, 1786–1801), I, 33 Henry VIII session 1, *c.* 1.
23. Sidney to Walsingham, 15 May 1577, Titus BX fol. 92r.
24. Rapple, *Martial Power*, pp. 192–3.
25. McLaren, *Political Culture*, pp. 59–68 in particular.
26. See P. Collinson, 'The Monarchical Republic of Queen Elizabeth I', in Collinson, *Elizabethan Essays* (London: Hambledon, 1994), pp. 31–58; and Alford, *Early Elizabethan Polity*.
27. Sidney to Walsingham, 15 May 1577, Titus BX, f. 92r.
28. P. Sidney, 'Discourse on Ireland', June 1577, Cotton MSS Titus BXII, London, British Library, fols 577–9.

29. See Q. Skinner, *The Foundations of Modern Political Thought*, 2 vols (Cambridge: Cambridge University Press, 1978), vol. 2, pp. 284–301, and Q. Skinner, 'From the State of the Prince to the Person of the State', in Q. Skinner, *Visions of Politics*, 3 vols, vol. 2: *Renaissance Virtues* (Cambridge: Cambridge University Press, 2002), pp. 368–413, on pp. 387–99.
30. See B. Worden, *The Sound of Virtue: Philip Sidney's 'Arcadia' and Elizabethan Politics* (New Haven, CT: Yale University Press, 1996), p. 47.
31. See A. Cromartie, *The Constitutionalist Revolution: An Essay on the History of England, 1450–1642* (Cambridge: Cambridge University Press, 2006), pp. 179–233.
32. Sidney to Walsingham, 20 June 1577, TNA SP63/58/50.
33. See A. Lyall, 'Snagge, Thomas (1536–1593)' and Crawford, 'White, Sir Nicholas (*c.* 1532–1592)', *ODNB*. Also Snagge to Walsingham, November 1577, TNA SP63/59/52.
34. Cromartie, *Constitutionalist Revolution*, pp. 112–14.
35. Brady, *Chief Governors*, p. 154.
36. See 'Commonwealth Thought' in chapter 1 of this study.
37. Murray makes similar observations about the fact Sidney made use of the royal prerogative in the actions discussed above – J. Murray, *Enforcing the English Reformation in Ireland: Clerical Resistance and Political Conflict in the Diocese of Dublin* (Cambridge: Cambridge University Press, 2009), p. 298.
38. 'The Contents of a Commission Granted for Faculties in Ireland and a Brief Note of Certain Defects', 20 December 1578, The National Archives SP63/63/49.
39. 'The Contents of a Commission Granted for Faculties in Ireland and a Brief Note of Certain Defects', 20 December 1578, The National Archives SP63/63/49.
40. 'The Contents of a Commission Granted for Faculties in Ireland and a Brief Note of Certain Defects', 20 December 1578, The National Archives SP63/63/49.
41. 'Certain Notes Delivered by Robert Garvey Touching the Commission for Faculties', 2 January 1579, TNA SP63/65/2.
42. See G. R. Elton, *The Tudor Constitution* (Cambridge: Cambridge University Press, 1960), p. 332. For a wider discussion of the constitutional intentions of Henry VIII and Thomas Cromwell see G. R. Elton, 'Henry VIII's Act of Proclamations', *English Historical Review*, 75:294 (1960), pp. 208–22 and R. W. Heinze, *The Proclamations of the Tudor Kings* (Cambridge: Cambridge University Press, 1976), p. 59.
43. 'The Answer of Adam Archbishop of Dublin to Mr Garvey his Justification of the Commission for Faculties', 6 January 1579, TNA SP63/65/8.
44. 'The Answer of Adam Archbishop of Dublin to Mr Garvey his Justification of the Commission for Faculties', 6 January 1579, TNA SP63/65/8.
45. Garvey to Burghley, 7 January 1579, TNA SP63/65/9.
46. Murray, *Enforcing the English Reformation in Ireland*, pp. 303–13.
47. J. Guy, 'The Elizabethan Establishment and the Ecclesiastical Polity', in Guy (ed.), *The Reign of Elizabeth I*, p. 131. See 'Epilogue: Beyond the 1590s' in this volume.
48. T. Smith, *De Republica Anglorum* (London: Henry Middleton for Gregorie Seton, 1583), p. 47.
49. *Calendar of the Patent and Close Rolls of Chancery in Ireland*, ed. James Morrin, 3 vols (Dublin: A. Thom and sons, for H. M. Stationery Office, 1861), vol. 1, p. 370. Letters patent took a standard form and the above quote is taken from the letters patent issued to Lord Deputy Sussex in 1556/7. The text of the various letters patents issued to Sidney were not recorded by Morrin, and the originals were destroyed with the destruction

of the Four Courts in Dublin in 1922. Also see D. Edwards, 'Ideology and Experience: Spenser's *View* and Martial Law in Ireland', in H. Morgan (ed.), *Political Ideology in Ireland, 1541–1641* (Dublin: Four Courts, 1999), pp. 127–57, on pp. 130–3.

50. *Calendar of the Patent and Close Rolls of Chancery in Ireland*, vol. 2, p. 520.
51. Smith, *De Republica*, p. 44.
52. R. Rapple, *Martial Power and Elizabethan Political Culture: Military Men in England and Ireland, 1558–1594* (Cambridge: Cambridge University Press, 2009), p. 181.
53. Rapple, *Martial Power*, p. 183.
54. See V. P. Carey, 'Atrocity and History: Grey, Spenser and the Slaughter at Smerwick (1580), in D. Edwards, P. Lenihan and C. Tait (eds), *Age of Atrocity: Violence and Political Conflict in Early Modern Ireland* (Dublin: Four Courts Press, 2007), pp. 79–94.
55. Lord Justices to Walsingham, 7 March 1584, The National Archives SP63/108/8.
56. Lord Justices to Walsingham, 10 December 1583, SP63/106/7.
57. Lord Justices to Walsingham, 7 March 1584, TNA SP63/108/8.
58. Neither the 1570 act, which made it illegal to bring in bulls, nor the 1581 act, which made it illegal to seek to convert Elizabeth's Irish subjects, had been discussed in parliament in Ireland. They were not therefore on the Irish Statute Book. It was this lacuna in legislation Perrot sought to rectify in his 1585–6 parliament – but with no success. We discussed aspects of Perrot's parliament in 'Papistry and Penal Legislation' in chapter 2, and will return briefly to this problem near the end of 'From "Broken State" to Abstract "State"' in chapter 4 and 'Local Office Holding and the Old English Gentry' in chapter 5. It is also noted in V. Treadwell, 'Sir John Perrot and the Irish Parliament of 1585–6', *Proceedings of the Royal Irish Academy*, section c 85 (1985), p. 371, that a proposed bill 'for trial of offences committed outside the Irish jurisdiction of the crown' may also have been a direct response to the O'Hurley problem.
59. Lord Justices to Walsingham, 7 March 1584, TNA SP63/108/8.
60. P. Collinson, 'The Monarchical Republic of Queen Elizabeth I', in P. Collinson, *Elizabethan Essays* (London: Hambledon, 1994), pp. 31–58, on pp. 32–9.
61. Collinson, 'Monarchical Republic', pp. 32–8.
62. *The Statutes at Large Passed in the Parliaments Held in Ireland*, I, 33 session 2 Henry VIII, *c*. 2.
63. Edward Fenton to Walsingham, 16 October 1579, The National Archives SP63/69/64.
64. Lords justices to Walsingham, 6 August 1583, TNA SP63/104/7.
65. Wallop and Loftus to Burghley, 5 September 1583, TNA SP63/104/62.
66. Malby to Walsingham, 16 April 1583, TNA SP63/101/29.
67. Queen to lords justices, 9 September 1583, TNA SP63/104/64.
68. J. G. Crawford, *Anglicizing the Government of Ireland: The Irish Privy Council and the Expansion of Tudor Rule, 1556 to 1578* (Dublin: Irish Academic Press, 1993), final chapter.
69. Elizabeth to Irish council, 26 February 1586, The National Archives SP63/122/81.
70. Loftus to Burghley, 4 December 1586, TNA SP63/127/4.
71. Loftus to Burghley, 4 December 1586, TNA SP63/127/4.
72. Loftus to Burghley, 4 December 1586, TNA SP63/127/4.
73. Fenton to Burghley, 4 December 1586, TNA SP63/127/6.
74. Mr Chief Justice Gardiner to Burghley, 6 December 1586, TNA SP63/127/13.
75. Mr Chief Justice Gardiner to Burghley, 6 December 1586, TNA SP63/127/13.
76. See H. Morgan, 'The Fall of Sir John Perrot', in J. Guy (ed.), *The Reign of Elizabeth I* (Cambridge, Cambridge University Press, 1995), pp. 109–25.

77. Taken from Morgan, 'The Fall of Sir John Perrot', p. 121. Also see Willis MS 58, Oxford, Bodleian Library, fols 247–8, 263–305.
78. 'A True Note of the Articles against Sir John Parrett the XXVII of April 1592', Sloane MS 2172, London, British Library, fols 37–38. Hiram Morgan generously provided me with numerous copies of his full transcriptions of various documents relating to Perrot's trail.
79. The form of government set out in *Utopia* was anti-monarchical and it heavily critiqued contemporary civil society. See B. Bradshaw, 'More on Utopia', *Historical Journal*, 24:1 (1981), pp. 1–27. It might be added, with regard to increasing interest in renaissance reading habits, as found in Jardine's and Grafton's work on Gabriel Harvey's Livy, or even in the comments Bradshaw makes in his article on More's *Utopia*, that Perrot provides us with a conscious account of how he read or understood *Utopia*. See L. Jardine and A. Grafton, '"Studied for Action": How Gabriel Harvey Read his Livy', *Past and Present*, 129 (1990), pp. 30–78.
80. Northumberland Papers, VI no. 30, Alnwick Castle, fol. 59. Hiram Morgan pointed me to Perrot's reference to More's *Utopia*.

4 The End of an Irish Mixed Polity

1. Q. Skinner, *The Foundations of Modern Political Thought*, 2 vols (Cambridge: Cambridge University Press, 1978), vol. 2, in particular 'The Context of the Huguenot Revolution', pp. 241–301. Also M. van Gelderen, *The Political Thought of the Dutch Revolt 1555–1590* (Cambridge: Cambridge University Press, 1992), in particular pp. 62–165.
2. C. Brady, 'Conservative Subversives: The Community of the Pale and the Dublin Administration, 1556–86', in P. J. Corish (ed.), *Radicals, Rebels and Establishments: Historical Studies* XV (Belfast: Appletree Press, 1985), pp. 11–32; and J. Murray, *Enforcing the English Reformation in Ireland: Clerical Resistance and Political Conflict in the Diocese of Dublin* (Cambridge: Cambridge University Press, 2009), in particular his discussion of the papal bull *Laudabiliter*, pp. 56–65.
3. Skinner, *Foundations*, vol. 2. Also see 'Inverting Resistance Theory' and 'Potential Irish Radicalism' in chapter 1 of this book, where the elision between a constitutional position and a grace- and conscience-based view of political relationships is addressed to some degree.
4. van Gelderen, *Political Thought of the Dutch Revolt*, pp. 68–73, pp. 110–14 and in particular pp. 167–80 and pp. 213–56. Van Gelderen identifies an emerging notion of negative freedom or liberty in the Netherlands. Precisely how this relates to the notion of 'the state' and freedom in Ireland will be discussed further in this chapter in relation to the emergence of an embryonic notion of negative liberty amongst members of the Old English community – see 'From "Broken State" to Abstract "State"' and 'The Language of "the State" and the Possibility of Toleration'.
5. J. G. A. Pocock, *The Machiavellian Moment: Florentine Political Thought and the Atlantic Republican Tradition* (Princeton, NJ: Princeton University Press, 1975), pp. 83–113.
6. Q. Skinner, *The Foundations of Modern Political Thought*, 2 vols (Cambridge: Cambridge University Press, 1978), vol. 2, pp. 284–301. Also J. H. Franklin, 'Sovereignty and the Mixed Constitution: Bodin and his Critics', in J. H. Burns and M. Goldie (eds), *The Cambridge History of Political Thought* (Cambridge: Cambridge University Press, 1991), pp. 298–328, on pp. 298–9, 307.
7. A. McLaren, 'Rethinking Republicanism: *Vindiciae, Contra Tyrannos* in Context', *Historical Journal*, 49:1 (2006), pp. 23–52. Once again, aspects of the elision between

a constitutional position and a grace- and conscience-based view of political relationships are addressed in 'Inverting Resistance Theory' and 'Potential Irish Radicalism' in chapter 1 of this study.

8. See S. J. Brutus, the Celt, *Vindiciae, Contra Tyrannos*, ed. G. Garnett (Cambridge: Cambridge University Press, 1994), pp. xix–liv.
9. See 'Henry Sidney and the Levying of Cess' in chapter 3.
10. B. Worden, *The Sound of Virtue: Philip Sidney's 'Arcadia' and Elizabethan Politics* (New Haven, CT: Yale University Press, 1996), passim and in particular pp. 89–114. The sense in which, in a post-reformation world, there was a wider search for new vocabulary in order to articulate and unite the nation is discussed in R. Helgerson, *Forms of Nationhood: The Elizabethan Writing of England* (Chicago, IL: Chicago University Press, 1992), pp. 1–18 and passim. For a different view on Philip's intellectual background see, R. E. Stillman, *Philip Sidney and the Poetics of Renaissance Cosmopolitanism* (Ashgate: Aldershot, 2008), in particular pp. 35–62. Stillman suggests Philip adheres more to the intellectual outlook of Philip Melanchthon. In short, for both Philips, fallen man did not lack the capacity to act well through his own volition – though the cultural and intellectual context presented here would suggest Philip's intellectual leanings are more those of a Calvinist.
11. P. Sidney, 'Letter to Queen Elizabeth, 1580', in W. Gray (ed.), *The Miscellaneous Works of Philip Sidney, Knight* (Boston, MA: T. O. H. P., 1880), p. 289.
12. Sidney, 'Letter to Queen Elizabeth, 1580', p. 289.
13. Sidney, 'Letter to Queen Elizabeth, 1580', p. 289.
14. Sidney, 'Letter to Queen Elizabeth, 1580', pp. 289–90.
15. Sidney, 'Letter to Queen Elizabeth, 1580', p. 290.
16. For a discussion of the relationship between Stubbs's Gaping Gulf and Philip Sidney's letter see N. Mears, 'Counsel, Public Debate, and Queenship: John Stubbs's "The Discoverie of a Gaping Gulf", 1579', Historical Journal, 44:3 (2001), pp. 629–50. Mears suggests that there was no direct connection between Philip's letter and any possible briefing given to Stubbs by members of the privy council. For Mears, therefore, Stubbs's pamphlet/treatise is actually evidence of an English public opinion and public sphere.
17. J. Stubbs, *The Discovery of a Gaping Gulf*, (London: H. Singleton for W. Page, 1579), fol. 2r.
18. Stubbs, *The Discovery of a Gaping Gulf*, fol. 3r.
19. Stubbs, *The Discovery of a Gaping Gulf*, fols 3r, 6v, 7r.
20. Stubbs, *The Discovery of a Gaping Gulf*, fol. 16v.
21. Stubbs, *The Discovery of a Gaping Gulf*, fol. 19r.
22. Stubbs, *The Discovery of a Gaping Gulf*, fol. 22v.
23. Stubbs, *The Discovery of a Gaping Gulf*, fols 23v, 40 r.
24. For more biographical details on Fenton and Bryskett, see A. Hadfield, 'Fenton, Sir Geoffrey (c. 1539–1608)', *ODNB* and R. A. McCabe, 'Bryskett, Lodowick (*c.* 1546–1609x12)', *ODNB*.
25. For a broader discussion of the influence of French political thought in England see J. H. N. Salmon, *The French Religious Wars in English Political Thought* (Oxford: Oxford University Press, 1959), in particular 'Elizabethan Reception', pp. 15–38.
26. G. Fenton, *An Epistle of Godlie Admonition* (London: Henry Bynneman, 1569), fol. 1r. Also see A. Gordon, 'Antonio del Corro', *ODNB*.
27. Fenton, 'A Prayer to Jesus Christ, for peace and unitie in the Church, by Geffray Fenton', in *An Epistle of Godlie Admonition*, fol. 7r.

28. Fenton, *An Epistle of Godlie Admonition*, fol. 7r.
29. G. Fenton, 'To the Right Honorable and Virtuous Ladie, Anne Countesse of Oxenforde', in *Golden Epistles* (London: Henry Middleton for Rafe Newbery, 1575), fols 2v, 3r.
30. Verifying the accuracy of Fenton's translation (since the original source is not given) was made possible by the help of Dr Jennifer Browne, University College Cork, and her expert knowledge of Pierre Bayle's *Dictionnaire Historique et Critique* which supports the narrative provided by Fenton.
31. G. Fenton, 'A Preface Conteyning the Occasions of the Conference', in *Actes of Conference in Religion* (London: H. Bynneman for William Norton and Humfrie Toye, 1571), fol. 3v.
32. Fenton, 'A Preface Conteyning the Occasions of the Conference', in *Actes of Conference in Religion*, fol. 5v.
33. Fenton, *Actes of Conference in Religion* (1571), fol. 2r.
34. G. Fenton, *A Discourse of the Civile Warres and Late Troubles in Fraunce* (London: Henry Bynneman for Lucas Harrison and George Bishop, 1570), fol. 1v.
35. Fenton, *A Discourse of the Civile Warres and Late Troubles in Fraunce*, p. 2.
36. Fenton, *A Discourse of the Civile Warres and Late Troubles in Fraunce*, p. 4.
37. Fenton, *A Discourse of the Civile Warres and Late Troubles in Fraunce*, p. 18.
38. Fenton, *A Discourse of the Civile Warres and Late Troubles in Fraunce*, p. 27.
39. Fenton, *A Discourse of the Civile Warres and Late Troubles in Fraunce*, pp. 39, p. 42.
40. Fenton, *A Discourse of the Civile Warres and Late Troubles in Fraunce*, pp. 102–3.
41. Fenton, *A Discourse of the Civile Warres and Late Troubles in Fraunce*, p. 114.
42. Fenton, *A Discourse of the Civile Warres and Late Troubles in Fraunce*, fol. 3v.
43. Fenton, *A Discourse of the Civile Warres and Late Troubles in Fraunce*, pp. 24, 40.
44. Fenton, *A Discourse of the Civile Warres and Late Troubles in Fraunce*, p. 42.
45. Fenton, *A Discourse of the Civile Warres and Late Troubles in Fraunce*, pp. 103, 109. The edict of Nantes as promulgated in France is seen in classic historiography as a crucial step towards a concept of religious toleration – however, this position has now been challenged to a degree. See R. A. Mentzer, 'The Edict of Nantes and its Institutions', in R. A. Mentzer and A. Spicer (eds), *Society and Culture in the Huguenot World 1559–1685* (Cambridge: Cambridge University Press, 2002), pp. 98–116.
46. See L. Racaut, 'Nicolas Chesneau, Catholic Printer in Paris during the French Wars of Religion', *Historical Journal*, 52:1 (2009), p. 35. Dr Jennifer Browne at University College Cork helped in comparing the original French treatise with Fenton's translation.
47. G. Fenton, *A Forme of Christian Pollicie* (London: H. Middleton for Rafe Newbery, 1574), p. 23. The arguments set out here are similar to Calvin's insistence that the preacher and magistrate work together. See also from the current study 'European State Theory' in the introduction, 'Inverting Resistance Theory' in chapter 1 and 'Hooker, Grindal and Norton' in chapter 2 of this book.
48. Fenton, *A Forme of Christian Pollicie*, p. 23.
49. Fenton, *A Forme of Christian Pollicie*, pp. 35–6.
50. Fenton, *A Forme of Christian Pollicie*, p. 94.
51. Fenton, *A Forme of Christian Pollicie*, fols 2-3.
52. G. Fenton, *The Historie of Guicciardin* (London: Thomas Vautrollier, 1579), p. 1.
53. Fenton, *The Historie of Guicciardin*, p. 3.
54. Fenton, *The Historie of Guicciardin*, p. 2 and passim.
55. Fenton, *The Historie of Guicciardin*, fol. 2r.
56. M. Viroli, *From Politics to Reason of State: The Acquisition and Transformation of the*

Language of Politics 1250–1600 (Cambridge: Cambridge University Press, 1992), pp. 178–200.

57. Bryskett's *Discourse* will be discussed in detail in the first section of chapter 5.
58. For the confessional and more religious response to these risings see chapter 2.
59. For more detail, and a slightly alternative analysis of events, see C. Maginn, 'The Baltinglass Rebellion, 1580: English Dissent or a Gaelic Uprising', *Historical Journal*, 47:2 (2004), pp. 205–32.
60. 'Interrogatories to be Ministered to the Earl of Kildare', [19 July] 1581, The National Archives SP63/84/36; and 'Interrogatories to be Ministered to Baron Delvin', [19 July] 1581, TNA SP63/84/37.
61. Loftus to Walsingham, 24 October 1581, TNA SP63/86/30 I.
62. C. Brady, *The Chief Governors: The Rise and Fall of Reform Government in Tudor Ireland, 1536–1588* (Cambridge: Cambridge University Press, 1994), p. 235; and C. Lennon, 'St Lawrence, Christopher, Seventh Baron Howth (d. 1589)', *ODNB*.
63. Grey to Walsingham, 30 May 1582, TNA SP63/92/112.
64. Irish council to Walsingham, 29 August 1582, TNA SP63/94/106.
65. 'An Estimate of the Dep: Charges', TNA SP63/106/45.
66. 'Proclamation of General Pardon' [Draft], 1581, TNA SP63/87/84.
67. 'Proclamation of General Pardon' [Draft], 1581, TNA SP63/87/84.
68. Grey to Walsingham, 9 June 1581, TNA SP63/83/43.
69. 'Instructions Given by her Servant Sir N. Malby Knight to Be Communicated to her Deputy and Council in Ireland', 3 April 1582, TNA SP63/91/4.
70. Grey to English privy council, 12 April 1582, TNA SP63/91/22.
71. Grey to English privy council, 12 April 1582, TNA SP63/91/22.
72. 'Touching Nicholas Nugent', [8 April] 1582, TNA SP63/91/18.
73. White to Burghley, 23 December 1581, TNA SP63/87/55.
74. White to Burghley, 23 December 1581, TNA SP63/87/55.
75. White to Burghley, 23 December 1581, TNA SP63/87/55.
76. Kildare to Leicester, 23 December 1582, TNA SP63/98/53.
77. Grey to Walsingham, 22 May 1582, TNA SP63/92/52: 'The earl of Kildare and the baron of Delvin are now to be sent over as directed'; also see D. Finnegan, 'Fitzgerald, Gerald, Eleventh Earl of Kildare (1525–1585)', *ODNB* and C. Lennon, 'Nugent, Christopher, Fifth Baron Delvin (1544–1602)', *ODNB*.
78. White to Burghley, 2 February 1581, TNA SP63/80/48.
79. Q. Skinner, *Liberty Before Liberalism* (Cambridge: Cambridge University Press, 1998), pp. 63–72.
80. White to Burghley, 23 December 1581, TNA SP63/87/55.
81. 'Baron Delvin's Plot', 26 March 1584, TNA SP63/108/58. Also see Valerie McGowan-Doyle's recent study which suggests there was a far broader project to establish the customary opposition of the Old English gentry. See V. McGowan-Doyle, *The Book of Howth: Elizabethan Conquest and the Old English* (Cork: Cork University Press, 2011), in particular ch. 3.
82. Wallop to Walsingham, 16 and 18 June 1583, TNA SP63/102/85.
83. M. Braddick, *State Formation in Early Modern England* (Cambridge: Cambridge University Press, 2000), pp. 9–10. Also see S. G. Ellis, 'Tudor State Formation and the Shaping of the British Isles', in S. G. Ellis and S. Barber (eds.), *Conquest and Union: Fashioning a British State 1485–1725* (London: Longman, 1995), pp. 40–63.
84. Fenton to Burghley, 14 September 1581, The National Archives SP63/85/41.

85. Fenton to Burghley, 21 September 1581, TNA SP63/85/54.
86. Bryskett to Burghley, 7 April 1581, TNA SP63/82/19; Bryskett to Walsingham, 21 April 1581, TNA SP63/82/45; Bryskett to Burghley, 25 April 1581, TNA SP63/82/53; Bryskett to Walsingham, 1 February 1582, TNA SP63/89/5; and Bryskett to Walsingham, 10 May 1582, TNA SP63/92/29.
87. Grey to Walsingham, 15 January 1581, TNA SP63/80/10.
88. W. St Leger to Burghley, 26 January 1581, TNA SP63/80/29.
89. Fenton to Burghley, 2 May 1582, TNA SP63/92/3.
90. 'Notes Touching the Well Doing of the Earl of Clanrickard', TNA SP63/99/17 I.
91. Fenton to Burghley, 23 December 1582, TNA SP63/98/51.
92. N. Canny, 'Edmund Spenser and the Development of an Anglo-Irish Identity', *Yearbook of English Studies*, 13 (1983), special issue: *Colonial and Imperial Themes Special*, pp. 1–19, on p. 14. Also White to Burghley, 23 December 1581, TNA SP63/85/55.
93. Wallop to Burghley, 10 June 1582, TNA SP63/93/17.
94. Wallop and Loftus to Burghley, 8 December 1582, TNA SP63/98/23.
95. Loftus and Wallop to English privy council, April 1583, TNA SP63/101/31.
96. Loftus and Wallop to English privy council, 24 July 1583, TNA SP63/103/37.
97. Fitzwilliam to Burghley, 31 July 1588, TNA SP63/135/96.
98. Wilbraham to Walsingham, 6 October 1588, TNA SP63/137/8.
99. Russell to Burghley, 17 August 1594, TNA SP63/175/55.
100. Fenton to Walsingham, 16 January 1583, TNA SP63/99/27.
101. Fenton to Walsingham, 17 April 1583, TNA SP63/101/33.
102. Fenton to Walsingham, 17 April 1583, TNA SP63/101/33.
103. See '"Papistry" and Penal Legislation' of chapter 2.
104. Brady to Burghley, 5 November 1582, TNA SP63/97/19.
105. Fenton to Burghley, 22 September 1592, TNA SP63/165/62.
106. This is discussed in part in 'Papistry and Penal Legislation' in chapter 2 of this study.
107. Long to Walsingham, 8 July 1585, TNA SP63/118/12.
108. Long to Walsingham, 8 July 1585, TNA SP63/118/12.
109. Loftus to Walsingham, 30 September 1586, TNA SP63/126/34; Lord deputy and council to the English privy council, 28 January 1586, TNA SP63/122/47; and Perrot to Hatton, 21 August 1584; J. Perrot, 'The Perrot Papers: The Letter-Book of Lord-Deputy Sidney Sir John Perrot between 9 July 1584 and 26 May 1586', ed. C. McNeill, *Analecta Hibernica*, 12 (1943), pp. 3–65, on pp. 6–7.
110. Perrot to Walsingham, 18 June 1585, TNA SP63/117/36.
111. Perrot to Walsingham, 18 June 1585, TNA SP63/117/36.
112. Lord deputy and council to the English privy council, 28 January 1586, TNA SP63/122/47.
113. Lord deputy and council to the English privy council, 28 January 1586, TNA SP63/122/47.
114. Perrot to Walsingham 18 June 1585, TNA SP63/117/36.
115. Perrot to Walsingham, 18 June 1585, TNA SP63/117/36.
116. Perrot to Elizabeth, 12 September 1585, Perrot MS 1, Oxford, Bodleian Library (hereafter Perrot MS 1), fol. 122.
117. Perrot to Burghley, 24 September 1585, TNA SP63/119/32; Perrot to Burghley, 10 April 1586, TNA SP63/123/39.
118. See, for example, Malby to Burghley, August 1572, TNA SP63/37/34. The letters sent by Geoffrey Fenton discussed in this chapter, as well as the letters detailed in 'An Irish

View of "Civil Obedience" Restated' in chapter 2 of this book also provide evidence of a pejorative use of the term 'liberty'.

119. See C. Ballériaux, 'The Idea of Freedom in the Missionary Writings about the New World', in Q. Skinner and M. van Gelderen (eds.), *Freedom and the Construction of Europe*, 2 vols (Cambridge: Cambridge University Press, 2013), vol. 2, pp. 247–65.
120. Perrot to Walsingham 18 June 1585, The National Archives SP63/117/36.
121. Walsingham to Long, December 1585, TNA SP63/121/50 [Draft]; and Perrot to Burghley, 24 September 1585, TNA SP63/119/32. Perrot makes reference in his letter to Elizabeth's instructions. Perrot's use of the oath of supremacy is discussed in both '"Papistry" and Penal Legislation' in chapter 2 and 'Gaelic Political and Religious Vocabulary' in chapter 5 of this book.
122. Long to White, July 1586, TNA SP63/125/12 I.
123. Long to White, July 1586, TNA SP63/125/12 I.
124. Long to White, July 1586, TNA SP63/125/12 I.
125. T. Clavin, 'Walsh, Sir Nicholas', *Dictionary of Irish Biography*.
126. N. Walsh, 'Oration', 14 May 1586, TNA SP63/124/24. See N. Walsh, 'Nicholas Walsh's Oration to the Irish House of Commons, May 1586', ed. M. A. Hutchinson, *Analecta Hibernica*, 45 (2014), pp. 35–47 for a full annotated transcription of, and commentary on, Walsh's oration.
127. Walsh, 'Oration', 14 May 1586, TNA SP63/124/24. fol. 45 r.
128. See J. Bodin, *On Sovereignty*, ed. J. H. Franklin (Cambridge: Cambridge University Press, 1992), pp. 89–109.
129. Walsh, 'Oration', fol. 46v.
130. J. Hooker, 'Order and Usage', in V. F. Snow ed., *Parliament in Elizabethan England: John Hooker's Order and Usage* (New Haven, CT: Yale University Press, 1977), p. 124; and J. Ponet, *A Short Treatise of Politike Powe*r (Strasbourg: by the heirs of W. Köpfel, 1556), fol. 6r.
131. Walsh, 'Oration', fol. 46 v.
132. Q. Skinner, 'Machiavelli on *Virtù* and the Maintenance of Liberty', in *Visions of Politics*, 3 vols, vol. 2: *Renaissance Virtues* (Cambridge: Cambridge University Press, 2002), pp. 160–85, on pp. 260–8.
133. Walsh, 'Oration', fol. 47 r.
134. Walsh, 'Oration', fol. 47 r.
135. Walsh, 'Oration', fol. 47 r.
136. Walsh, 'Oration', fol. 48 r.
137. van Gelderen, pp. 260–8.
138. The continued health of aspects of Collinson's gentry-republic in England, past Elizabeth's reign, has been pointed to by M. Goldie, 'The Unacknowledged Republic: Office-Holding in Early Modern England', in T. Harris (ed), *The Politics of the Excluded* (New York: Palgrave, 2001), pp. 153–94.

5 Ireland's Lordships and an Absolutist State

1. Aspects of this more gradual and blurred transition have been discussed, for example, in D. Starkey (ed.), *The English Court from the Wars of the Roses to the Civil War* (London: Longman, 1987). Also see S. Adams, *Leicester at the Court: Essays on Elizabethan Politics* (Manchester: Manchester University Press, 2002). Furthermore, L. Stone, *The Crisis of the Aristocracy* (Oxford: Clarendon Press, 1965), discusses the erosion of the

economic position of lordships as a post-feudal economy took over. A wider discussion of the changing condition of society can be found in S. Hindle, *The State and Social Change in Early Modern England, c. 1550–1640* (Basingstoke: Palgrave, 2000). The pressure exerted by economic and social change can be set beside the more specific developments discussed here, where social change, in part, provided the imperative for the construction of new structures and institutions.

2. It is noted in D. Edwards, 'Beyond Reform: Martial Law and the Tudor Re-conquest of Ireland', *History Ireland*, 5:2 (1997), pp. 16–21, that under Perrot and then Fitzwilliam's second deputyship, due to prohibitions from the queen, the number of commissions issued fell, as compared to Sidney and Grey. In 1597, however, with the Nine Years War, martial law was again endorsed by the crown. Moreover, as this chapter argues the tone of debate had by the 1580s altered significantly.
3. M. Peltonen, *Classical Humanism and Republicanism in English Political Thought 1570–1640* (Cambridge: Cambridge University Press, 1995), pp. 54–118. Peltonen's specific discussion of Beacon and John Hooker will be addressed in chapter 6.
4. Again this is discussed more fully when addressing Beacon and Spenser in chapter 6.
5. See R. A. McCabe, 'Bryskett, Lodowick (*c.*1546–1609x12)', *ODNB.*
6. L. Bryskett, *A Discourse of Civill Life* (London: [R.Field] for William Aspley, 1606), p. 1.
7. R. A. McCabe, *Spenser's Monstrous Regiment: Elizabethan Ireland and the Poetics of Difference* (Oxford: Oxford University Press, 2002), p. 236.
8. McCabe, 'Bryskett, Lodowick'.
9. Bryskett, *Discourse*, fol. 3v.
10. Bryskett, *Discourse*, p. 21.
11. Bryskett, *Discourse*, pp. 21-2.
12. Q. Skinner, 'Machiavelli on *Virtù* and the Maintenance of Liberty', in Q. Skinner, *Visions of Politics*, 3 vols, vol. 2: *Renaissance Virtues* (Cambridge: Cambridge University Press, 2002), pp. 160–85.
13. Bryskett, *Discourse*, p. 22.
14. Bryskett, *Discourse*, p. 41.
15. Bryskett, *Discourse*, pp. 67, 70.
16. Bryskett, *Discourse*, p. 72.
17. Bryskett, *Discourse*, p. 102
18. Bryskett, *Discourse*, p. 90.
19. Bryskett, *Discourse*, p. 140.
20. Bryskett,*Discourse*, p. 62.
21. See R. Tuck, 'Scepticism, Stoicism and Raison D'etat', in Tuck, *Philosophy and Government* 1572–1651 (Cambridge: Cambridge University Press, 1993), pp. 31–64; and P. Burke, 'Tacitism, Scepticism, and Reason of State', in J. H. Burns and M. Goldie (eds), *Cambridge History of Political Thought* (Cambridge: Cambridge University Press, 1991), pp. 479–98. The specific argument over the corruption of courtly life and the need for political action is clearly expounded in A. Gajda, *The Earl of Essex and Late Elizabethan Political Culture* (Oxford: Oxford University Press, 2012), pp. 18–25, 226–8, 239–40. Also see P. Kewes, 'Henry Saville's Tacitus and the Politics of Roman History in Late Elizabethan England', *Huttington Library Quarterly*, 74:4 (2011), pp. 515–51; and J. H. L. Salmon, 'Stoicism and Roman Example: Seneca and Tacitus in Jacobean England', *Journal of the History of Ideas*, 50:2 (1989), pp. 199–225.
22. E. H. Shagan, *The Rule of Moderation: Violence, Religion and the Politics of Restraint in Early Modern England* (Cambridge: Cambridge University Press, 2011).

23. Bryskett, *Discourse*, p. 168.
24. Bryskett, *Discourse*, p. 170.
25. Bryskett, *Discourse*, p. 186.
26. McCabe, *Spenser's Monstrous Regiment*, pp. 236–8. There is a sense in which the first part of the *Faerie Queene* published in 1590 is more confident and optimistic in its task of exploring how man can self-fashion, whilst the second half published in 1596 is less optimistic and self-assured.
27. 'Sir John Perrot on the Government of Ireland', Sloane MS 2200, London, British Library (hereafter 'Perrot on the Government of Ireland'), fol. 2r.
28. C. Brady, *The Chief Governors: The Rise and Fall of Reform Government in Tudor Ireland, 1536–1588* (Cambridge: Cambridge University Press, 1994), pp. 219–300.
29. See R. H. Tawney, *The Agrarian Problem in the Sixteenth Century* (London: Longmans Green and Co., 1912), pp. 27–40.
30. Brady, *Chief Governors*, pp. 219–300.
31. 'Perrot on the Government of Ireland', fol. 9r.
32. 'Perrot on the Government of Ireland', fol. 7r.
33. Comment is appended to 'A Discourse for the Repressing of the Rebellions Stirred up in Ireland', July 1581, Harleian MS 3292, London, British Library, fol. 12v.
34. R. Rapple, *Martial Power and Elizabethan Political Culture: Military Men in England and Ireland, 1558–1594* (Cambridge: Cambridge University Press, 2009), pp. 179–93.
35. 'Perrot on the Government of Ireland', fol. 5v. Some form of this proposal was adopted by Mountjoy in the midst of the Nine Years War in an attempt to lower costs. See F. M. Jones, *Mountjoy 1563–1606: The Last Elizabethan Deputy, 1563–1606* (Dublin: Clonmore and Reynolds Ltd., 1958), p. 105.
36. See H. Morgan, *Tyrone's Rebellion: The Outbreak of the Nine Years' War in Tudor Ireland* (Woodbridge: Royal Historical Society, 1993), pp. 34–6.
37. Perrot to English privy council, August 1585, Add. MS 4785, London, British Library (hereafter Add. MS 4785), fol. 182r.
38. Perrot and Irish council to English privy council, August 1585, Add. MS 4785, fol. 183v.
39. Morgan, *Tyrone's Rebellion*, pp. 34–6.
40. See K. Nicholls, *Gaelic and Gaelicized Ireland in the Middle Ages* (Dublin: Lilliput, 1972), p. 26.
41. Perrot to English privy council, 23 October 1584, The National Archives SP63/112/41.
42. Perrot to English privy council, October 1584, SP63/112/41.
43. Perrot to English privy council, October 1584, in J. Perrot, 'The Perrot Papers: The Letter-Book of Lord-Deputy Sidney Sir John Perrot between 9 July 1584 and 26 May 1586', ed. C. McNeill, *Analecta Hibernica*, 12 (1943), p. 10.
44. Perrot to English privy council, October 1584, in 'The Perrot Papers', pp. 36–9; also see Perrot to Burghley, 22 October 1584, TNA SP63/112/28.
45. Morgan, *Tyrone's Rebellion*, p. 36 and p. 38.
46. Perrot to Walsingham 15 and 30 August 1584, Add. MS 4785, fol. 201v.
47. Perrot to Elizabeth, 1 April 1585, TNA SP63/116/1.
48. Perrot to Queen, 27 September 1585, Perrot MS 1, fol. 139r.
49. Perrot to Burghley, 3 September 1586, Perrot MS 1, fol. 172v.
50. Wallop to Burghley, 15 November 1586, TNA SP63/126/82. Also William Herbert, who will be discussed in this chapter at the start of 'The State, Connacht and Munster', in reference to the Munster plantation, described how his fellow planter

Edward Denny could not control his passions. See Herbert to Norris, 12 July 1588, TNA SP63/135/81. Also Fenton to Burghley, 1 July 1586, TNA SP63/135/1. Fenton described how an individual 'smelleth of passion' when he was involved in a particular dispute. Beside this, in the more general comments on Perrot's behaviour, there is the broader sense given that the lord deputy simply cannot control himself.

51. A. Gajda, *The Earl of Essex and Late Elizabethan Political Culture* (Oxford: Oxford University Press, 2012), pp. 18–25, 225–9, 239–40.
52. Perrot did attempt to further church reform and evangelism, similar to Sidney's godly agenda – see 'An Irish Preaching Ministry' in chapter 1.
53. N. Machiavelli, *The Prince*, ed. Q. Skinner (Cambridge: Cambridge University Press, 1998), in particular 'How Contempt and Hatred Should Be Avoided', pp. 63–71, and 'The Civil Principality', pp. 34–6.
54. See the first note to chapter 5.
55. Elizabeth to Sidney, 24 February 1568, The National Archives SP63/23/51. Also see C. Brady, 'The O'Reillys of East Breifne and the Problem of Surrender and Regrant', *Breifne* 6 (1985), pp. 233–62.
56. 'O'Reilly's Submission', 9 December 1579, TNA SP63/70/52.
57. H. Morgan, *Tyrone's Rebellion: The Outbreak of the Nine Years' War in Tudor Ireland* (Woodbridge: Royal Historical Society, 1993), pp. 41–3; also see S. J. Connolly, *Contested Island: Ireland 1460–1630* (Oxford: Oxford University Press, 2007), p. 217. 'Indenture Sir John O'Reilly', 28 November 1584, TNA SP63/112/92.
58. Perrot to Burghley, 4 December 1584, TNA SP63/113/ 9.
59. Elizabeth to Perrot, 30 December 1584, SP63/113/40.
60. Perrot to Burghley, 4 December 1584, TNA SP63/113/ 9.
61. Denization is a process whereby a foreign subject is naturalized.
62. Fenton to Burghley, 14 June 1586, TNA SP63/124/76.
63. Indenture between Lord Deputy Perrot and council and Sorley Boy, 18 June 1586, TNA SP63/124/83.
64. Wilbraham to Burghley, 9 July 1586, TNA SP63/125/11.
65. Indenture between Lord Deputy Perrot and council and Sorley Boy, 18 June 1586, TNA SP63/124/83.
66. Wilbraham to Burghley, 9 July 1586, TNA SP63/125/11.
67. 'The Information of Sir Henry Bagenal Touching her Majesty's Service in the North of Ireland', 7 June 1586, TNA SP63/124/66.
68. Loftus, Bagenal and Bingham to Burghley, 28 January 1587, TNA SP63/127/20.
69. W. MacCaffrey, *Elizabeth I: War and Politics, 1588–1603* (Princeton, NJ: Princeton University Press, 1994), pp. 349–71 and Morgan, *Tyrone's Rebellion*, pp. 62–4.
70. R. Rapple, 'Taking up Office in Elizabethan Connacht: The Case of Sir Richard Bingham', *English Historical Review*, 123:501 (2008), pp. 277–99, argues that Bingham was wilfully attempting to bait O'Rourke into rebellion and that whilst he acted as though an absolutist, he lacked a conscious ideological intent. The argument as set out in this study would suggest otherwise – that Bingham did have a clear ideological intent.
71. Bingham to Burghley, 8 September 1589, TNA SP63/146/32.
72. Bingham to Walsingham, 23 May 1589, TNA SP63/144/55.
73. See 'Mr John Bingham's Declaration', 16 July 1591, TNA SP63/159/13; John Bingham to Burghley, 8 August 1591, TNA SP63/159/30; and 'Note of the Charges against O'Rourke', November 1591, TNA SP63/161/24. See H. Morgan, 'The Fall of Sir John Perrot', in J. Guy (ed.), *The Reign of Elizabeth I* (Cambridge, Cambridge University

Press, 1995), pp. 109–25, on p. 119. Morgan writes concerning the incident that 'the original incident had been a charivari, the ritual humiliation of someone who breaks the rules of communal behaviour or acts against the prevailing moral code'.

74. Lord deputy to Burghley, 11 December 1591, TNA SP63/161/36.
75. Merbury to Burghley, [27 September] 1589, TNA SP63/146/60.
76. J. G. A. Pocock, *The Ancient Constitution and the Feudal Law: A Study of English Historical Thought in the Seventeenth Century: A Reissue with a Retrospect* (Cambridge: Cambridge University Press, 1987), pp. 30–57.
77. 'Burghley's Remembrances of Irish Causes', 26 March 1584, TNA SP63/108/60.
78. Gardiner to Walsingham, 4 January 1590, TNA SP63/150/4.
79. 'Fiants of the Reign of Queen Elizabeth', in *The Sixteenth Report of the Deputy Keeper of the Public Records in Ireland* (Dublin: Alex. Thom & Co., 1884), appendix 2, pp. 30, 81, 91 111.
80. See D. Edwards, 'Beyond Reform: Martial Law and the Tudor Re-conquest of Ireland', *History Ireland*, 5:2 (1997), pp. 16–21. Gardiner to Walsingham, 4 January 1590, TNA SP63/150/4. 'Draft Proclamation to Restrain Martial Law in Ireland', TNA SP63/150/4 I.
81. Arthur O'Tool to Elizabeth, June 1591, TNA SP63/158/65.
82. Arthur O'Tool to Elizabeth, June 1591, TNA SP63/158/65.
83. 'Answer of Phelim O'Tool to the Bill of Complaint of Arthur with Geneological Notes', June 1591, TNA SP63/158/72; and 'State of the Controversy between Felim O'Tool, of Powerscourt, and Arthur Tool for the Tools' country', TNA SP63/159/8.
84. Arthur O'Tool to Elizabeth, June 1591, TNA SP63/158/65.
85. A. J. Sheehan, 'Official Reaction to Native Land Claims in the Munster Plantation', *Irish Historical Studies*, 22:92 (1983), pp. 297–317.
86. MacCaffrey, *War and Politics*, pp. 349–71 and Morgan, *Tyrone's Rebellion*, pp. 62–4. Also 'Information against Sir William Fitzwilliam during his Deputation', 13 September 1594, TNA SP63/176/19.
87. Lord deputy to privy council, 2nd March 1590, TNA SP63/151/2.
88. H. Morgan (ed.), 'The Deputy's Defence: Sir William Fitzwilliam's Apology on the Outbreak of the Nine Years War', *Proceedings of the Royal Irish Academy*, section c 114 (2014), p. 19.
89. H. Morgan, *Tyrone's Rebellion: The Outbreak of the Nine Years' War in Tudor Ireland* (Woodbridge: Royal Historical Society, 1993) and K. Nicholls, *Gaelic and Gaelicized Ireland in the Middle Ages* (Dublin: Lilliput, 1972). R. A. McCabe, *Spenser's Monstrous Regiment: Elizabethan Ireland and the Poetics of Difference* (Oxford: Oxford University Press, 2002) also attempts to see the poet responding to a Gaelic cultural and a poetic world ignored by other Spenser scholars, pp. 5–6 and passim.
90. Morgan, *Tyrone's Rebellion*, p. 212
91. 'Earl of Tyrone's Answer to the Actions wherewith the Privy Council Charge him', The National Archives, March 1590, SP63/151/20.
92. S. J. Connolly, *Contested Island: Ireland 1460–1630* (Oxford: Oxford University Press, 2007), p. 232. Concerns over Maguire were expressed by Fenton in November 1593, TNA SP63/172/17 and December 1593, TNA SP63/172/33.
93. Bingham to Burghley, 25 September 1592, TNA SP63/165/66.
94. Bingham to Burghley, 25 September 1592, TNA SP63/165/66.
95. 'Declaration by Patrick McArt Moyle [McMahon]', January 1592, SP63/169/23 III.
96. See M. C. Questier, *Conversion, Politics and Religion in England, 1580–1625* (Cam-

bridge: Cambridge University Press: 1996), pp. 98–125.

97. 'Declaration by Patrick McArt Moyle [McMahon]', January 1592, SP63/169/23 III.
98. Lord deputy and council to privy council, 16 September 1593, TNA SP63/171/34.
99. 'Treatise on Ireland by Sir George Carew', SP63/174/13 I.
100. Fenton to Burghley, December 1594, SP63/177/31.
101. H. Morgan, 'Hugh O'Neill and the Nine Years War in Tudor Ireland', *Historical Journal*, 36:1 (1993), p. 22.
102. H. Morgan, 'Hugh O'Neill and the Nine Years War in Tudor Ireland', *Historical Journal*, 36:1 (1993), p. 24.
103. H. O'Neill, 'Articles Intended to be Stood upon by Tyrone, Nov–Dec 1599', in 'Faith and Fatherland or Queen and Country', ed. H. Morgan, *Duiche Neill: Journal of the O'Neill Country Historical Society*, 11 (1994), pp. 21–2.
104. R. A. Mentzer, 'The Edict of Nantes and its Institutions', in R. A. Mentzer and A. Spicer (eds), *Society and Culture in the Huguenot World 1559–1685* (Cambridge: Cambridge University Press, 2002), pp. 98–116.
105. O'Neill, 'Articles', pp. 21–2.
106. H. Morgan, 'Policy and Propaganda in Hugh O'Neill's connection with Europe', in M. A. Lyons and T. O'Connor (eds), *The Ulster Earls and Baroque Europe: Refashioning Irish Identities, 1600–1800* (Dublin: Four Courts, 2010), pp. 28–30.
107. D. Edwards, *The Ormond Lordship in County Kilkenny, 1515–1642: The Rise and Fall of Butler Feudal Power* (Dublin: Four Courts, 2003), ch. 4.
108. S. J. Connolly, *Contested Island: Ireland 1460–1630* (Oxford: Oxford University Press, 2007), pp. 179–80.
109. Herbert to Burghley, 30 April 1587, The National Archives SP63/129/42.
110. See A. Sheehan, 'Official Reaction to Native Land Claims in the Munster Plantation', *Irish Historical Studies*, 23:92 (1983), pp. 297–317. Also M. MacCarthy-Murrough, *The Munster Plantation: English Migration to Southern Ireland, 1583–1611* (Oxford: Oxford University Press, 1986).
111. Herbert, [July?] 1588, TNA SP63/135/81 II.
112. Herbert, [July?] 1588, TNA SP63/135/81 II.
113. Herbert, [July?] 1588, TNA SP63/135/81 II.
114. Herbert, [July?] 1588, TNA SP63/135/81 II.
115. N. Doggett, 'Denny, Sir Edward (1547–1600)', *ODNB*. R. Rapple, *Martial Power and Elizabethan Political Culture: Military Men in England and Ireland, 1558–1594* (Cambridge: Cambridge University Press, 2009), pp. 61, 179–80.
116. Herbert to Burghley, SP63/137/31, 20 October 1588.
117. B. Cunningham, 'The Composition of Connacht in the Lordships of Clanrickard and Thomond, 1577–1641', *Irish Historical Studies*, 24 (1984), p. 4.
118. 'A True Discourse of Cause of the Late Rebellion of the Burkes', 18 November 1586, TNA SP63/126/83.
119. Wilbraham to Burghley, 9 July 1586, TNA SP63/125/11.
120. Lord deputy and Irish council to Elizabeth, 24 October 1585, Perrot MS 1, fol. 124r. Despite a lack of success, the various composition agreements made had laid a broader base for government funding.
121. See C. Brady, *The Chief Governors: The Rise and Fall of Reform Government in Tudor Ireland, 1536–1588* (Cambridge: Cambridge University Press, 1994), pp. 149–54, 157 for an account of this aspect Sidney's composition plans.
122. M. Braddick, *The Nerves of State: Taxation and the Financing of the English State,*

1558–1714 (Manchester: Manchester University Press, 1996), in particular pp. 13–18, 76–87.

123. See J. Bodin, *On Sovereignty*, ed. J. H. Franklin (Cambridge: Cambridge University Press, 1992), p. 1.
124. Perrot to Leicester, September 1585, Perrot MS 1 fol. 135 v. Also see Treadwell, 'Sir John Perrot and the Irish Parliament of 1585–6', p. 277.
125. Cunningham, 'The Composition of Connacht', pp. 1–14.
126. Wilbraham to Burghley, 9 July 1586, TNA SP63/125/11.
127. 'Fiants of the Reign of Queen Elizabeth', in *The Sixteenth Report of the Deputy Keeper of the Public Records in Ireland* (Dublin: Alex. Thom & Co., 1884), appendix 2, pp. 30, 33, 38, 80.
128. 'A True Report Made by the Bishops of Meath and Kilmore, Sir Robert Dillon, Sir Nicholas White, and Sir Thomas Le Strange [concerning Bingham's actions in Connacht]', 13 May 1589, SP63/144/34 I. Also Jones to Burghley, 13 May 1589, SP63/144/30.
129. 'A True Discourse of Cause of the Late Rebellion of the Burkes', 16 November 1586, TNA SP63/126/83.
130. 'A True Discourse of Cause of the Late Rebellion of the Burkes', 16 November 1586, TNA SP63/126/83.
131. 'A True Discourse of Cause of the Late Rebellion of the Burkes', 16 November 1586, TNA SP63/126/83, and 17 November, 1586, SP63/126/84.
132. This can be found in many of the letters sent by Robert Weston, Adam Loftus and other clerics as cited in chapters 1 and 2.
133. See for example Bagenall to Burghley, 9 June 1586, TNA SP63/124/70; Fenton to Burghley, 22 August 1586, TNA SP63/124/60; Fenton to Burghley, 14 September 1586, TNA SP63/126/11; Wallop to Burghley,15 November 1586, TNA SP63/126/82; Wallop to Burghley, 13 December 1586, TNA SP63/127/27; and Wallop to Burghley, [13] July, TNA SP63/130/41.
134. See the epilogue and H. S. Pawlisch, *Sir John Davies and the Conquest of Ireland: A Study in Legal Imperialism* (Cambridge: Cambridge University Press, 1985), pp. 103–9.
135. N. P. Canny, 'Edmund Spenser and the Development of an Anglo-Irish Identity', *Yearbook of English Studies*, 13 (1983), special issue: *Colonial and Imperial Themes Special*, pp. 1–19; and N. P. Canny, 'The Permissive Frontier: Social Control in English Settlements in Ireland and Virginia', in K. R. Andrews et al. (eds), *The Westward Enterprise* (Manchester: Manchester University Press, 1978), pp. 17–44.
136. P. Collinson, 'The Monarchical Republic of Queen Elizabeth I', in Collinson, *Elizabethan Essays* (London: Hambledon, 1994), pp. 31–58.
137. See the discussion in '"Papistry" and Penal Legislation' in chapter 2.
138. Perrot to Burghley, 21 September 1585, The National Archives SP63/119/32.
139. Perrot to Burghley, 24 September 1585, TNA SP63/119/32.
140. See V. Treadwell, 'Perrot and the Irish Parliament of 1585–6', *Proceedings of the Royal Irish Academy* section c 85 (1985), pp. 259–308 and 'Note of English Statutes to Be Enacted in Ireland', TNA SP63/112/36.
141. Rosyer to Burghley, 25 September 1586, TNA SP63/126/22.
142. Trollop to Burghley, 26 October 1587, TNA SP63/131/64.
143. Fitzwilliam and Loftus to Walsingham and Burghley, 26 February 1590, TNA SP63/150/74.

144. R. White to Burghley, 8 May 1590, TNA SP63/152/15.
145. 'Book Set Down in Writing by the Archbishop of Cashel by her Majesty's Express Commandment', 30 May 1592, TNA SP63/164/47.
146. See 'Commission to Sir William Fitzwilliam, Appointed Lord Deputy', 17 February 1588, TNA SP63/133/53.
147. White to Burghley, 10 July 1586, TNA SP63/125/12.
148. Loftus to Burghley, 22 September 1590, TNA SP63/154/37.
149. Delvin to Burghley, 17 May 1593, TNA SP63/169/42 – 'touching accusations against Sir Robert Dillon for practising with O'Rourke'.
150. See Epilogue in this volume.
151. C. Condren, *Argument and Authority in Early Modern England: The Presupposition of Oaths and Offices* (Cambridge: Cambridge University Press), p. 20 and passim.
152. N. P. Canny, 'Identity Formation in Ireland: The Emergence of the Anglo-Irish', in N. P. Canny and A. Pagden (eds), *Colonial Identity in the Atlantic World 1500–1800* (Princeton, NJ: Princeton University Press, 1987), pp. 159–212; and C. Brady, 'Reform Government and the Community of the Pale', in Brady, *The Chief Governors: The Rise and Fall of Reform Government in Tudor Ireland, 1536–1588* (Cambridge: Cambridge University Press, 1994), pp. 209–44.
153. N. Younger, *War and Politics in the English Counties* (Manchester: Manchester University Press, 2012), pp. 36–46.

6 An Irish State Theory

1. M. Peltonen, *Classical Humanism and Republicanism in English Political Thought 1570–1640* (Cambridge: Cambridge University Press, 1995), pp. 54–118.
2. This is part of the thesis set out by Q. Skinner in *Hobbes and Republican Liberty* (Cambridge: Cambridge University Press, 2008), ch. 5.
3. J. Hooker, *A Pamphlet of the Offices, and Duties of Everie Particular Sworne Officer, of the Citie of Excester* (London: Henry Denham, 1584), pp. 2, 16–17.
4. A. McLaren, *Political Culture in the Reign of Elizabeth I: Queen and Commonwealth 1558–1585* (Cambridge: Cambridge University Press, 1999), pp. 164–71. This is also discussed in more detail in chapter 2 'Hooker, Grindal and Norton' and in 'Re-interpreting State Theory' in the introduction to this study.
5. J. Hooker, 'The Supplie of this Irish Chronicle ... until this present yeare 1586', in R. Holinshed, *Chronicles*, 2nd edn (London: [Henry Denham], 1587), pp. 111, 114, 140.
6. See discussion in 'An Irish View of "Civil Obedience" Restated' in chapter 2. A. Patterson, *Reading Holinshed's Chronicles* (Chicago, IL: Chicago University Press, 1994), actually points to the controversial nature of Holinshed's project where both the first and second editions were called in and censored by the English privy council, pp. 11–12, 234–63. This also relates to Stanihurt's earlier contribution, which favoured a rehabilitated earl of Kildare and so potentially attractive some censorship.
7. Hooker, 'The Supplie of this Irish Chronicle', p. 117.
8. Hooker, 'The Supplie of this Irish Chronicle', p. 133. Isaiah 59:8.
9. Hooker, 'The Supplie of this Irish Chronicle', p. 141. Matthew 12:43.
10. Hooker, 'The Supplie of this Irish Chronicle', p. 140.
11. Hooker, 'The Supplie of this Irish Chronicle', p. 160.
12. Hooker, 'The Supplie of this Irish Chronicle', pp. 133, 153–83. Here an account is also given of the second Desmond rebellion, where the behaviour of Viscount Baltinglass

and wider opposition to Sidney's attempt to commute cess is noted. Also another dimension to Hooker's account here concerns a protestant apocalyptic outlook. See A. Ford, 'The Irish Historical Renaissance and the Shaping of Protestant History', in A. Ford and J. McCafferty (eds), *The Origins of Sectarianism in Early Modern Ireland* (Cambridge: Cambridge University Press, 2005), pp. 133–40.

13. Hooker, 'The Supplie of this Irish Chronicle', pp. 118, 119, 150, 165.
14. See the 'The Evangelical Difficulties of Derricke and Others' in chapter 2 of this volume.
15. Hooker, 'The Supplie of this Irish Chronicle', p. 162.
16. Hooker, 'The Supplie of this Irish Chronicle', p. 120.
17. See the 'The Stanihursts and Some Ambiguities Concerning God's Grace' in chapter 1 in this volume.
18. Patterson, *Reading Holinshed's Chronicle*, pp. 7–8.
19. Hooker, 'The Supplie of this Irish Chronicle', p. 139.
20. Hooker, 'The Supplie of this Irish Chronicle', pp. 140–1.
21. See *The Great Charter of the Liberties of the City of Waterford* (Kilkenny: J. Reynolds, 1806); and Hooker, 'The Supplie of this Irish Chroncile', p. 139.
22. Hooker, 'The Supplie of this Irish Chronicle', p. 145.
23. Hooker, 'The Supplie of this Irish Chronicle', pp. 116, 143, 150-3.
24. Hooker, 'The Supplie of this Irish Chronicle', pp. 110, 112, 114, 119, 135, 140, 141, 144.
25. Hooker, 'The Supplie of this Irish Chronicle', pp. 111, 119, 141.
26. M. Peltonen, *Classical Humanism and Republicanism in English Political Thought 1570–1640* (Cambridge: Cambridge University Press, 1995), pp. 56–7.
27. Hooker, *Pamphlet*, p. 3.
28. Hooker, 'The Epistle Dedicatorie', in *Pamphlet*, p. 6.
29. Hooker, 'The Epistle Dedicatorie', in *Pamphlet*, pp. 6–7.
30. This is not, however, to question the overall trajectory of Peltonen's argument or his identification of an early civic republicanism.
31. M. Peltonen, *Classical Humanism and Republicanism in English Political Thought 1570–1640* (Cambridge: Cambridge University Press, 1995), pp. 75–102.
32. R. Beacon, *Solon his Follie; or, A Politique Discourse Touching the Reformation of Common-Weales Conquered, Declined or Corrupted*, ed. C. Caroll and V. Carey (Binghampton, NY: Medieval and Renaissance Texts and Studies, 1996). See in particular, pp. xxiii–xxiv.
33. Beacon, *Solon*, p. 18.
34. Beacon, *Solon*, pp. 19–20.
35. Beacon, *Solon*, p. 39.
36. Beacon, *Solon*, p. 43.
37. Beacon, *Solon*, pp. 44–5.
38. Beacon, *Solon*, p. 44.
39. Beacon, *Solon*, p. 84.
40. J. P. Sommerville, 'Early Modern Absolutism in Theory and Practice', in C. Cuttica and G. Burgess (eds), *Monarchism and Absolutism in Early Modern Europe* (London: Pickering & Chatto, 2011), pp. 118–20. This section of the study also follows the general observation made by D. Alan Orr in 'Inventing the British Republic: Richard Beacon's *Solon his Follie* (1594) and the Rhetoric of Civilization', *Sixteenth Century Journal*, 38:4 (2007), pp. 975–94, on p. 975 – that *Solon* was more about the 'consolidation of royal sovereignty in Ireland'. However, I would disagree with the assertion that this undermines Beacon's civic republicanism. Instead, it simply adds to its complexity or

difficulty. In effect, those with a civic republican outlook took up office in an emerging absolutist state in Ireland, thus both these languages clash at a level.

41. Beacon, *Solon*, p. 84
42. See 'Bryskett, Italian Republicanism and *Fortuna*' in chapter 5 of this book.
43. Beacon, *Solon*, p. 87.
44. Beacon, *Solon*, p. 22.
45. Beacon, *Solon*, p. 34
46. Beacon, *Solon*, p. 29.
47. Beacon, *Solon*, p. 27–8.
48. Beacon, *Solon*, p. 119 and the corresponding n. 72.
49. J. Lipsius, *Sixe Bookes of Politickes or Civil Doctrine* (London: Richard Field for William Ponsonby, 1596), pp. 1–15 and passim. See G. Voogt, 'Primacy of Individual Conscience or Primacy of the State? The Clash between Dirck Volckertsz Coornhert and Justus Lipsius', *Sixteenth Century Journal*, 28:4 (1997), pp. 1231–49 which contextualizes part of Lipsius's work within a fraught debate over the position of conscience in a functional political community.
50. Beacon, *Solon*, p. 113.
51. Beacon, *Solon*, p. 132.
52. Beacon, *Solon*, pp. 134, 137–9.
53. Beacon, *Solon*, p. 51.
54. This may be indicative of a wider shift in a conception of preaching, where oratorical skills began to be favoured. See A. Hunt, 'Tuning the Pulpits: The Religious Context of the Essex Revolt', in P. McCullough (ed.), *The English Sermon Revised: Religion, Literature and History, 1600–1750* (Manchester: Manchester University Press, 2001), pp. 86–114. Beacon, *Solon*, pp. 52–3.
55. Beacon, *Solon*, p. 86.
56. Beacon, *Solon*, p. 68.
57. Beacon, *Solon*, pp. 123, 125.
58. Beacon, *Solon*, p. 121
59. This interpretation is supported by Vincent Carey's apt suggestion that *Solon* should be seen as a hybrid text mixing both Machiavellian advice to the prince on how to govern successfully and more straightforward republican sentiment. V. Carey, 'The Irish Face of Machiavelli: Richard Beacon's *Solon his Follie* and Republican Ideology in the Conquest of Ireland', in H. Morgan (ed.), *Political Ideology in Ireland, 1541–1641* (Dublin: Four Courts, 1999), pp. 83–109, on pp. 85–6, 107.
60. A. Hadfield, *Edmund Spenser: A Life* (Oxford: Oxford University Press, 2012), p. 336.
61. E. Spenser, *A View of the State of Ireland*, ed. A. Hadfield and W. Maley (Oxford: Blackwell, 1997), pp. 68, 88, 112, 117, 138, 160, 161.
62. Spenser, *View*, p. 11
63. Spenser, *View*, p. 13
64. Spenser, *View*, p. 30.
65. C. Brady, 'Spenser's Irish Crisis: Humanism and Experience in the 1590s', *Past and Present*, 111 (1986), pp. 17–49
66. Nicholas Canny suggests that a *View* should be read in a colonial context, arguing that Spenser appropriated the positions and language of his New English contemporaries. Whilst I think the text should be read beyond the confines of a colonial context, this does support the contention, in line with Skinner's methodology, that Spenser's thought needs to be understood within the limits of available normative vocabulary

and ideas. Brendan Bradshaw has also pointed to the complicated aspects of Spenser's humanism. He suggests that in a colonial context, a *View* departs from earlier humanist optimism and rejects the viability of reform by condemning the Irish, despite deploying certain modes of humanist analysis and critique. This follows Bradshaw's more general emphasis on the dark side of reformed protestant involvement in Ireland. But as argued throughout this study, Spenser's position is more complicated, since in reality a tension remains between condemnation and a hoped for redemption; and this encompasses not simply Irish society, but a far broader conception of an English godly community. See N. P. Canny, 'Edmund Spenser and the Development of an Anglo-Irish Identity', *Yearbook of English Studies*, 13 (1983), special issue: *Colonial and Imperial Themes Special*, pp. 1–19, on p. 1; and B. Bradshaw, 'Robe and Sword and the Conquest of Ireland', in C. Cross, D. Loades and J. J. Scarisbrick (eds), *Law and Government under the Tudors: Essays on his Retirement Presented to Sir Geoffrey Elton* (Cambridge: Cambridge University Press, 1988), pp. 139–62.

67. Spenser, *View*, p. 30.
68. Spenser, *View*, p. 31.
69. Spenser, *View*, pp. 31–2.
70. Spenser, *View*, p. 32.
71. See 'Inverting Resistance Theory' in chapter 1. The breakdown in common law and mixed polity values in Ireland is also discussed in 'Hooker, Grindal and Norton' in chapter 2, and in 'Arthur Grey's Proto-absolutism and the Irish Mixed Polity' and 'From "Broken State" to Abstract "State"' in chapter 4, as well as throughout chapter 5.
72. Spenser, *View*, p. 34.
73. See '"Papistry" and Penal Legislation' of chapter 2, 'From "Broken State" to Abstract "State"' in chapter 4, and 'Local Office Holding and the Old English Gentry' in chapter 5.
74. Spenser, *View*, p. 21.
75. Spenser, *View*, p. 21
76. Spenser, *View*, pp. 82–3.
77. A. Hadfield, 'Briton and Scythian: Tudor Representations of Irish Origins', *Irish Historical Studies*, 28:112 (1993), pp. 390–408. Also see Spenser, *View*, pp. 44–78 where Scythians are mentioned at different points and a general account is provided of the cultural and conditional reasons for degeneracy.
78. See, for example, N. P. Canny, *Making Ireland British* (Oxford: Oxford University Press, 2001).
79. Spenser, *View*, p. 71. See 'Bryskett, Italian Republicanism and *Fortuna*' in chapter 5 in this volume. Also R. A. McCabe, *Spenser's Monstrous Regiment: Elizabethan Ireland and the Poetics of Difference* (Oxford: Oxford University Press, 2002), pp. 236–9.
80. Aspects concerning Spenser's views on the location of sovereignty in the Irish kingdom, as well as those of Beacon and Herbert and the wider intellectual context, are to some extent addressed in the first two chapters of A. Hadfield, *Spenser's Irish Experience: Wilde Fruit and Salvage Soyl* (Oxford: Oxford University Press, 1997). Also see A. Hadfield, 'Spenser, Ireland and Sixteenth Century Political Theory', *Modern Language Review*, 84:4 (1994), pp. 1–18.
81. Spenser, *View*, p. 103.
82. Spenser, *View*, p. 15.
83. Spenser, *View*, pp. 21–3.
84. Spenser, *View*, p. 24.
85. Spenser, *View*, p. 22.

86. Spenser, *View*, p. 67 and pp. 112–3.
87. Spenser, *View*, pp. 159–60.
88. This is part of the argument advanced by C. Brady, 'Spenser's Irish Crisis: Humanism and Experience in the 1590s', *Past and Present*, 111 (1986), pp. 17–49, where it is suggested that Spenser is attempting to trick or manipulate the reader into agreeing with a position Spenser knows to be morally untenable because of its brutality. Spenser, *View*, p. 135.
89. Spenser, *View*, pp. 95–100.
90. Spenser, *View*, p. 100.
91. Spenser, *View*, pp. 136–7.
92. Spenser, *View*, p. 81.
93. Spenser, *View*, pp. 147–8.
94. Spenser, *View*, p. 85.
95. See W. Herbert, *Croftus Sive de Hibernia Liber*, ed. A. Keaveney and J. Madden (Dublin: Irish Manuscripts Commission, 1992), in particular pp. 85–95. The treatise also demonstrates a clear awareness of contemporaneous European political philosophy, including Justus Lipsius.
96. See McCabe, *Spenser's Monstrous Regiment*, p. 5, which discounts the validity of talking about Spenser as republican. Here McCabe is responding to A. Hadfield, 'Was Spenser a Republican?', *English*, 47 (1998), pp. 169–82.

Epilogue: Beyond the 1590s

1. J. Guy, 'The 1590s: The Second Reign of Elizabeth I?', in J. Guy (ed.), *The Reign of Elizabeth I* (Cambridge, Cambridge University Press, 1995), pp. 1–19.
2. S. Alford, *The Early Elizabethan Polity: William Cecil and the British Succession Crisis, 1558–1569* (Cambridge: Cambridge University Press, 1998), pp. 209–22; P. Lake, *Anglicans and Puritans? Presbyterianism and English Conformist Thought from Whitgift to Hooker* (London: Unwin Hyman, 1988), pp. 37–53; and P. Lake, 'The Politics of "Popularity" and the Public Sphere: The "Monarchical Republic" of Elizabeth I Defends Itself', in P. Lake and S. Pinus (eds), *The Politics of the Public Sphere in Early Modern England* (Manchester: Manchester University Press, 2007), pp. 59–94.
3. Guy, 'The 1590s: The Second Reign of Elizabeth I?', p. 12.
4. Guy, 'The 1590s: The Second Reign of Elizabeth I?', p. 12.
5. J. Guy, 'The Elizabethan Establishment and the Ecclesiastical Polity', in Guy (ed.), *The Reign of Elizabeth I*, pp. 126–49, on pp. 131–4.
6. Guy, 'The 1590s: The Second Reign of Elizabeth I?', pp. 12, 18.
7. H. O'Neill, 'Faith and Fatherland or Queen and Country', ed. H. Morgan, *Duiche Neill: Journal of the O'Neill Country Historical Society*, 9 (1994), pp. 9–65, on pp. 5–11, 23–49.
8. A. Ford, *James Ussher: Theology, History and Politics in Early-Modern Ireland and England* (Oxford: Oxford University Press, 2007), chs 5 and 6.
9. A. Gajda, *The Earl of Essex and Late Elizabethan Political Culture* (Oxford: Oxford University Press, 2012), pp. 164–74. Also see P. E. J. Hammer, 'Patronage at Court, Faction and the Earl of Essex', in Guy (ed.), *The Reign of Elizabeth I*, pp. 65–86. The view set out here of factional disorder could be read in terms of the breakdown in Christian or protestant unity in the polity.
10. T. Wilson, 'The State of England anno dom. 1600 by Thomas Wilson', ed. F. J. Fisher, *Camden Miscellany*, 3rd Series, 52 (London: Camden Society, 1936), p. 33.

11. Wilson, 'The State of England anno dom. 1600 by Thomas Wilson', p. 18.
12. Wilson, 'The State of England anno dom. 1600 by Thomas Wilson', pp. 18–26, 37–43.
13. Hadfield, *Edmund Spenser: A Life* (Oxford: Oxford University Press, 2012), p. 335.
14. Gajda, *Earl of Essex*, pp. 166–7
15. Gajda, *Earl of Essex*, pp. 127–40.
16. F. Bacon, *Sir Francis Bacon his Apologie, in Certain Imputations Concerning the Late Earle of Essex* (London: [Richard Field for] Felix Norton, 1604).
17. J. P. Sommerville, *Royalists and Patriots: Politics and Ideology in England 1603–1640* (Abingdon: Routledge, 1986).
18. L. Levy Peck, 'Beyond the Pale: John Cusacke and the Language of Absolutism in Early Stuart Britain', *Historical Journal*, 41:1 (1998), pp. 121–49.
19. M. P. Holt, *The French Wars of Religion, 1562–1629* (Cambridge: Cambridge University Press, 1995), pp. 153–72.
20. R. A. McCabe, *Spenser's Monstrous Regiment: Elizabethan Ireland and the Poetics of Difference* (Oxford: Oxford University Press, 2002), pp. 272–5.
21. F. M. Jones, *Mountjoy 1563–1606: The Last Elizabethan Deputy, 1563–1606* (Dublin: Clonmore and Reynolds Ltd., 1958), p. 150–5.
22. K. Simms, *From Kings to Warlords* (Woodbridge: The Boydell Press, 1987), p. 35.
23. C. Maginn, 'Blount, Charles, Eighth Baron Mountjoy and Earl of Devonshire (1563–1606)', *ODNB*.
24. N. P. Canny, 'O'Neill, Hugh, Second Earl of Tyrone (*c.*1550–1616)', *ODNB*.
25. N. P. Canny, *Making Ireland British* (Oxford: Oxford University Press, 2001), ch. 4.
26. H. S. Pawlisch, *Sir John Davies and the Conquest of Ireland: A Study in Legal Imperialism* (Cambridge: Cambridge University Press, 1985), p. 103.
27. Pawlisch, *Sir John Davies and the Conquest of Ireland*, p. 104.
28. Pawlisch, *Sir John Davies and the Conquest of Ireland*, p. 104.
29. Pawlisch, *Sir John Davies and the Conquest of Ireland*, p. 109.
30. Pawlisch, *Sir John Davies and the Conquest of Ireland*, p. 109.
31. M. Ó Siochrú, *God's Executioner: Oliver Cromwell and the Conquest of Ireland* (London: Faber and Faber), pp. 69–70, 81–2, 229–30
32. J. P. Sommerville, '*Leviathan* and its Anglican Context', in P. Springborg (ed.), *The Cambridge Companion to Hobbes's Leviathan* (Cambridge: Cambridge University Press, 2007), p. 364. Interestingly, the continuation of a notion of a godly commonwealth into the civil war, and the rhetoric of godly virtue, is explored in J. Scott, 'The Cause of God' and 'Discourses of a Commonwealth', in Scott, *Commonwealth Principles: Republican Writing of the English Revolution* (Cambridge: Cambridge University Press, 2004), chs 2 and 3. Milton, for instance, couched his actions with reference to obedience to God, see pp. 58, 170, 201.

INDEX